Although Hilary Gallo spe[...] [...] complex negotiations for big [...] [...]s [...] Clifford Chance, Accenture and Capge[...] [...] he really is a bit of [...] softie. It wasn't always this wa[...] [...] [...]y on in his career he wore a nice suit and negotiated everything with an iron fist as if his blessed life depended on it. Slowly he worked out that this wasn't him and that being hard didn't actually work that well. Years of trying things out, some great mentors, some of the world's best and worst training, a bit of therapy and quite a few good books helped him to find a better way. Hilary learned how to combine the power of soft with a strong, principled core. Hilary now coaches people who are either dealing with leadership challenges or dealing with life's perennial question: 'What am I going to do next?'

www.thepowerofsoft.com

the power of soft

hilary gallo

SO

THE POWER OF

FT

How to get what you want without being a ****

unbound

This edition first published in 2016

Unbound
6th Floor Mutual House 70 Conduit Street London W1S 2GF
www.unbound.co.uk

Special thanks to:
From *The Empathic Civilization* by Jeremy Rifkin, copyright ©2009 by Jeremy Rifkin. Used by permission of Tarcher, an imprint of Penguin Publishing Group, a division of Penguin Random House LLC.

While every effort has been made to trace the owners of copyright material reproduced herein, the publisher would like to apologise for any omissions and will be pleased to incorporate missing acknowledgments in any further editions.

Typesetting by Bracketpress

Illustrations by Alice Smith

Art direction by Mecob

A CIP record for this book is available from the British Library

ISBN 978-1-78352-139-5 (trade edition paperback)
ISBN 978-1-78352-141-8 (ebook)
ISBN 978-1-78352-140-1 (limited edition hardback)

Printed and bound in Great Britain by Clays Ltd, Elcograf S.p.A.

2 3 4 5 6 7 8 9

To Ina, Lucas & Anna

Dear Reader,

The book you are holding came about in a rather different way to most others. It was funded directly by readers through a new website: Unbound.

Unbound is the creation of three writers. We started the company because we believed there had to be a better deal for both writers and readers. On the Unbound website, authors share the ideas for the books they want to write directly with readers. If enough of you support the book by pledging for it in advance, we produce a beautifully bound special subscribers' edition and distribute a regular edition and e-book wherever books are sold, in shops and online.

This new way of publishing is actually a very old idea (Samuel Johnson funded his dictionary this way). We're just using the internet to build each writer a network of patrons. Here, at the back of this book, you'll find the names of all the people who made it happen.

Publishing in this way means readers are no longer just passive consumers of the books they buy, and authors are free to write the books they really want. They get a much fairer return too – half the profits their books generate, rather than a tiny percentage of the cover price.

If you're not yet a subscriber, we hope that you'll want to join our publishing revolution and have your name listed in one of our books in the future. To get you started, here is a £5 discount on your first pledge. Just visit unbound.com, make your pledge and type SOFT in the promo code box when you check out.

Thank you for your support,

Dan, Justin and John
Founders, Unbound

Water is fluid, soft and yielding.
But water will wear away rock, which is rigid and cannot yield.

As a rule, whatever is fluid, soft and yielding
will overcome whatever is rigid and hard.

This is another paradox: what is soft is strong.

Lao Tzu (604–531 BC)

CONTENTS

CHAPTER I

EXPLORING
PARADOX

It was as I was returning home one Saturday afternoon from a long work week that I realised my negotiation model was broken. This was the mid 1990s and I was working for Electronic Data Systems (EDS), a technology services company. We were at the leading edge of outsourcing deals, taking over an organisation's technology and offering it back to them under contract for a multi-year term with a big cost saving. From pretty much a standing start, we had just outsourced all the IT of the DVLA (the UK's Driver and Vehicle Licensing Agency), Her Majesty's Revenue and Customs and also global giant Rank Xerox. We were now being offered a big deal with a large UK-based industrial conglomerate. Not only would we run their computing systems globally but we'd also buy two consulting and technology businesses they owned. My boss and I were the two in-house lawyers; he ran the legal side of the outsourcing deal while I looked after the purchase of the two companies. To do the deal we had to base ourselves in Coventry for weeks on end and somebody smart negotiated a good price for us all to stay in a huge rural gothic hotel outside Coventry. This was 'being sent to Coventry' in style.

I distinctly remember coming home that Saturday night after a particularly hard week, as the negotiations came to a climax. Even though it was a long drive home, I was still pumped full of adrenalin. We had just put our final positions to our client across both deals. What struck me was how horrified my then partner was at my behaviour. She first remarked on my language, which she said was pretty foul and unlike me. It went deeper, though: my whole attitude had become abrasive and even abusive in her eyes. She was shocked at how confrontational I was. This was the first I knew of it, but instinctively I felt she was right. I went from proud to slightly defensive and then more slowly to slightly sheepish.

From that point I knew something deep down that I only later acknowledged consciously. I knew that we were not going to win the deal. We hadn't acted as we might, we hadn't got the right relationship, we hadn't done the best we could. The following week I was there to help in the briefing when our managing director was due to go to a meeting with the client's CEO, ostensibly to wrap things up. I remember seeing him off with gusto but he came back later with no deal. We heard a week later that our major competitor had been invited in. Subsequently they won the deal. We understood that it was a loss leader for them and the client was subsequently absorbed in a huge merger. We took consolation in all of that, but the fact remained that we had lost.

As I reflected on this deal I realised that it was a turning point in my career as a lawyer. I had focused on getting the best possible deal for my employer. I had been an advocate for some strong positions and argued hard for them. We had taken these positions because we believed they were right. As the lawyer I had ended up leading the active part of the deal team, the negotiations with the client. The rest of the team, external lawyers from a top City law firm, financial experts and our technical team, were taking the lead from me. We stoked each other up and believed our own publicity. The client's team was structured in the same way, and as a result we ended up being highly confrontational. There was also a lot of ego involved. In hindsight it didn't feel good.

I subsequently left EDS and also fundamentally shifted my focus. I could see that there was a much larger picture than a positional fight for the technically right answer. We felt we'd made compromises when we presented our final deal to our Coventry client, but they were just that, compromises. They weren't creative solutions to fully understood problems that we had worked on together. I also wasn't happy that my work and home personas could be so different, particularly without my being aware of it. I knew that I needed to work on understanding both the commercial and human challenge more broadly to achieve more in future. The challenge was mine but I also knew that I needed to shift environment to find the answers. If I had known what to do, I could have done it at EDS. Not knowing what to do was a good reason to move somewhere else where I was more likely to get some help. By luck as much as judgement, I was right. The firm I joined, Andersen Consulting,[1] were pioneers in understanding a new thing they called 'Relationship Management'. At its core, this was about understanding more, both about the client but also about yourself. What drew me in was the professionalism, profitability and image of the organisation. I would find out more about what that was driven by in due course.

The first thing I want to be clear about is that I think negotiating with dominant power is relatively easy. If you hold the thing people want, you can demand the best terms. You can tell people what you think and you can define what is right. Big supermarkets have often pulled business from suppliers because they won't agree to their prescribed terms. So many of our ways of thinking and our systems are built around a prevalence of dominant power that runs at least through the past 2,000 years or so of history. In it the bullies prosper. For my part, I was bullied at work and I in turn bullied. The fruits of my labours contained seeds of sustenance but also of destruction. Once after a bad day at work I got stopped for speeding and realised that there was no sense in taking my frustration out on others. What was the point of intimidating other road users, scaring pedestrians and ultimately defiling the quietly ever-giving natural world around me that gave me sustenance? We hate being victims ourselves, but at the same time it is easy to become part of a pattern where we take our revenge for being bullied by also taking a part-time role as the villain. The problem is that through this approach we don't grow. The good suppliers give up and go elsewhere. Creativity and new product thrive in an atmosphere of trust, not fear. Sooner or later the bully will be left sitting in his vast but now empty palace, as the last cronies desert.

While we wrestle with this situation, we are living at a time of opportunity. As the dust of two world wars continues to settle we have the opportunity, in an environment of unprecedented transparency, to reach back to a different way of negotiating everything in our lives. In our hearts we know it is possible, it is just that the way things have been organised for so long makes it difficult to see the way. All that it requires is to see beyond 'fighting' for things and to understand how we achieve much more through 'creating' opportunity. As ever, the surface language we use is an indicator of the deeper attitudes at work. This is about moving from a coercive model steeped in dominant power to a co-optive model based on higher distributed power and choice. It's not an easy change to make because the prevailing model, however nice we are individually, sits deeply in us systemically.

In the technology services industry we learnt to operate this way because we had very little if any dominant power. As a supplier in a busy industry we were one of many and had to seek differentiation from others to succeed. We could not simply dominate or demand. This was our, my, mistake in Coventry. Punching out or back when we didn't get what we want didn't work for us. Much as that solution appealed to part of our ruffian selves, our truly creative deeper self knew a better way.

It was years later when I finally realised that my approach to fatherhood and relationships was also going to change. Full awareness can take a while to set in and so it was in me as I hid behind many layers of habit and belief. My wife had just given birth to our son, our first child, and was exhausted. I had taken our days-old baby from his cot to calm him late at night and had laid his small soft form on my chest as I lay on our bed. Slowly he calmed and slowly I understood what was happening. He was taking comfort from my warmth but also from my heartbeat beneath and around him. In that moment I truly realised how deeply all my models were broken. In that moment I listened to what was really there. I listened to what he was telling me and knew then and there that I wanted to be a different father from the one I had expected to be. Child had spoken to child, and a different man emerged. This man could no longer carry forward the rather Victorian approach to parenting and relationships that I had had. I did still need strength but I also needed to be true to the gentle softness I felt. That was the base from which I built.

The problem with holding things within is that they tend to find their own way out. Often the thing will get us physically. In my case, I had a sudden bout of bad back pain which took the best part of a year to get better. Then, a year later it recurred. When I had first had the problem I had been busy with an intense deal at work and after a doctor's appointment, where surgery had been discussed, I had dealt with it myself, taking the pain and managing my way through it. I just didn't have the time to deal with it properly, I told myself. This first time it had been tough; too tough to want to repeat. I had learnt a lot but hadn't really asked for much help. This time had to be different and I immediately booked an appointment with a physiotherapist and talked to friends about their experiences. Of all the advice I took I knew surgery was at the very wrong end of the scale for me. A friend had taken this option and it had not gone well. I felt this strongly but wasn't sure why.

The solution I found, through the sports clinic that I attended, was Pilates. I got a few basic exercises and after a Pilates introduction on holiday I bought a book and followed a daily programme at home.[2] Within weeks I felt different and within six weeks my body was different. Pilates helped me build a strong core, slowly from the inside. Instead of looking at things from the surface and wondering what to do, something very different emerged from within. Living muscle was now working in concert with my skeletal structure to provide this strong core. In the next few years my bad back recurred once or twice briefly but could be managed away in days not months. Since picking up a bit of yoga to add flexibility and Feldenkrais[3] to boost my bodily and structural awareness, my back problems have disappeared.

This question of core and spine came to mind one sunny afternoon when I watched a horse roll in a field. I couldn't help noticing firstly how much the horse enjoyed the act of rolling on the ground, but also how for the horse there was no simple roll from side to side. We might think of a horse as having a rounded back and that, like us, a roll through its back is straightforward. This isn't the case. This horse lay on its side for some time, moving and scratching, and then with a great wriggled push went for a roll. At first it failed and fell back on the side it had started from. On the second try, the horse put in more effort. By force of its swing into the roll through legs, head and neck it achieved a full roll to the other side. As the horse finally got up, I noticed what I had never really thought about: the prominence of the horse's spine along the top of its back and the fact that this horse, at least, couldn't simply lie on its back. It very definitely had to be on one side or the other. A horse's spine is effectively on top and its soft organs are underneath, much more protected.

As we humans progressed from a four-limbed to an upright stance, one of the huge immediate issues must have been the movement of the spine to the back part of the body, as we face forward. For any animal standing on four limbs, its soft organs are naturally underneath, shielded from exposure or attack. Standing on two legs, they are immediately exposed at the front. Some organs like the heart are protected by the rib cage but many, including the stomach and in particular the genitals, are not protected at all. As my daughter says when I express any concern for her safety on her own: 'Don't worry, I know how to bring a man down very quickly.' As a direct result of this exposure, we often take action to protect the softness we thus expose. Historically we have the codpiece as a form of adornment as well as protection. In the trenches of the First World War it was even noted that as a soldier went over the top he tended to lean forward to protect his genitals.[4] Male cricketers wear a protective box when they go out to bat.

Overreliance on outward trappings can become a strong shell that protects and hides. A tortoise carries its heavily armoured shell but without it the tortoise cannot live. Naked tortoises only exist in cartoons. I was reminded of this as I watched a chauffeur-driven limousine pull up on a street in Hamburg. A well-dressed middle-aged man emerged first, followed by a female colleague in a crisp, expensive suit with sunglasses, high-heels and scarf. I contrasted this with a man I'd observed the previous day in the German countryside drawing up in a light-weight electric-powered trike. Neither situation was remarkable but the differences were significant. The trike driver emerged in a leap from his flimsy machine, casually dressed and in search of a place to plug in his vehicle. He was slim and looked highly approachable. Neither his clothing nor his vehicle provided much protection. The couple in Hamburg were by contrast out-wardly impressive. They reminded me of Russian matryoshka dolls as they emerged from a luxury car dressed in smart clothes. They certainly looked the part but I couldn't help noticing that this man was carrying a great deal more weight beneath his business suit. The contrast between the two situations was marked. The man in the lightweight trike had the wheels of a car but no need for a carapace. In London a few days later I reflected on this as I watched people speed about on bicycles. At unarmoured risk yes, but with the ability to stop and smell the air; freedom as the payback.

This process of adding armour both has its limits and works against our core direction of growth. We know armour has its limits because in physical form we can see that the heavier the suit of armour gets the more it restricts us and weighs us down. In both evolutionary and practical terms, the lobster is trapped in its shell and so it is cooked. The simplest way in which the shell stops development can be seen in ammonite fossils,[5] whose beautiful spiral shells reveal how chamber was added on chamber as the structure grew. In furtherance of this basic strategy ammonites sought to protect themselves with more and more elaborate forms of shell protection, adding spines and other extensions which made them even more unpalatable to predators. This same protection ultimately became too great a burden, allowing other adaptations and rival species to take over. Although ammonites were highly successful in the Jurassic and

Cretaceous seas, they are now extinct partly, it is thought, because of a failed reproductive strategy. The over-armoured shell may literally have stopped them connecting.

We have many situations where this physical limit to our armour can be seen. A good example is the Halifax bomber during the Second World War when Leonard Cheshire, who went on to found the Leonard Cheshire Foundation, was a squadron leader. Cheshire became frustrated with the number of bombers that were being lost. He realised this was partly because the aircraft had been weighed down with extra equipment, thus losing power and manoeuvrability. The last straw was the addition of cowls to blanket the exhaust fumes from night fighters. Cheshire ordered the removal of the cowls along with some gun turrets and other non-essential equipment, which transformed the performance of the bombers allowing them to fly faster and higher.[6] Losses soon fell and morale improved.

The parallel problem is that the more time we spend exploring the limits of armour, the less time we spend in developing better co-operative solutions. After the war, Cheshire moved into working with people with disabilities. Like Cheshire, once we step out of armour we can apply our energy to far better ends; developing our awareness of the situation, our trust of others and our creativity. Instead of spending, indeed wasting, energy on armouring ourselves to protect our separateness, we can spend on relationships with others to build on our connectedness.

Ultimately this is about being happy to be naked, metaphorically or literally. As humans we tend to dress up. There's no problem with this, unless we are actively hiding something. If we feel uncomfortable naked, why is that? It can often be because we impose impossible expectations on ourselves and as a result lack confidence. We think that our bodies should be different in some way, closer to our image of perfection. We compare ourselves with others who are, by the way, secretly making exactly the same comparison. It's a judgement we make of ourselves and it takes us away from the reality of what is. To refuse to accept what we are is disrespectful; firstly to ourselves but also to others and, ultimately, to the natural order of things. The only way to start any journey properly is to accept where we really are and to build from there. Thus, even if we do need to change, we must still get comfortable with our current state first. If we are in Birmingham there is no point in planning a journey to Cardiff believing we are in Bristol.

The child inside

The poet Ted Hughes was a complex and brilliant man with a controversial private life. In 1986 he wrote a powerful letter to Nicholas, his son from a previous marriage to Sylvia Plath, whom he had left when Nicholas was a baby.[7] In the letter (which is available in full on-line) Hughes talks about the child he saw inside all of us. We are, he says, only aware of this child as a general crisis of inadequacy, helpless dependence, pointless loneliness or simply a sense of not having a strong enough ego to deal with the turmoil of the external world. This sense is one that most people seem to feel, however frequently or infrequently, throughout their lives, whether or not they can admit it to themselves or their closest friends.

What we have done, Hughes explains, is to build from an early age and then hide behind an armoured secondary self that deals with the outer world and protects the inner child. The problem, Hughes goes on to say, is that that child is the only part of us that really matters. It holds what makes us human and is where our truth and inspiration come from. In Hughes's view, the bits that don't come from the inner child are worthless. This is exactly where the issue lies. What we hold at that emotional, sometimes slightly scared and incredibly vulnerable core is the very heart of our being. We surround it with armour, but that armour has a cost.

The paradox, father explains to son, is that the only time people really feel alive is when they are suffering; when the external everyday armour is overwhelmed by a challenge and the naked inner child is exposed and made visible. This emotional, existential paradox is completed when we find ourselves fighting desperately hard to prevent this essential experience from happening. We instinctively know that we need to invest more heart to truly live and to grow, yet we find ourselves building approaches, structures and lives that protect us from the risk of our exposed nakedness being seen in public.

It is this inner core that we need to get to know and to nurture. The paradox that Hughes talks of sits at the core of the work that needs to be done. Close connection with this inner self holds many of the essential clues. In this inner sanctum we also hold the drivers behind many of the behaviours that can limit us. Exposure of the child is hard and makes us feel vulnerable but through it we grow in confidence. As in the completion of a physical challenge, pushing ourselves to do something we are most fearful of can be our route to growth.

This duality is not just a poet's way of seeing things, it is echoed in much of modern psychology, from Freud's ego and id through Jung's development of persona, front and shadow. The conflict also appears in Erik Erikson's 'identity crisis' and Alfred Adler's 'inferiority complex', and in drama where character is based on the struggle between what the character really is inside and what they project as a front. Think David Brent in *The Office* or Basil Fawlty in *Fawlty Towers*. In both the comedy comes from the way the conflict between the front and the core is made visible to us and exploited for entertainment. Basil's veneer of gentility fails to hide a desperate and hopeless sense of inadequacy in the same way that Brent's bouncy playfulness covers up his loneliness and insecurity.

Front can be a useful tool but put up unwittingly it becomes simply a lack of self-awareness. The danger then, is that we don't understand or control it. Psychoanalyst Stephen Grosz relays a warning story told to him by a woman he met on a flight who was going to visit her mother for the first time in nearly 16 years. The Jewish woman's father had so taken against her blond Catholic boyfriend that he had threatened, and then when she married the man carried out the threat, to stop speaking to her; a lead which her mother had been obliged to follow. The reunion of mother and daughter was only taking place because the mother was divorcing the father. She'd found out that her husband had, all along, been having an affair with his receptionist, who was Catholic and blonde. The daughter's take on the situation was 'the bigger the front, the bigger the back'. The protest made was in direct proportion to the real but hidden issue. Did projecting his own guilt onto his son-in-law really help the father? This unwitting externalisation of our own stuff onto others is a fertile source of conflict. If we don't see what we are doing, transferring the conflict onto someone not only stokes up our anger, but prevents us from dealing with it.

As the stakes get higher the armour, the skin we put over things, looks thicker but the reality can be very different. As we are more successful the risks go up. Business leaders often admit to their executive coaches that they are insecure. Many of us aim for the top in our careers but once we get there we often feel lonely. Insecurities don't get easier as the role gets bigger, they get worse. A friend once asked his father what was the best thing about being retired and was shocked at the answer. 'I no longer have to worry about someone walking into my office and telling me I have been found out,' came the reply. His father, who ended up as MD of a large company, had been chronically insecure all the time. Once, faced with a similar frank admission from a world-weary CEO, I asked a room of senior executives on retreat to put up their hands if they felt this way. Everyone, including myself and the other facilitator, raised their hands in quiet salute to this largely unspoken but prevalent fact. The important thing is dealing with our feelings of uncertainty and harnessing them appropriately. US architectural critic Paul Goldberger even came up with a saying, known as Goldberger's Law, when he reflected on architect Zaha Hadid's suing a journalist over an allegedly libellous book review: 'The greater the success the thinner the skin.'[8]

Two of everything?

> If you want the truth to stand clear before you, never be for or against. The struggle between 'for' and 'against' is the world's worst disease.[9]
> Seng-ts'an, c. 700 BC

> You are either with us or against us in the fight against Terror.
> George W. Bush, 2001

One of the many paybacks of standing up is that we can take advantage of our hands. In primitive times these would have been engaged in the act of walking, balancing, climbing and getting about. In time, bi-pedal man also developed art and language which allowed us to express ourselves more openly to each other, face to face. This is fine up to a point. We each have experiences, stories and then opinions, but the rub is, that they tend to differ. As a result, we tend to polarise. In groups we are even more tribal. We see 'them and us' distinctions in our behaviour. Leaders, reinforce the choices we make. Without necessarily knowing it we daily negotiate this space: we do it in our families, in our organisations, in politics and in our relationship with the rest of the natural world. The way we see the opportunities and the way we negotiate them becomes a crucial life skill.

An expression that I notice and use frequently is that of 'on the one hand this' and 'on the other hand that'. It is both a form of language but also, more importantly, of behaviour. I'd like to introduce this as a way of seeing the paradox. It is our freed up hands in play. Here it is in its simplest form.

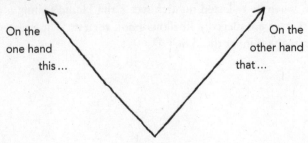

On the
one hand
this …

On the
other hand
that …

Perhaps this is a challenge that comes out of our bi-pedal and bi-modal nature; we do tend to see things as polarities and to feel that one or another must be right. The challenge that *The Power of Soft* seeks to address, is the extra value available to us in the reconciliation of this paradox, at least in part. If each polarity does have its own value, what greater value might be available to those who can successfully combine the most valuable component parts? Physicist Niels Boehr pointed out that although the opposite of a measured fact is a falsehood, the opposite of a profound truth may well be another profound truth. The joy of creative living in this space is to be able to see the best parts of each opposing paradox and to meld them together to shoot forth something new that captures the positive energy of each.

Part of the duality behind the power of soft came clear when I changed roles in a new organisation. The new company was struggling commercially and was not winning as much new business as it wanted to. As I talked to people, the picture I saw had elements in that I recognised from previous experience. This organisation had been a dominant player and tended to take quite aggressive positions with its customers. Once the customers pushed back, the organisation conceded and usually gave way more than it needed to. It was like a parent who at one moment shouted at or argued with their child but later smothered them with kisses. Like the mixed up child, that might grow up from extremes of parenting, the company's customers and even more so, its potential customers, were left feeling confused. The company thought everything was all right because it had ultimately given the customer what it wanted but the customers, when I asked them how they felt, said that we were 'commercially difficult'. What they meant was that they didn't know where they stood with us or what we really wanted. They were also put off by the aggressive signals we were inclined to give off, particularly early on. The overall result was distrust, lack of understanding and a feeling of insecurity in the relationship.

Later, when we were discussing the issue, I stood up, took a pen and used a series of symbols to explain the problem as I saw it. The first symbol I drew represented the positional front we tended to take. It was tough and felt 'spiky' to others. It was almost a weapon we chose to wield. The shape was a simple crude arrow-head:

This spiky armoured front wasn't the whole picture though. What I was seeing here was all the strength being projected forward. What had happened to the back? The answer was clear. This was the duality. We easily flipped from one polarity to the other, as our sales team got more involved. Initially we wanted to protect ourselves then, when push came to shove, we dismissed these initial concerns in order to win the deal. At core, we had very little structure. Behind the strong, position-taking front, there was a lack of self-knowledge. We bent to what we felt at the time. So, to the strong front I added a jelly shape behind it:

The package as a whole looked like it had strength but this was mostly held in the front rather than in the core. Our armour was keeping us upright. If we were a person, we would have had a weak, and thus a medically bad back. What we achieved, we achieved mostly by chance. Our profitability showed this unstructured approach. By not knowing what we really needed we were failing in the most important ultimate measure for a business; our numbers were also poor.

As we talked about the challenge I started to draw an alternative picture of what quickly became a 'strong core' combined with a 'soft front'. Here the shapes were different. Here the core has a structure that builds on the idea of a strong central spine; reminiscent of the old adage: 'get a backbone'. Because of this core strength, the shape was able to change out front to a softer form, represented by a more circular shape, more open to the world:

What we are seeing here is a need to bring the strength back into the core, similar to my own experience with the bad back. If we build our strength from our core, we have more flexibility in how we solve challenges out front in the world, in our dealings with customers and suppliers. This is no different to the challenges experienced by the parent with the child. By setting strong boundaries in the right areas, we can in turn, allow more flexibility. Having core strength allows us to release the full benefits of the softer, more open front. It is only with strength at core that we can really get the best of our softness. This duality is both the paradox of the power of soft itself but also its contribution to exploring and making the best of all the paradoxes we face.

Over time, the componentry of the strong core and the soft front became clearer. Into these shapes, everything I had learned and struggled with over the years, fitted neatly. The Core itself has two major parts, which make up the next two chapters.

Breaking away from position-taking to focus on underlying needs is the subject of Chapter 2. This approach builds on one of the most important breakthroughs in negotiation philosophy, the idea of Principled Negotiation that came out of the Harvard Negotiation Project and which was popularised by Roger Fisher, William Ury and later Bruce Patton in their book *Getting to Yes*, first published in 1981.

To get things really working, the power of soft requires a re-boot of the way we understand power. Power is a critical component that is less stable now than it has been for thousands of years. In Chapter 3 we take the Humpty Dumpty of power off its wall, take it apart and put it back together again.

These first two moves, understanding our real needs and our real power, together make up the substance of the strong core. How they come together and how we build this strength with appropriate boundaries is also key. Chapter 4 starts with a small boy on a train and ends with the errors of Goldfinger.

Once we have attended to our core, the harder, more structural aspects, we can turn our attention to the softer Front. This is where we truly unleash the Power of Soft. There have been a lot of developments in psychology and neuroscience in recent years and there is much benefit to be taken here. Chapter 5 focuses firmly on people and relationships and picks up poets and taxi-drivers on the way. The other component of the Softer Front is our Awareness: how we see things; the power of observation and the dangers of assumption and judgement. Chapter 6 shows what clear perception can do for us, while Chapter 7 brings the soft front together with a focus on listening and being heard. The problem is that our eager mouth tends to tug at the leash. We look at why that is so and introduce the Inner Interrupters. Finally, in Chapter 8 we connect up the rest of the paradox that is the full Power of Soft and see how a little boy and a tree can widen the question still further.

CHAPTER 2

KNOWING THE MOUNTAIN

Corporate team building days can be a time of mixed emotions. This one was no exception. A few days out at a French château had been quite an appealing thought. Now I was here, the truth slowly seeped through to my bones. I was eighteen months into working for this global but Europe-based organisation and was coming to the end of my first assignment. The deal I was working on was the largest loss-making deal anywhere in the company by a country mile. Our job was to get it back to break-even from a position where it was losing tens of millions a year. To say someone had sold us a puppy was an understatement. This one also had systemic family problems and dodgy bowels. The puppy was now doing well, however, and after making a decent impact in my first role in this organisation, I wanted a change. The prospect of catching up with colleagues and working out what I was going to do next drew me into the corporate love-fest. That was until I found out what we were doing. In our rooms we had all found team rugby shirts with our names on the back. Word slowly filtered around that we were going to be expected to wear the shirts to take part in a team building exercise where we'd be taught the Maori Haka. Our hearts fell. With mates this might have been fun; with work colleagues this sort of thing can be quite painful. We donned our shirts and approached the lawn in front of the château with trepidation only to find our CEO already pulling the faces and doing the movements like a native. In for a penny, I thought. Breaking ranks against that backdrop can be a dangerous strategy.

That night at drinks, I got wind of my next assignment, a new deal worth a few hundred million pounds over several years. We were going to be bidding for it against all our major competitors in the IT sector. The deal was with a public educational body. We had some good consulting work in the sector but no big deals. I was told this was a 'must win'. My role was to be the commercial lead. It sounded perfect so I started to ask what the problem was. The issue we needed to fix was our win rate. We were tending to lose deals for commercial reasons: price and terms. At the same time clients were making deals tougher and tougher to win. In the law of supply and demand, power had shifted to the customers, and the suppliers hadn't yet caught up. I was being asked to fix the problem.

Back in the UK we met as a team to prepare for the bid. We were fortunate in having a bid director and a sales lead who not only saw but practised the benefits of planning. They had the idea of getting us together to write a bid response to a request that we had not yet received from the customer. This set the tone. We were already ahead. At that meeting we came up with a strategy in our commercial and legal team that caught the rest of the team's imagination. This was 'The answer is yes, now what is the question?' This might sound mad but we came up with it as a strategy because the negotiation process was going to be limited. The customer's contract was going to be issued to us and we would have to mark it up with our required changes. Any deviations they didn't like would be scored against us. We wanted to change the normal way of looking at things, so instead of starting with what we wanted we would start from what we thought the customer would want. It sounded great in principle so we set it as a strategy.

A few weeks later I got the first mark-up of the contract back from our legal team. It was about 100 pages long and had a similar number of pages of technical and financial appendices. As I looked at the legal comments my heart sank. There were hundreds of things that, according to our legal team, needed to change: a sea of red ink. This was, however, the process that we had committed to as a team.

We then spent days going through the contract again and again. The process was one of hearing, as a team, exactly why we were objecting to something our customers wanted. We had to ask ourselves much more deeply what lay behind our objections. If we wanted to stop the customer coming on our premises, we had to ask ourselves why that was. We then had to look elsewhere in the contract and in the supporting documents and see if something there gave us comfort. If there wasn't we had to ask ourselves if it really mattered. 'Would you die in a ditch over this?' was a question we commonly asked. What I realised again and again was that as an organisation we had got in the habit of taking positions on certain matters and not really understanding why. The things that mattered ran deeper and we weren't currently facing them. If we had all been in a room discussing the fundamental need and challenge with the customer, we would have started to expose real issues. We pushed to explore that difference. This was about building real honesty and self-knowledge.

The other clear issue was that conditions in the market were changing. We needed to find a way to engage the core of our organisation with what customers really wanted now. This was a challenge, as many key decisions were taken centrally by people who rarely meet customers. We needed to find a way to connect our decision-makers to our customers. So, we set up a process of briefing the people who would be involved in the internal approvals for the deal. A small team travelled to head office to brief our heads of functions and to start this process.

Back in the UK office, as we continued to pore over the contract, we grouped concerns together where possible.

In the final week before the bid, our list still contained a couple of hundred assumptions, so I spent a few very long days and nights whittling the list down and negotiating the assumptions internally with the team. Eventually they fitted on half a page of A4. We had consolidated a heap of positions that we had taken as an organisation to produce a shortlist of principle statements that it was difficult to disagree with. The one about staff simply stated the number we expected to take on together with an overall statement about their suitability for the provision of the service. This expressed our need in minimum terms that could be defended to our customer.

We also brought our consolidated list of real issues to the wider team. It was too easy for all of us to operate in silos, with opinions from legal, financial, technical and delivery perspectives not always being reconciled. We found that as we shared more concerns openly in the group, we found more solutions. One person would be worried about an issue but by steering the group to look on the positive side, to consider how big an issue it really was, whether it would really happen and how we'd solved it before, an answer would emerge. By holding clear positive intent, this forum solved many issues in creative ways.

Elsewhere in the discussions on the contract we learnt to get inside the customer's thinking. When they took a position we thought about why. Often I had to challenge a presumption that something had been asked for because the customer wanted to gain advantage over us. Instead, we came to see that all the customer was trying to do was to protect themselves, however inelegantly. Their intent was surely good and I pushed for a team presumption that this was so, rather than its opposite.

The other thing that the process forced us to do was to challenge ourselves and to recognise which points were most important to us. Hundreds of points became a top ten. Eventually we only raised one change on the contract itself; everything else either joined the assumptions list, became a change in technical approach or was something we decided to live with. The work we put in to understand what we really needed is what ultimately helped us be a successful team. By taking the time to challenge ourselves and to grow our self-knowledge, we grew stronger. This is a lesson that is applicable anywhere, in a team or individually.

We won the deal, and looking back is instructive because in the last ten years the industry has changed so much that many of these things now seem normal. Then, they were radical. We spent days going through the reasons why things were problems, reducing them to their bare issues and finding a way through. The time spent doing this hurt. Previously we'd been rebelling against the change in positions without working out what we needed. In a way it was easier for us to stay as we were: fixed, positional. Change had been hard but ultimately it was worthwhile.

One of the accusations we faced on this deal and on others subsequently was the reaction that somehow we had gone 'soft'; we had simply given in. This was a corporate concern that we needed to deal with because whenever anything went wrong it was easy to blame the 'soft' contract. Things did go wrong from time to time and it was important to still recognise and deal with these risks. We hadn't gone soft in the way they meant it, instead we'd rigorously assessed what we needed, asked for it and then made sure that we were easy to deal with.

The facts were that we had not only won the deal, we also made money from day one, which in this industry was unusual. We'd also found ways to protect ourselves. Instead of staying with the hard process of the organisation and the existing ways of doing things, our people- and team-based way of talking everything through, of going over it and reordering it so it worked better had been the key component in our success. I later found out that our win had been extremely narrow. If it hadn't been for one of the pricing mechanisms that we created in our discussions and the customer's favourable interpretation of it, we would not have won at all.

One of our key learnings was that the accusation of being commercially out of step we had previously faced wasn't just to do with the positions we took. It was also to do with the feeling that the customer could never really pin us down. Our strong front hid a soft core that didn't know what it wanted. This meant that although we might take a tough position on an issue, we'd often given in if we were pushed. This was confusing to our customer. It was OK to still hold out for key principles, but we needed to be clear what they were. We also needed to be prepared to explain our reasons and be consistent.

Nothing better summarises the journey we all face in the quest to get what we need, without relying on strong front, than the work of Nan Shepherd. Nan is not a negotiator and has never worked in the corporate world. She was a lecturer in English at Aberdeen University for over forty years and spent much of her spare time walking, especially in the Cairngorm mountains of Scotland. Nan wrote a book, *The Living Mountain*, about her experiences. This is, it seems, a rare thing, as most mountain literature is written by men. What marks Nan out is that she is not interested in the peaks of the mountains. What interests her is the 'being' she gets from the mountains, not the 'doing'. Nan wants to explore the core of the mountain, the part that we never see, where the bulk of the mountain is. Mont Blanc may be 4,810 metres high but the road tunnel that goes through it is 11.6 kilometres long. For Nan the mountain is what's inside, not the summit. Something may push us to the top but it also disconnects us from the core of the mountain, the connection with other mountains and the energy-carrying streams that make their way down to connect and join. Life is in the lower borders. Nan has a fascination with depth and detail: 'The more one learns of the intricate interplay of soil, altitude, weather, and the living tissues of plant and insect … the more the mystery deepens.'[1] In Nan's words, 'The thing to be known grows with the knowing', or as Patrick Kavanagh, the Irish poet, says, 'In the world of poetic experience it is depth that counts, not width'.[2] This is a preparedness to accept and a joy to explore the intimate. It is an acceptance of connectedness that Robert Macfarlane beautifully summarises in an introduction to a 2011 edition of Nan's book: 'We are co-natural with the world and it with us, but we only ever see it partially.'[3]

To use the mountain metaphor, what we so easily do in our negotiations is scale the peaks. We take positions which we believe in. In solid corporate surroundings, in our team meetings and the hard policy structures that follow them, we can end up reinforcing and solidifying these positions. This feels good and gives us comfort. What we come to realise eventually, though, is that this 'top of the mountain' position is isolated from the people we need to understand, to live with and do business with. They are either on the tops of their own mountains, or are waiting for us in the valley below. It is the valley where the community between us exists and where we both need to go. Shouting from the top of the mountain is no way to communicate towards a shared solution. Being able to zoom out and see the topography for what it is can help. If we were able to get up in a helicopter above both positions, we would probably see that there are paths through the mountains either established or still to be explored. It is this wider view of the terrain taken in a selfless or independent way that helps us see the way forward. It is what William Ury calls 'going to the balcony': a place from which we can see things clearly, removed from the action and the emotional charge of the moment.

From the perspective of the balcony we can see both our shared intent and the true objective of what we are trying to achieve. This reminder of true intent is pointed out in the ancient Chinese treatise on military tactics, *The Art of War*, attributed to Sun Tzu. The simple but so easily forgotten truth is that the objective of war is actually to achieve peace. Battles are all very well but are they serving the overall objective? In negotiation the trick is to step back and ask both parties 'What is our common objective?' In the mountain example it is a question of moving down into the valley, the area between mountains, where the mountain structures actually meet and finding out what we have in common rather than how we differ. Starting with communality is the key lesson. It's one of the reasons why the English talk about the weather. We are not interested in what the weather actually is. We are interested in exploring viewpoints through the medium of the weather. Seeing the same things in the physical world helps us see similar things in the more complex ones we work in. Noting a difference in the way we see the weather might also explain other differences. Once, in a difficult negotiation, I asked my opposite number where she was going on her holidays. She explained that she was spending time in a deep, wet, dark Scottish wood. She enjoyed cold and damp weather. In that moment I had even more of an understanding as to why we were struggling to agree.

The Art of War has also inspired another model of levels useful in leadership, both organisationally and in negotiation. The ancient text has been translated to say:

> All men can see these tactics whereby I conquer, but what
> none can see is the strategy out of which victory is evolved.

This produces a simple and very useful hierarchy of thinking that I was introduced to by journalist and writer Gavin Esler. Esler proposes this as a key way of thinking for leaders and cites it as the model used by Alastair Campbell to guide Labour's 1997 General Election victory in the UK.[4] It was also used to produce a strategy to sustain power for Tony Blair, at least initially. Used consistently, the model helps give clarity between the tactical, strategic and overall objective levels. It serves as a useful reminder as to why we are doing things and allows a leader to set context and objective while allowing the wider team who will execute tactically to participate in developing a series of strategic initiatives that support the objective.

The model looks like this:

Objective – Our overall purpose – the *Why*?

Strategy – *How* are we going to achieve this?

Tactics – *What* we do, day to day

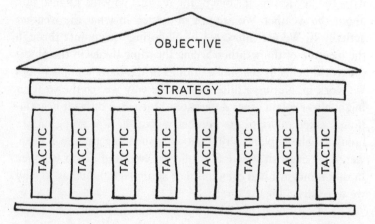

This simple model is sometimes referred to as 'OST' and often gets added to. Its key value is as a constant alarm system of the essential linkage between what is happening on the ground right now and how it links to our overall objective. There is little point in winning a small, tactical provision in the contract if it doesn't link to your overall aim of achieving a profitable, worthwhile deal overall or achieving a sustainable and valuable relationship. This is true not only for yourself or your organisation but also for the other party. It is also true of your joint endeavour. Does what you are doing now serve the objective you are really aiming for? In difficult times it can be beneficial to force ourselves to pull back to that objective either in our own minds or in open conversation. Could we, for example, say: 'Thank you for that, Jack. I can see that this would be a possible solution but do you feel it is something that would encourage us to work together successfully over the longer term'? Being able to move between levels like this, to move out of the merely tactical, can be the lifesaver that rescues a situation as we appeal to someone's higher motives.

'Right idea, Mr. Bond...'
'...But wrong pussy.'

In simple terms, my job in the first days of my career as a lawyer was to find ways to further my client's position. If we wanted to get out of an existing relationship or to guarantee commitment to a new one, we found ways to argue for what we wanted. We then set up contracts to secure it. Our focus was always on building a robust position for our side. Protection and rights were at the core of this. We built contracts that secured everything we wanted or worried about and issued letters of advice telling clients about their rights under old contracts that hadn't worked out. Over time the measure of success was the weight of the armour and it became a more heavily armoured process as we built more protection and ever greater armour for our clients. It felt like we were always building an attack or a defence. The things we built felt a bit like these:

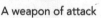

A weapon of attack   or a protective structure

The main effect of this was to provoke a Newtonian opposite and equivalent reaction in the people our clients were aiming to do business with. If you start to build weapons, the other side's armourers also will be set to work. If we build a castle, the enemy's siege weapons generally improve soon after. Such are the simple dynamics of warfare. We could often see it even in the letterheads as opposing lawyers changed. Law firms are employed to do the serious business of armouring but also to give the reassuring whiff of reputation, available funds and seriousness of intent. Many times over the small firm was ditched and the other side employed a big name, either as a reaction or as a pre-emptive strike. There was one particular firm that everyone feared in any serious litigation. If the other side appointed them it was like finding out that Voldemort or Darth Vader was now facing you. The investments we made were in weapons and armour, attack and protection against failure; our own special effects. We were no longer investing in relationships; we promoted hostilities. In that situation it's only the armourers who get rich.

I'd long since realised this approach was overly simplistic and that it could be rather antagonistic. For a while I'd been thinking about what I could do to change it. One day a test came along. My client was a partner in a large consulting firm and the battle of the day was over ownership of some software the firm was developing for a customer. Ralph, the partner, explained that the customer wanted to own this software because they were paying for it. On the other hand, he very much wanted to own the software because he wanted to use it as a base for developing further products for other customers. It was also the policy of the consulting firm to retain ownership of their product wherever possible. Ralph was conflicted. He knew that it was often not possible to retain ownership of products the firm developed for its customers and yet he felt obliged to fight for it.

What we were facing looked like this:

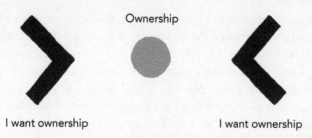

Ownership

I want ownership   I want ownership

This time there was a particular object in the middle and it had a clear name.

What had happened is that both the consulting firm and the client had become fixed on the thing that stood between them: ownership of the software. As a result, stronger and stronger arguments were being put by either side. The customer's biggest argument revolved around the money they were paying. The consulting firm argued that their policy was not to give customers ownership of software they developed. This incensed the customer, who didn't see why the firm's policy should take priority over their needs. The consulting firm argued that if they weren't going to own the fruits of their labours, then they would have charged higher fees. At this the customer laughed. 'Higher fees! You must be joking, you are already ripping us off.' As the arguments mounted, trust was suffering. The positions each were taking, particularly the consultants', were damaging the relationship.

Against this backdrop, Ralph asked 'What can I do?'.

My response was to ask Ralph if he knew why they wanted to own the software. He replied, 'Yes, of course I do, they feel it's theirs because they are paying for it.' 'OK,' I said, 'I get that, but have you asked them what are the things they want to achieve by owning it?' Ralph eventually conceded that he didn't know the answer. He was also reluctant to ask. So we hatched a plan to go and talk to the customer and find out. This made Ralph nervous and he was also quite sceptical. My sense was that this was largely because he didn't know the answer and didn't really know where this was headed. This uncertainty was alien to the firm and to Ralph.

What resulted was a conversation with the customer at which we sought to change the dynamics. We started the meeting on neutral ground and then stressed our joint interests in getting the job done. We eventually came to the main question and asked what it was that the customer hoped to get out of owning the software. It took a while to get to the bottom of it. What they wanted most was to have exclusive use of the product that they had paid for in order to be ahead of their competitors. When we asked more questions about what this really meant, it became clear that this applied for a limited period and only to particular elements of the software. As a result, we started talking about giving them commitments that would meet these needs. We could see a route through where we would agree not to license these elements of the software to others for a limited period. In return they were happy that we kept the ownership. Suddenly the game had changed.

It became clear that they had never thought about what ownership meant for them. There were downsides to what they wanted that they hadn't considered. When we asked them how they would go about protecting their rights against others, who might copy the software, they soon decided that they would not want that hassle. They also had no desire to develop the software. The more we talked about the detail the clearer it became that discussions to date had focused on a goal that was too simplistic. They were now happy to give us ownership because they saw elements of it to be a burden to them. What we did in this situation was to change the nature of the discussion. Instead of focusing on the frontal position each side was taking we concentrated on the core of what each side really needed; we took the time to step back and to consider what that really was for each of us. This gave us a way forward. That way forward was not obvious from the beginning; it emerged as we learnt more about what we each needed.

When we adopt positions we are not only moving away from other's needs, we are also disconnecting from our own needs. Positions are wants. In a consumer society based on economic growth we have begun to see little difference between the two. We are encouraged to fulfil needs by acquiring things to fulfil our desires. We may seek the latest fashion. The item of clothing we buy is not a need. Honesty is to acknowledge that the underlying need is something else: a desire to fit in, to be appreciated or noticed, to be loved. Without that understanding we can go on searching for its fulfilment. Our real needs are often more modest. In scaling the peak we can leave a large a gap of dishonesty between the position we take and the truth, the real need, behind it. The psychologist Carl Jung called this gap the 'shadow' – the space between our true self and the mask or persona we adopt. The bigger the gap between the front, the mask, and the true self, the bigger the shadow. Shadows tend to come with a cost.

Failing to understand our real needs is also a sure recipe for depression. The person who doesn't know what they need is on a directionless journey of stumble and wander. Unfortunately, many of us have had to accept that not getting our needs met is a normal situation. As we grow up we are often taught that somehow we are 'good' if we can deny our needs. This might be true for our wants but it is not for our needs. We need what we need. If we really need love, to be denied it hurts. This is something which the process of Non-Violent Communication pioneered by Marshall Rosenberg focuses on.[5] It was borne out by a situation a friend of mine found himself in. Some years previously, he had lost the love of his life when their relationship ended abruptly. Ever since then he had flitted from relationship to another, but none lasted more than a few months. As I listened to my friend talk I began to wonder what he really needed. On the surface he said he was looking for a woman to marry and settle down with. We talked more and with some of Rosenberg's key questions in my head I asked my friend what he really need-ed that he wasn't getting. I also asked him what he needed to have in this moment that he didn't have. We went through a process of unpeeling several layers and I asked the questions a number of times before we finally got to the real answer. What he needed was people, ideally someone but most importantly family and close friends near to him, who cared about him and loved him. He'd lacked unconditional love as a child and this is what he was seeking. As we talked he realised that in the short term he was more likely to get this from the close friends and family that he had than from any new relationship. Because he hadn't really understood his need he was focusing on the wrong strategy. The women he met also found him overly 'needy' because he always wanted too much from them. He was depressed because he wasn't meeting his needs. This process of focusing on defining what our real needs are and then building a strategy to meet them can't be beaten for its simplicity or effectiveness. The problem is that it is so simple and basic that many of us fail to do it.

There is also something both these examples reveal about how we can take our needs and misunderstand them. We then externalise them into a relationship with an object. The solution we grab at is to simply see that object as the solution. This needs displacement is going on all around us in the fog of a lack of truth between wants and needs. Ownership, a new partner or a new acquisition becomes what we focus on. If that object is a person, we tend to objectify them, which causes its own problems. We will come back to how we objectify people in Chapter 5. The realisation of the displacement is like the classic example of getting a miser to talk about his money and realising that the problem he has isn't the money at all. The miser suffers because of his relationship with money and what it substitutes for. No amount of money will satisfy him. What he is really after is something else entirely.

Many of the early Bond films feature the arch villain Ernst Stavro Blofeld, head of SPECTRE, known for his habit of stroking his white Persian cat. The stroking is not just for the cat's benefit. In *You Only Live Twice* the cat tries to escape Blofeld's clutches: he wants to hold the cat more than the cat wants to be held. If you follow this theory, the cat-stroking is probably a better clue to Blofeld's real needs than his ambition to take over the world. The terror, revenge and extortion that SPECTRE specialises in is like the outward face of many villains, a reactive expression of a thwarted inner need. Blofeld's cat provides the route to the real answers but it's not a straightforward one. In *Diamonds are Forever*, faced with a number of Blofeld clones, Bond takes the extreme measure of kicking the cat to see which Blofeld it runs to. The cat reacts as expected and Bond, with his single shot, dispatches the villain. Moments later another cat, Blofeld's actual feline, appears. Unfortunately, Bond has shot the wrong Blofeld because there is also more than one cat. The answers to knowing what people need aren't always as obvious as they might seem.

Mapping and charting

One of the jobs here is to be able to explore territory. It's a difficult one because all we see on the surface is a position taken by someone: 'I want ownership', 'I want a girlfriend' or 'I need to take over the world'. It's usually quite a directive expression of a definite solution to our needs. This simple starting request seems like it is the answer. What we've realised is that this position can be a front which represents a deeper need or needs. What we initially see is the pointy bit at the top of the mountain. It's rare that anyone voluntarily and initially shares with us the real needs that underlie the position they have taken.

To get over this superficial, surface way of seeing things we esentially need to dig around and look. Digging technique comes later. The part that we can develop further here is helping to create a map of the territory so we can start to navigate through it more confidently and knowledgeably.

The best-known mapping tool for needs is still Abraham Maslow's Hierarchy of Needs,[6] first published in 1943. This is now mostly represented as a triangle but in his initial paper explaining his theory Maslow used no distinct shape. His levels are as follows:

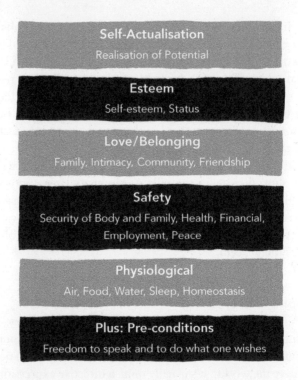

In simple terms what Maslow showed was that we first need satisfaction of basic levels of need. We need air, food, water and sleep before anything else. Then we move on to our safety needs, the roof over the head, before we progress to love and belonging. Maslow believed that people moved through the hierarchy in stages; so that at any given time their needs at each level might be partly met. He gave an example in which an individual might be 10 per cent Self-Actualised but still have 40 per cent Esteem, 50 per cent Love, 70 per cent Safety and 85 per cent of their Physiological needs being met. If that is so, it is the movement of the individual through the hierarchy that might be triangular rather than the hierarchy itself. Each person's shape in the hierarchy is likely to be different. The question becomes one of focussing on the individual and the distribution of their needs rather than simply placing someone on the hierarchy.

Maslow's model is useful in helping to identify where a particular person's interests lie. A managing director with pictures of himself with celebrities all over his office may be heavily focused on his self-esteem and status needs. If we want this MD to get interested we need to find something that matches his needs. The fact that our project is good for the environment may not be enough. If the project could connect him with a celebrity campaigner then suddenly we might have his interest. The photo that we take with the celebrity becomes a thing that can be shown in the office and mentioned to friends. On the other hand another MD may be turned off by anything so showy. The model might be simplistic but often these basic things are what we need to attend to in the moment. They are also an honest truth about what motivates us that we are unlikely to want to admit openly.

Understanding simple human needs is also important in the most complicated negotiations. Yes, the deal is important but so is refreshment, rest and civility. We get so involved in the matter at hand that we can easily forget the basics. If someone is tied up in a complex negotiation, what they might really need is as simple as someone booking a hotel for the night for them or the suggestion of a toilet break. Such things may be quietly bugging someone and giving them consideration shows respect for the person.

The messages we get from people about their needs are also frequently confusing. In answer to this, I see Nan Shepherd's focus on the heart of the mountain to be critical. If we make the hierarchy our model, our focus too easily becomes getting to the peak. The lofty peak blinds us to the importance of the stable, connected base. In truth, the base of the mountain again holds the clues to many of the questions we face. Maslow wisely observed the effect that sustained satisfaction of their basic needs has on people, particularly when these needs are met early in their lives:

> It is just the ones who have loved and been well loved and
> who have had many deep friendships who can hold out
> against hatred, rejection or persecution.

This links to John Bowlby's theory of Attachment,[7] which was revolutionary after the Second World War. Bowlby showed that the secure attachment to their caregiver achieved by around two thirds of young children in early life was what allowed them to navigate the world confidently and safely. It is not the distancing of a mother figure that creates the child's ability to go forth safely alone but rather the security that is unconditionally provided as an initial base. The secure base allows confidence to travel. The child needs to journey but forcing that travel without creating a secure base does not work.

Maslow answers what is now a frequent question on his model: the frequent imbalance between love and esteem, where esteem seems to be more important to a person than love. What Maslow says is that:

> Such people, who lack love and seek it, may try hard to put
> on a front of aggressive, confident behaviour. But essentially
> they seek high self-esteem and its behaviour expressions more
> as a means-to-an-end than for its own sake; they seek self-
> assertion for the sake of love rather than for self-esteem itself.

Thus, in the hierarchy model what we might notice is that a stage (love in this case) has been missed, causing imbalance in the next layer. This is the same imbalance that manifests in a Strong Front and indicates a weakness in the core. This front to back imbalance is a key feature of the way we work. What you see on the surface isn't necessarily the thing itself. It can be (and if it is on the surface it is likely to be) a reaction to an opposite happening, in the core. As Jeremy Rifkin puts it:

> Is it possible that human beings are not inherently evil or
> intrinsically self-interested and materialistic, but are of a very
> different nature – an empathic one – and that all the other

drives that we have considered to be primary – aggression, violence, selfish behaviour, acquisitiveness – are in fact secondary drives that flow from repression or denial of our most basic instinct?[8]

Rifkin's point explains a key confusion that many expressed needs are actually inversions of missing needs, so what is expressed as one thing might only really be met by a more basic need that has been denied. This flow of primary to secondary, back to front, can easily catch us out. Perhaps Maslow as well as Blofeld has a cat to trick us. In particular, in Maslow's model, deficiencies in the Esteem layer can be well explained by structural imbalaces in the Love and Belonging layer below. We seek esteem in satisfaction of love and connection.

Changing chairs

It's all well and good talking about moving from positions to understanding needs but in practice pulling back from or changing a position is more complex. First we have to see our position like a chair that we are sitting in, to be able to get up, move around and assess it from the point of view of others; knowing something and doing something about it are two different things. What is more, the advice we get can be confusing. Consider these quotes:

> The reasonable man adapts himself to the world: the unreasonable man persists in trying to adapt the world to himself. Therefore all progress depends on the unreasonable man.
> George Bernard Shaw, *Man and Superman*

> When we are no longer able to change a situation … we are challenged to change ourselves.
> Victor E. Frankl[9]

In 1961 Dr Seuss published a compilation of stories that I was lucky enough to be given by my uncle on my third birthday in

1968. I'm not sure what I made of it at three but this book has stayed with me all my life. I recommend all four stories in *The Sneetches and Other Stories*, but particularly the second: 'The Zax'. This is a story of not one Zax but two. They seem identical except in one key characteristic: one is a North-Going Zax and one is a South-Going Zax. The two Zax, making tracks, meet one day, foot to foot and face to face, in the prairie of Prax. The North-Going Zax protests first with the claim that he always goes north and demands that the South-Going Zax gets out of his way. The South-Going Zax inevitably responds that he always goes south. He points out that the North-Going Zax is in his way and asks him to move to let him go south in his 'south-going groove'. At this the North-Going Zax announces proudly that he never takes a step to one side and to prove that he won't change his ways he promises to stand where he is for fifty-nine days. The South-Going Zax ups the ante by offering to stand where he is for fifty-nine years and cites a rule he learnt as a boy never to budge, 'Not an inch to the west! Not an inch to the east!' The South-Going Zax's final threat is to stay here not budging even if it makes both of them and the whole world stand still.

The rest of the world does not stand still. It merely accepts the fixity of the Zax and works its way around them. A highway comes through and the Zax are seen still facing each other in the centre of a roundabout, and underneath a bypass. This is one of the great paradoxes of life. As humans we seek towards pattern, order and certainty. As such, the built and planned environment becomes our norm. In the natural world, change is continual. The pace of change is different but everything is moving. Some plants can be seen to grow by the day and a flower can open to and then move to face the sun. A glacier may appear not to move, then fracture and crash. Land masses look permanent but many are still moving, carried by the convection currents beneath them or recovering from the pressure caused by the last ice age. Even the Universe, is apparently still expanding after the Big Bang. It is not the world that is fixed. It is human behaviour that imposes fixed structure on natural change. Indeed the more we like nature the more we tend to occupy and build on it. We build suburbs to enjoy space, freedom and access to nature and by doing so compromise the very thing that we prize.[16] The things we build tend not to be changeable and have to be defended from change by maintenance. If we don't weed the path, cut the grass and prune the trees they will become overgrow and our structures will suffer. Change is natural, fixity isn't.

There is something about getting up before sunrise that helps with creativity. Before the sun gives light and shape to things there is less structure in the world, the mind is more free. The conscious structuring mind is perhaps less awake and less likely to impose its agenda. So it is early in life. The educationalist Sir Ken Robinson, in his now famous TED talk and in a subsequent lecture at the Royal Society of Arts, has famously attacked the factory nature of the schooling process to which we subject our children. Instead of allowing children to flower softly at their own pace, encouraging their creativity and curiosity, we subject them to a hard year group 'Class of ...' model that has features of the Victorian factory. As Robinson puts it, 'in place of curiosity, we have a culture of compliance'.[10] At school children are expected to comply and many of our memories of school are of hard structure and discipline. By the time we are adults very few of us believe that we are creative. A scary test is simply to ask children of different ages whether they are creative. As children progress through school the proportion who claim to be creative declines rapidly. This is a sobering thought. Creativity is a process not only of noticing, recalling and coming up with ideas but of connecting, selecting, crafting and promoting them. Creativity is something we were born with as part of our birthright and is an ability that grows with use. In using our creativity we also learn which parts of the process we are particularly good at as individuals. Without creativity, growth and change we lose an important part of who we are and what we can offer.

Fixity and fluidity

An Australian friend told me a story about his travels in search of both learning and culture in Australia.[12] Like most non-native Australians he had grown up with strong connections with European culture, such as children's stories and myths. One of the things that perplexed him was the idea of the castle. In Europe these are not just the stuff of legend; they are part of the landscape. Our history is one of attack and defence, and the castle has played a part in that. The castle is both a real taking of a position and a symbol of position-taking and defence.

Australia's history is very different and there are no castles. Or so we thought. One day on my friend's travels he spotted what he thought must be a castle. The overall shape was similar and the battlements impressive. The area around it had been kept clear and there were means of patrolling the direct vicinity, in case of a breach of its fortifications. As someone who had never seen a castle, he was fascinated. He investigated further, and imagine his surprise when the castle turned out to be Pentridge Prison.

The difference between a castle and a prison is obvious. One is designed to keep people out and the other to keep people in. Their effect is the same, however: a rigid control of the entry and exit of people. In a castle, your focus is on protection but by focusing on keeping others out you are effectively locking yourself in. As soon as you have something to protect there is a potential downside of wanting to defend it. Holding tends to go hand in hand with having. If you hold something, you are less open to other possibilities. As native American-trained tracker Tom Brown Jr. says:

> The white man builds a shelter, and it becomes his prison ...
> he separates himself from the earth and refuses to budge.
> Therefore he is always sick.[13]

The problem is that in subjecting projects in life to hard discipline we lose fluidity. This is something easily seen in disputes. A dispute starts as a difference in opinion or position. At the time it starts there is a degree of fluidity to it. Actions could easily be taken both to find a solution to the hard problem and to catch any softer human differences that might be occurring between the parties. Over time a dispute that is not caught in such a way tends to escalate and solidify. At a certain point legal or other external advice might be taken. An investment is made in establishing or confirming the positions taken and more people come on board to support each of the positions. What was fluid becomes fixed and difficult to move. The traditional method of resolving the situation is to continue the investment in fixity and ultimately to ask a third party, judge, court or arbitrator to decide the answer. The process is expensive and disempowering. There may be a winner but there is also a loser and usually more loss on both sides than we like to admit.

This increase in fixity is similar to building a house. When we start a building project the parameters are quite open. We might have a plot of land that enables a property of a certain size and aspect to be built. We also have a budget that may be limited or flexible. In many other respects the project has fluidity: construction method, layout, materials and fittings are all things that we can make choices about. As we progress things become more and more fixed. We choose a builder, we plan the layout, we fix the plumbing and electrics, we choose the tiling. At a certain point we may encounter a problem with an aspect of the build that we would not have had earlier. In the later stages the fact that the special (and as it now turns out, rare) tiling that we have carefully selected is delayed by two months becomes a huge problem. Whereas a few months previously we would simply have changed it, now we have a contract for it. At problem points we have to ask ourselves what has caused the fixity and whether we can regain some of the earlier fluidity.

This movement from fluidity to fixity doesn't always have to be the case. In the fast-changing world of IT, 'agile' systems building has been carried out for years now. The idea of developing a complex system by starting with a simple operational one and fleshing it out as required is something developers are now able to do. The development team of a new online retail bank are doing exactly that. They start with simple procedures and design solutions according to the practical needs that emerge rather than going through a long planning process to define and deal with every possibility before they start. This is also the approach some planners take with 'desire paths'. Instead of pre-planning where paths will run, the architect allows paths to be created by people as they travel from place to place, say across a park. After a while such a path can be adopted with more formal paving. We thus get the path people would choose, if their choice was unfettered. In construction terms it is the equivalent of returning to the style of building that was practised hundreds of years ago before building became more of a planned or even factory style process.

Instead of planning a scheme and perhaps specifying and shipping in complex components such as windows from factories hundreds or even thousands of miles away, houses used to be built from locally sourced components by either its eventual occupiers and their friends or local craftsmen or a combination. If a beam that had been forested or found didn't quite fit it was cut to shape. Walls were made, wattle and daub from natural materials found locally. Flexibility was present throughout and people necessarily played a much greater part in the construction. Instead of hard structured and planned process, a soft fluid approach is taken. People have a different role in this system.

This approach is not just something that is rooted in the past. Contemporary buildings can take this route, as was proven by woodsman Ben Law in an episode of Channel 4's *Grand Designs* programme. Ben built his wooden cruck-framed house in this fluid manner for £28,000 with the help of friends and ended up not only being voted by viewers as the best Grand Design ever but also presenter Kevin McCloud's favourite project. There is a quiet message in our choice when we privately applaud this type of approach. We like this fluid attitude in others even though we might struggle to do it ourselves. The insight here is that this hard, fixed approach has its limits. The idea of rock gives us certainty but rock itself shows us that hard is just soft that has given in to pressure. It is the shortness of time we have, that

deceives us. Heat and pressure forms rock from soft components; in the form of mud, sediment, sand and liquid. Over time
things simply change and rock will also. Even the land we live on
changes, most of it was once covered in water and likely will be
again. Life is soft.

In organisations this idea of fixity contrasts with the fluidity
of change present in the day to day. To try to capture this, the
man who invented the term 'mid-life crisis', Elliot Jaques, also
invented the idea of 'Requisite Organisation' which leadership
consultant and author Warren Bennis further developed into
four ways of looking at an organisation: the manifest, the
assumed, the extant and the requisite. At one end of the scale the
manifest is the system as it is designed; the org chart, if you like.
Then there is the assumed, that which people believe really
exists. Next there is the extant, what it really is. Finally, there is
the requisite, what it would be if it were in accord with reality.
The four elements put in a scale from controlled to more open
are as follows:

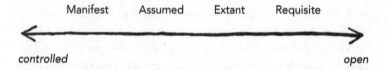

This throws up at least two points. Firstly, there must be a tie
between organisational and individual effectiveness if there is a
close match between the ends of this spectrum. Strong identity
depends on coherence between these viewpoints. An organisation that sees itself as one thing but needs to be another will not
benefit from that schism. Secondly, 'requisite' has a growing
draw. Increasingly this is where organisations are going with
evolving systems of management rather than imposed ones.
Why would anything want to be other than what it needs to be?
In order to secure maximum evolutionary advantage from
everyone who is able to contribute to an organisation or a
challenge, we have to ask ourselves which end of the scale is
more likely to give us good answers. How open are we going to

be to inputs from the external world, such as the desire path, when we design?

Fixity undoubtedly has its place. It is more justified if we are talking about a simple system, such as a thermostatic control. The thermostat has a fixed governing framework we want it to operate in. If the temperature goes up beyond a certain point, we want the heating system to cut out. A challenge to the thermostatic system is probably not something we want to encourage. Organising a large crowd to perform a task consistently may also occasionally require this approach. If we want people to move towards a particular fire exit, we need to be clear on the instruction. In a complex organisation or discussion this may not be the answer we want. Everything around us is changing faster and faster. We desperately need to encourage people to look for new information and to test our existing assumptions and beliefs. Today we have to challenge and be prepared to disrupt our models all the time or we will fall behind.

Writer, professor and business guru Roger Martin calls this place of not budging 'contented model defence' and contrasts it to a freer place of 'optimistic model seeking'.[14] In this move to fixity the key shifts are from optimism to contentment and from seeking to defence. We become happy with what we have and we defend it. In this move we stop our seeking and our efforts go into building defences. This is the castle exactly. In a castle you are safe but there is a danger that there is no longer any journeying or seeking. To be aware of just how dangerous this can be for us is the first step. Then, the trick is to notice it and rediscover the option of flexibility. Instead of worrying about that feeling of uncertainty that can paralyse us all, ask yourself, whether you'd prefer to be fixed or fluid in your approach. Then consider whether the fearful frisson of uncertainty you might feel is such a bad thing. Might it not help to keep us on our toes?

Finally, if you still need to, think about what is stopping any change. The simple fact is that change involves loss. If you ever struggle to make a change or see someone else is struggling, ask yourself what it is that you or they are losing. Coming to terms with what we fear losing is the final key to change. What comforts does the castle hold? The comfort of the castle might be nice but what are we not seeing in the wide lands outside that might enrich us more?

A crack in everything?

In the commercial sphere and in procurement particularly a new generation of leaders are emerging who negotiate differently. Instead of doing what is often described as 'screwing suppliers into the ground' they openly look for opportunity and value. Key to this approach is an engaging curiosity, a low sense of ego and a belief that people are actually good, and if you let them they will do good things. David Wyer is such a leader and one of the most inspirational people I have ever spoken to: in the time I spend with David more new ideas emerge than I can usually cope with. Fundamental to David's approach is his openness to new thinking and his willingness to change his view based on what he hears. When I asked why David was like this he told me that he made a major breakthrough in the early 2000s when he watched the BBC programme *Child of Our Time*. This series follows the lives of twenty-five children, all born in 2000. What David noticed was the quality of relationship one mother in particular had with her child. Although she had fewer advantages than others, her son's love for her was unconditional and unquestioning. She knew that she was flawed and made sure her son realised that she knew this. She had a drink problem and was clear that she didn't know everything and couldn't provide everything. As a result, her son knew there was space for him to grow into, perhaps to compensate.

David saw a contrast with other parents in the programme who were trying to be perfect. They seemed less real, more two-dimensional. Watching this he realised that he didn't want to be a leader who tried to be perfect. Instead he decided that he would be honest about his strengths and admit that he wasn't good at and didn't know everything. David admitted, even today, that many people do not understand this approach and that he is often criticised for not attending to the details that he knows he is not good at. Fortunately his approach gets results in negotiations. He is also someone who people want to work with and for. David is interested in what others bring and provides them with the opportunity to grow.

David also admitted to me that it is not always easy for him to follow this model. In a pressurised environment being an expert who knows the answer is what people expect, particularly at a senior level. David notices that occasionally when he starts to give greater direction his behaviour is incongruent with his beliefs and he starts struggling to engage people. At that point he has to remind himself that he is not and does not want to be the person who stands up and knows it all. Instead of being a fountain of all knowledge David wants to continue to be a sponge. This way he can continue to learn more and, instead of fire hosing his audience with his point of view, invite more contributions from others.

The space David curates as a leader is ultimately a creative one. This approach of trusting to ourselves comes not with answers, but with encouragement and, crucially, belief in our own resources. Instead of being an imposition or an enforcement of any hard external answer it goes in the opposite, altogether softer direction, in search of the internally-sourced, vernacular product of our own experience and imagination, in the knowledge that by giving our support rather than our instruction, we will find the way.

Nowadays David cites Leonard Cohen as his musical guide. Cohen's wisdom in his song 'Anthem' is for us to forget the conceit of an externally sourced 'perfect' answer to our challenges but rather to know, as David has found, both that there is a hidden entrance – 'a crack' – in everything, and that it is through this crack that our greatest inspirations, 'the light', enter our lives.

This approach creates space to grow. Instead of occupying the space, it champions the possibility of there being plenty more space to grow into. It also works for each of us individually. There are echoes here of the words of the wise Greek stoic Epictetus:

If you want to improve, be content to be thought foolish and stupid.

Knowing we are not perfect is the acknowledgement we need to make. Crucially it also operates when we collaborate with others or lead teams. Physically, it appears as a stepping to one side together with an invitation to enter into the empty space. This contrasts with our tendency, as experts, to stand at the front and dominate the space, knowing all the answers. Expertise has its place but leading with it can create a dependent, limited frame of thinking, in others and ourselves.

Soul dreams

On the morning after Nelson Mandela's death, in December 2013, I was travelling by train and as I changed trains I was following a very well-dressed gentleman. I was curious about him and couldn't help but overhear part of his mobile phone conversation. I'll never know who he was or who he was speaking to but I distinctly remember what he said. In the characteristic manner of the eccentric he was running slightly counter to the mood of the country on this fateful morning. He was reminding his friend that Mandela hadn't always been such a hero. The interesting-looking stranger had a long memory and was recalling, with a degree of vigour, the fact that when Mandela first came to London after his release, he had not always been welcomed publicly at the front door of Downing Street, but rather ushered in quietly at the back.

This story is a quiet reflection on the paths of the really great. To be really great you don't start great, at least not externally in the world. To be the champion of a momentous change you don't usually get up most of the way through the change to join the bandwagon. It's more likely that you are there early and start the wagon rolling. When you first stand up it's likely to be pretty lonely. It's also likely that you will be standing there alone for some time. That takes inner strength and a degree of stubbornness. This is the situation into which George Bernard Shaw's words about the reasonable and unreasonable man can legitimately be played. We do depend on a degree of persistence in order to achieve progress.

Going against the flow is not a generic recommendation but rather a skill that we all need selectively from time to time, either to change our own ingrained habits or to challenge the group. Some people will always find this easier than others. My interesting fellow passenger fell firmly into this category, for even as the world went into mourning, he was not simply joining in but making a point about social change. There are characters who are good at this; they are often at one end of the scale, successful entrepreneurs or, at the other end, social pariahs.

The key here is that we hold our position at the right level. It should inspire rather than control. It is Martin Luther King's 'I have a dream' that sets others off to achieve their own solutions. It is not 'Hi, I am Martin, and this is my plan of what I think we should do'. This is a vision that we can commit to and hold at core. It is not a frontal position, it is part of the Strong Core. As we will find out, commitment to core principles is paradoxically essential to building the strong core.

CHAPTER 3

HARNESSING POWER

The Punch paradox

David Cameron, on his election as Conservative Party leader in December 2005, made a promise to end 'Punch and Judy' politics. Cameron acknowledged the colleagues he had beaten to the leader's job, set the tone for his leadership, and said:

> And we need to change, and we will change, the way we behave. I'm fed up with the Punch and Judy politics of Westminster, the name calling, backbiting, point scoring, finger pointing.

Many of the promises Cameron made then and in subsequent election campaigns are of course political ones, but the 'Punch and Judy' promise is not political. This promise is behavioural, it transcends politics and speaks to a desire we all have for a less confrontational world. The idea that our politicians might show leadership in achieving this is a very attractive one.

So how did things change? Over four years later, in May 2010, David Cameron became Prime Minister. In April 2014, just under four years after becoming PM and getting on for nine years as leader of his party, Cameron faced Ed Miliband, the then Labour Party leader, at Prime Minister's Question Time in the House of Commons. The subject that day was the flotation of the Royal Mail on the stock market. Ed Miliband's words of choice on that financially challenging occasion were that the PM was 'not so much the Wolf of Wall Street' as the 'dunce of Downing Street'. How did Cameron respond? He replied that he would not take lectures from Miliband and Ed Balls, the Shadow Chancellor of the Exchequer, and went on to brand Ed and Ed 'the two Muppets'. Cameron referred to the pair's advice to former PM Gordon Brown when he sold a large part of the country's gold reserves. The jousting carried on in that vein.

So how did we end up at this point? The leaders of the UK's traditional two major political parties had both said that they would like to end this style of confrontation. Even the organiser of this particular kid's party, the Speaker of the House, had made a vow to end the 'yobbery and public school twittishness'. In practice our political leaders were not making these changes. If the evidence is of a strong desire to change coupled with the gross failure to make that change, there is something we are clearly missing.

Behavioural change is difficult. However, there is a stronger issue at play here and the very idea of 'Punch and Judy' is itself a clue to what that might be. Viewed objectively, Punch is itself a paradox. Watch a performance at the British seaside and you will see parents standing at the back, pushing their children forward to sit, enthralled, watching a 'Punch Professor' perform with his puppets. Punch is a loud, aggressive, misanthropic wife- and baby-beating misogynist. All the things we abhor. Yet we love him. We set the police on him and he kills the policeman. We still love him. The children scream with laughter and the adults, safe at the back, enjoy the simplicity of his evil antics. What is going on here?

Like so many things in Britain that look 'British', Punch is an import.[1] He landed on these shores as an early migrant from Europe in the 1600s. His spiritual home in the UK is in Covent Garden where in 1662 Samuel Pepys watched then wrote about a show performed by Pietro Gimonde from Bologna. In Gimonde's performances Punch was a marionette controlled by strings rather than a glove puppet and had the Italian name of Pollicinella. Like any immigrant who arrived here initially looking for work but then stayed, Punch slowly cut his ties to his home country and made new connections. As a street performer, with a basic story but little script, Punch took on cultural clues from his environment. What worked for people stuck and what didn't got edited out. This is the amazing reflective power of a street performance that has grown up over centuries. Because it reacts to what we react to, it tells us something about our story. That is the secret to why it is so compelling.

On 9 May 2012 a birthday party was held for Mr Punch in Covent Garden, celebrating the 350th anniversary of this significant event in the history of the show that has gone on to be known as Punch and Judy. In the shows at the party, many characters in Punch's journey came to pay their respects. Among them was Bruno Leone, a modern puppeteer from Naples. One of Bruno's puppets has similarities to Punch. He is called Pulcinella, which Bruno explains means 'little chicken'. Little Chicken is more simply dressed in white robes gathered at the waist with a belt, but he has Punch's large nose and the main characters he plays with are a woman and a dog.

What is striking watching Bruno perform are both the similarities and the differences. In both there is a relationship with a woman. Here the woman is better dressed than Judy and stands her ground. Pulcinella asks for a kiss, is refused a number of times, then takes it anyway, then takes the kiss to excess and is rebuked. The contrast with Punch and Judy is the imbalance of power that occurs in the British show. We are used to Punch being a thug and violently taking what he wants from everyone. This extreme imbalance crept in because it plays to something in the audience. Originally the female character in Punch and Judy was known as Joan because that was the most popular name among the domestic classes at the time of the show's arrival in Britain. In the 19th century 'Judy' was the term for a tramp's woman. The status of the female character fell ever further and changed to Judy. The dynamics between Punch and Judy reflected the dominant power present in society. The same power that could be used to press-gang a man into the navy was being used by Punch against Judy.

Alongside dominant power runs fear. It's no surprise that the character's name may have its origins as 'little chicken'. Fear runs heavily into aggression. In the early shows, fear is explored in the relationship with the dog or monster. Punch is initially scared but manages eventually, in music and rhythm, to master his fear. With the help of a stick he beats off his oppressor. The stick is a representative baton of this sort of power. There are two instinctive responses to the stick: we can either pick it up or we can continue to get beaten by it. The third option, choosing to lay it aside, is much tougher. Having power and choosing to use it wisely requires wisdom and courage. It is not wisdom or courage that we want to see in this sort of simple theatre. In many shows Judy introduces the stick herself and then hands it to Punch who uses it. This giving of power is significant. Judy is at very least complicit. Punch, like any tyrant, has learnt to behave as he does from somewhere. The reaction of children to their parent's behaviour tends to follow a pattern. Either behaviour is adopted or it is rejected and inverted. An untidy parent can easily pass on their talent for untidiness to the next generation. Alternatively a child may react to the mess by becoming extremely tidy, making up for the deficiency. Having a healthy relationship to tidiness is more difficult when we start with extremes. So it is with brutality.

Punch now reflects a modern British stereotype very well, if in extremis. In a Punch and Judy show by Clive Chapman performed in Covent Garden in May 2012, Clive's Judy set out to give an insightful view of her husband. In Judy's words he is simply a lazy man who sits in a big chair and drinks beer. She henpecks her beer-swilling husband who kicks back at her, using the tools at his disposal. The relationship between the two is transactional. Punch is always saying he wants a kiss, then he suddenly grabs Judy bodily to satisfy his demands. Punch's needs do get met and are represented by the baby which is, of course, a joy to Judy but an encumbrance to Punch. The conflict between the pair now takes place over the baby. Judy asks the audience to make sure Punch looks after the baby and of course, in pantomime style, he fails to. It is all fun to watch but elements from our world are deeply sunk into the polarised fighting. Punch is a highly judgemental abuser and agent of dominant power whereas Judy, who is probably in the process of mothering another young Punch, is trapped in the cycle of abuse.

After Covent Garden I was fascinated by the clues Punch and

the success of the show held. Initially, two strong themes emerged which seemed to hold the crux of the problem. First, Punch's relationship with power. His approach is pretty simple: he uses violent force without hesitation. The other was how Punch meets his needs. There is no subtlety to it at all. He wants sex, he grabs Judy. This is a power to simply take what he wants to satisfy himself. The convention of marriage and the consequences of the baby are both things he effectively chooses to reject without compromise. Something about that brazen honesty makes the show compelling. It is an extreme show of needs, satisfied with raw power. I saw parallels in Punch in my own behaviour and much behaviour I had previously experienced. This type of behaviour has a draw for us. How few of us are really able to say that they are never attracted to the possibility of quickly acquiring what they need by the exercise of dominant power? Particularly as it is an easy strategy for a man to use force to get what he wants. Too easy.

Structure and power

Dominant power sits as an accepted structure in our society. We accept the *Cutty Sark*, the tea clipper in dry dock in Greenwich, as a symbol of our history and a thing of beauty. Since its extensive restoration after fire, *Cutty Sark* sits in its own 'sea' of glass allowing us to appreciate it as a ship but also to look inside the hull and see it as a vessel for men and trade. When we go on board we find that the *Cutty Sark* sits inside a bigger story. The ship was once part of a tea trade between England and China that led to the 'Opium Wars'. These wars took place when China insisted that the tea that it was exporting to Europe should be paid for in currency rather than with the return cargo of opium that the English demanded. This small matter of trade was ultimately decided by dominant power and war. The *Cutty Sark* is not only a thing of beauty, it is a reminder of a time in which dominance ruled. It created empire and systems like the slave trade. This power filtered all the way down from the very top of the empire to the streets. The dominant power that decided the Opium Wars is the same dominant power that Punch reflected in his early shows on the streets of London. If you were a man and in danger of being press-ganged by the navy to go to sea, you tended to live with this dominant power at the centre of your life. Small surprise if the same 'impressment' that the press gang might use on you finds its expression elsewhere, perhaps in your relationship with women. Punch used dominant power because it was the model all around him.

This is the problem at the heart of the matter. The model of dominant power is so heavily sunk into us that we don't even notice the depth of its effects. Actions of war and its fighting and taking are at the heart of dominance. At the May 2015 General Election Ed Balls lost his seat and Ed Miliband resigned as leader of the Labour Party. In his farewell speech even Balls still used the war metaphor, and in his, I suspect, rather more scripted resignation speech Miliband used the war metaphor heavily and the word 'fight' or 'fighting' no fewer than five times. This way of thinking is locked into our underlying behaviour and pops up in our language. Any politician will struggle to end 'Punch and Judy' behaviour if the dominant power paradigm is what guides them at core. This is why we still struggle to deal with bullying. It is wrong because it is an abuse of dominant power and yet in places it is still tolerated. At times of stress, difficulty or tiredness the behaviour will often get worse as the base instinct kicks in.

Riane Eisler in her book *The Chalice and the Blade* makes the point that it wasn't always this way. The Blade is the metaphor for a wave of dominance which took over from the previously settled and peaceful nurturing power of the Chalice. Eisler goes back as far as 7000 BC and looks at the creation of 'Old Europe' in the Neolithic period, in particular at the way this peaceful way of living flowed into Minoan culture on Crete. In summary, this was a time of plenty in which giving was prized far above taking. The power of women as life givers was prized and the goddess, the giver of life, was celebrated in worship and art. In this time people had what they needed and lived peacefully. What seems to have happened is that through a series of waves starting from around 4000 BC a dominant, taking culture took over. Like a quiet creative child attacked by an unrelenting vicious bully, the peaceable way was in no real position to resist. Power from this point has travelled with the blade of the dominant invader. In a time of perceived scarcity this 'power over/taking' model came to rule. Even today, many of our finest minds are focused on the blade. Our weapon systems continue to be our most prized technologies. Modern structures of power are also entangled with religious beliefs that serve the dominant culture. The word 'hierarchy' itself comes from the Greek *hieros* (sacred) and *arkhia* (rule).

What Eisler does by opening this door to the past is to alert us to an underlying knowledge that we have. Masculine, strength-inspired dominance does not have to be the governing model. A more balanced partnership is possible between the power that takes life and the power that gives it. Our ability to use our hands, minds and our propensity to fashion tools and schemes can be put in service of both life-enhancing and life-destroying ends. This is not just a male/female question either. The power here is something that both sexes can employ in a partnership model where one sex doesn't choose to dominate the other. This is an empowered and respectful model we are slowly moving back towards but sometimes in fits and starts. William Golding famously wrote *Lord of the Flies*, a novel about a group of boys who, stranded on a desert island, resort to some of the worst behaviour possible. What is less well known is that Golding's own favourite book was published a year later, *The Inheritors*, in which he describes a peaceful group of Neanderthals who face extinction at the hands of a more progressive invading group who we slowly realise are modern *Homo sapiens*. As the story develops it gradually dawns on the reader that these gentle Neanderthals are not us, as we might have assumed. This realisation contrasts with the recognition that these aware, respectful and loving people have qualities that we can cherish. This small surviving tribe are extinguished but their genes live on in the form of a child who survives from the group. *The Inheritors* thus sits in sharp contrast to *Lord of the Flies* in the same way that Aldous Huxley's final novel *The Island* sits in sharp contrast to his classic *Brave New World*. Both authors follow their classic dystopian novels with sequels that explore more utopian possibility. In both cases the paradox is there for us to experience.

Awareness of these possibilities is what drives choice. It is too easy to be in the story ourselves and not see it for what it really is. An outsider with a different frame of reference may notice what we, as the occupiers of the story, do not see. For example, on a short walk through central London a tourist will encounter many deeply impressive buildings from Buckingham Palace at one end of the Mall to Admiralty Arch, Horse Guards Parade and on down Whitehall towards Westminster Abbey. On Parliament Square a series of significant institutions are gathered: the Houses of Parliament on one side, the Treasury and the Whitehall machine of Government on another and the Supreme Court, our highest judiciary, on another. Looking out on all this is Westminster Abbey, founded by monks over 1,000 years ago. In this small space we have the legislature, the executive, the judiciary and the Church all facing one another. This focused distillation is unusual if not unique. The structure created by the concentration of power in London, the grand façades of the buildings and the impression it gives is great for tourists but this display of power also has an effect on the way we think. Never mind that nearby Green Park started its life as a burial ground for lepers, nowadays it's the effect that power has on us that matters. We know that what lies behind the buildings is often less impressive. A lot of the power is an illusion but we accept the reality of that illusion nonetheless. What we need is more plurality; a spread of power among the many, not a concentration in the few.

Even when power is not evident physically it plays a part and imposes its structure quietly on us. It can be like a swirl of leaves caught by the wind, in a corner between two buildings. The pattern may look haphazard but elements of it are not. The leaves trapped in the vortex go where they are blown, travelling in structures that repeat. Finding such structures and stories in everyday life, with real people, is easy. If you turn on the TV or radio news or pick up a newspaper, you will find stories that fit patterns in which people are trapped.[2] The most common are the victim story and the drama triangle. The victim story might be the ordeal of an innocent young mother trapped by border police in possession of drugs or the tragic final moments of a group of lost mountaineers. The victim story gets stronger when there is also a villain who can be blamed for what has happened. The innocent young mother has, after all, been set up by her cruel father-in-law. If we can find a reason why the mountaineers got lost, the story suddenly becomes more interesting than merely that of a trip gone wrong. If we share some dislike for the villain, the story gets stronger still. If, say, an overzealous bureaucrat has removed some vital service which results in the climbers getting lost, that would be perfect. The drama triangle consummates the situation and triangulates the simple victim and villain dynamic.[3] The lost walkers needs a rescuer as does the innocent young mother trapped in a foreign customs office, destined for jail. The drama is thus now more complex and three-sided: villain, victim and rescuer.

None of this would be worrying if elements of it didn't start to play out in life at large. Whenever something happens to us and we seek to blame someone else we are potentially setting ourselves up as a victim. If the banks are the ones to blame for the financial crisis, then we have externalised the problem. It's not us, it's them. We don't have to ask ourselves what we might have done, either as individuals, organisations or society, to contribute. The more we concentrate on what they did wrong, the less we consider what we did. We also don't have to ask what we can do to help sort it out. Externalising the problem is ultimately disempowering. Getting trapped in a structure like this and not realising it traps us in a wider sense. We lose power and we give it up to others. Being able to see the trap or to point it out to someone who is in the trap can be the start of their breaking a wider habit. If it's us who tends to cry out for rescuing, it's always good when someone helps us out, but if we put ourselves in the situation where we need that help, then we are accepting our own powerlessness and giving power to others. Consistently asking to be rescued is like being a battery on constant drain, a great way to lose power. Being helped occasionally is fine but it's different from constantly asking or searching for it. Anyone always needing help, creates dependency.

The parallel story that we can easily get drawn into is that of being the rescuer. If you are a member of one of the caring professions, say a doctor or a nurse, drawing clear boundaries is essential. Making a distinction between helping someone to get back on their feet as opposed to continuing to help them walk can be crucial. Proverbially teaching your friend to fish is very different to always going to the fishmonger for him. True care is helping our friend to build the courage first to want to make the journey and then to actually make it.

Stories take all forms, although the simple ones are the best. Journalists set up conflict as an easy way to tell a story, well aware that there is often an element of fun in the conflict. Radio 4's *Today* programme is particularly good at this. If someone is invited on with one opinion, someone else with an opposing opinion is often sought to appear alongside as a verbal counter-measure. Now this could be said to be a way of achieving balance but it's also a good way to set up a classic conflict story. Suddenly what we find engaging is not the subject itself but the humour inherent in the conflict story. What we have is a piece of drama between two opposing parties and that is good sport in itself. Unfortunately, the possibility of learning new information from the opposing points of view is substantially diminished. It's a theatre that perpetuates the conflict model as a way of reconciling difference rather than offering anything more creative or an understanding of that difference.

One of the things that great leaders excel at is the ability to see the structure and story of power and to play the game. BBC presenter Gavin Esler spent many years in Washington and particularly learnt to admire the way President Ronald Reagan, an ex-professional actor, was master of the story. Reagan knew that the story people believed, particularly the visual one which he and his advisers played to, is all powerful. Reagan, whose environmental record was not good, could appear in an open-necked cowboy shirt, perhaps against a mountain backdrop, and simply play the embodiment of the all-American hero and have people believe in that story. As Esler puts it, 'Reagan could have announced that the Grand Canyon was to be turned into a cement factory, but the pictures told a different leadership story.'[4]

It isn't simply a case of playing within the story, though. Great leaders also know when the story needs to be violated. Better to take this on explicitly than to simply be an unwitting victim of what people are already thinking. Esler also pays particular attention to Michelle Bachelet, Chile's first female President, who in her journey to the top had to take on many of the country's established hierarchies, including the successors of the generals who had murdered her father under the Pinochet regime. As defence minister, Bachelet apparently astonished the military leaders at her very first meeting with them by the way she introduced herself: 'I am a woman, a socialist, divorced and agnostic. All the sins together. But we will work together very well.' This shows the way to tackle the underlying story, by calling it out. Bachelet gets the story, takes control and thus is able to start writing the story herself. The story itself is not the problem, but being trapped in an unseen vortex and ending up as a leaf in a storm is. We need to be the subject of the stories we create, not unwitting objects of a story that someone else controls.

Dominant power's weak spot lies in its simplicity. At its extremes it is based on physical coercion but mostly it is based on fear. Once that fear is released it has limited hold over us. As the great critic of Soviet totalitarianism Alexander Solzhenitsyn tells us:

> You only have power over people so long as you don't take everything away from them. But when you have robbed a man of everything, he's no longer in your power, he's free again.

Freedom to shift

What we are seeing in the world at the moment is a slow but clear shift from dominant 'Punch' power back to emphasis on individual empowerment. Fredric Laloux in his 2014 turning-point book *Reinventing Organisations* sees this as a progression of stages, characterised by colours, that we are slowly moving through. Laloux cites a growing number of organisations that are operating at a new level he calls 'Teal' which is beyond the 'Orange' and 'Green' approaches that his research shows most commercial organisations use today. The 'Teal' level is driven by a new generation of leaders who want to empower, not to direct. In this new generation of approaches also sits 'Holacracy', a system where, instead of being directed, employees choose how things will be run. Included in the model is a new way of managing role allocations, responsibilities and conflict. In this model leadership emerges rather than is imposed.

Laloux's development stages for organisations can be summarised as follows:

Level	Character	Guiding metaphor
RED	Constant use of fear and violence to keep order	Wolf Pack
AMBER	Top down command over what and how. Fixed hierarchy	Army
ORANGE	Goal is to beat competition. Management by objectives	Machine
GREEN	Focus on culture and empowerment to achieve employee motivation	Family
TEAL	Self-organising and highly connnected with no need for central command	Nature

This shift has been quietly happening for a long time but dominant power still plays a huge part in the way we think. It also still plays a significant role in global politics and particularly in nations where the recognition of human rights is less well advanced. We are, after all, still relatively close to two world wars in which dominant power played a major role. These wars may seem far behind us, but in terms of generational thinking passed down from parent to child, nation to nation and in our societal and corporate hierarchical structural systems we are still significantly influenced by them. Sitting on the Tube in London recently, listening to students in their early twenties talking, I realised that this generation, born in the early 1990s, would not have experienced the punk explosion of my early teens in the late '70s. Thirty years is not much time. If I, at a similar age, had moved back three decades I would have been in a period just after the Second World War, experiencing the Cold War. In generational terms we are not far from a world in which violence and dominance was much more common than it is today.

The good news is that we may have passed our crisis point in October 1962 with the Cuban Missile Crisis.[5] At that point it became clear that two great world leaders, Kennedy and Khrushchev, both of whom had also experienced personal loss in the Second World War (Kennedy his elder brother and Khrushchev his eldest son), did not want to unleash their nuclear arsenals but instead found a way to quietly negotiate a solution. Whenever we hear about nuclear weapons we are told how many times more powerful the potential of those weapons is now compared to those dropped on Japan in 1945. That statistic is what stills us. New extremes of dominant power may exist but it has been proven that neither side rationally, on balance, wants to use it. President Kennedy's model of imposing a blockade and quietly negotiating through a trusted route instead of unleashing the weapons of war is the ultimate Strong Core, Soft Front strategy. In time the brutal reality of the atomic bomb drop may be seen as a turning point at which the dominant power model truly started its end phase.

Climate scientist, author and creator of the Gaia theory, James Lovelock, in a talk he gave in London on 1 April 2014,[6] put the change very nicely in context when he said, 'We no longer need inequality between men for growth.' In history things evidently were different. Power and inequality had a function and were frequently abused. Now, as Lovelock also said that night, 'We are the first species to turn sunlight into information'; mankind has now got to a state where we can fully realise our power. This is something our increasing connectivity, driven significantly by the internet and social media, is giving us. At the same time transparency cuts the ability of the oppressor to achieve dominant ends in a coercive manner. Our ability to judge and publicly shame has brought the issue out into the disinfectant clarity of sunlight and fresh air. In that light, who wants to be seen as a potential abuser?

Individual empowerment

In June 2008 the wizard behind Harry Potter, JK Rowling, gave her Commencement Address to the graduating students at Harvard. That anyone today can watch this humbling and compassionate speech at any time from anywhere marks a fundamental and crucial change in transparency of information access. Rowling, an introvert by nature, starts by acknowledging the weeks of fear and nausea that the thought of the speech has given her before taking us on a blazing journey of redemption. Rowling acknowledges the awfulness of poverty and her own sense of complete failure some seven years after her own graduation, then talks about the power this gave her. Poverty is one thing but climbing out of poverty through your own efforts is something to pride yourself on. She acknowledges this deprived state, of a realisation of failure as being her 'rock bottom'; a point where there was a 'stripping away of the inessential' to leave her, with her greatest fear realised, free to rebuild her life. Contrary to our expectations of failure, this 'stripping away' gave Rowling inner security and taught her the true power that she had. Secure in her ability to survive, she was able to create.

As Rowling puts it, 'had I really succeeded at anything else, I may never have found the determination to succeed in the one arena where I believed I truly belonged'.

Even beyond the ability to act, at a fundamental level we all have power over what we think. Intellectual freedom is the one thing that it is very difficult for anyone to take away from us. This is essentially where our personal power, resides. Viktor E. Frankl, the Austrian psychiatrist who has famously written about his experiences in Auschwitz and other concentration camps, provides a deep contemplation on this, very real final freedom, in *Man's Search for Meaning*. Frankl sees men walking among the camp huts comforting others, giving away their last piece of bread, and remarks that although they are few in number, the fact that they are able to do so is 'sufficient proof that everything can be taken from man but one thing: the last of the human freedoms – to choose one's attitude in any given set of circumstances, to choose one's own way'. Frankl found that even in these circumstances, choices remained. Even in the camp, every hour offers a decision where either you do or do not submit your inner freedom to external powers. This decision, Frankl writes, determines whether or not you 'become the plaything of circumstance, renouncing freedom and dignity to become molded', in his case, into the typical inmate.

Life in a concentration camp under constant threat of death sits in stark contrast with our lives of freedom today. Yet, in these moments of utter failure and restriction we get a clearer picture of what our power really is. Ultimately we each hold this power. Every day we choose how we give it up. Once we acknowledge that this is how power works and that it is actually held by each of us, we are better able to harness it.

An altogether more mundane turning point for me was a situation when I was, as a lawyer, working late on a deal. We were at the early stages of a transaction with a bank. If we won the deal it would be worth a good few hundred million pounds. The client partner of our organisation held a crucial relationship with the bank's financial chief. I had drafted a difficult letter of commitment that we needed at this early stage of the deal. It was a subtle balance, over the course of the day the letter had been through many drafts and was finally beginning to get a consensus from the team. Everyone was broadly happy with it. It was now gone 9pm and we were all getting tired. The letter needed to go to the client first thing the following morning. I was used to having to find a balance between people's competing wishes under time pressure and capturing something that worked grammatically and legally. It was no surprise when the client partner, renowned for having very high standards, asked to see me in his office to review the latest draft. Though he didn't say anything, he seemed to be pleased with it. Then he started to change some of the punctuation. Next, he queried minor points of grammar and finally he started redrafting parts. We'd been through the letter all day and I could feel tiredness and anger stirring in response. I am still glad about what I did next: I told him that it was late, that I was going home and that I'd be in early in the morning so that we could finish it off. I left the office without waiting for his response. The following morning the letter was on my desk, with a small grammatical change, approved to be sent out. After years of buckling to this sort of pressure, staying late and dealing with the anger it had caused me internally, I had made a different choice and it had worked. I had the simple power to leave. I could take that power and still have a job. Some 15 years later I still remember this moment as a crucial step on a journey towards taking back my own power. From this small situation I realised I had far more power in my gift than I was actually accessing.

Giving up our own power is an easy thing to do. At this moment we can all do exactly what we want. Given this ultimate power of self-determination, the fact that we do give a lot up is maybe not surprising. It is, after all, a big responsibility to have. Marianne Williamson observed:

> Our deepest fear is not that we are inadequate. Our deepest fear is that we are powerful beyond measure. It is our Light, not our Darkness, that most frightens us.

This light of possibility is crying out for some limitation. This is why we so easily succumb to structure. Asking us to name a colour is usually much easier than asking us to think of a word. We have become used to being hemmed in.

Relational soft power

A number of existing models are helpful in looking at power in a modern and relational context. The concept of 'soft power' was first developed by Joseph Nye in his 1990 book *Bound to Lead*. Nye has continued to develop the concept as it has become more popularised and followed up with a book itself entitled *Soft Power* in 2004. Nye defines soft power simply as the ability to get what you want through attraction rather than coercion. It is the goat-herder approach, relying on creating interested followers, rather than the sheepdog approach, nipping at reluctant heels. Nye's focus is on the exercise of power by states rather than individuals or organisations but the point is still valid: soft power creates something that results in people being drawn towards it. Cultural soft power works through music, ideas, art and brands. Rather than shutting down options by aggressively blocking the way or showing teeth, we can leave all options open but allow people to gravitate towards the option that attracts them. *Monocle* magazine now compiles a Soft Power Survey which, in 2013, was topped by Germany. In 2012 the UK led this index as a result of hosting the Summer Olympics. More recently Angela Merkel's diplomatic leadership in Europe has been the best soft power country role model. This indirect, softer approach is one that politicians often struggle with. Nye quotes Newt Gingrich, the former Speaker of the US House of Representatives, speaking out against the Bush administration's approach in Iraq and expressing well the crucial difference in strategy: 'The real key is not how many enemy do I kill. The real key is how many allies do I grow.' Killing is the extreme symptom in the field for a more subtle approach at home. In the *Monocle* index it is remarked that Italy was only able to join the top ten because Silvio Berlusconi had been removed from power allowing a more culturally indirect form of power to emerge. How many leaders of that type do we still tolerate because they somehow get results?

It is traditionally said that power comes in three forms: we can be coerced, induced with money or co-opted. There is a potential problem in these three categories in that the middle one is neither beast nor fowl. Money is just a currency that can be used in a positive as well as a negative way, a construct that we use to ease our transactions. It is not motivation itself, at root. If money is a consequence of the labour we freely choose and is sufficient for our economic needs, then it is no inducement at all. We do the work because we are attracted to it and take the money as our reward. If on the other hand we need the money and thus the job in order to pay for our wants, then the deal starts to be more one of coercion than inducement. This is the danger of money; it can easily become fuel to a system of dominant power.

This change in seeing money merely as currency for other means is subtle but it leaves two simple forms of power in relationships: coercion and co-option. Co-option is the idea of creating things that we go towards willingly whereas coercion involves a push or pull. As we have seen, both of these involve a giving up of power, either to a demon we fear or a saint we follow. If what we are talking about is how we choose to give up some of our power to others, this bi-modal choice is simply the decision we make when we give it up. Seeing how we do this personally and organisationally can help the way we think of power when we negotiate. True power is us taking control of the story and making informed choices as to how we use it or give it away. In negotiation we can use this understanding to our advantage.

Philosopher A.C. Grayling talks of the contrast between 'agonic' and 'hedonic' systems and uses the example of two different types of primate, baboons and chimps, to illustrate this. Agonic baboons display the dominant, coercive model of behaviour where conflict and fear rules. Fun-loving hedonic chimps are more into pleasure. When an alpha male baboon makes a dominance display, others flee. When an alpha male chimp does so, the others settle down to watch. These are extremes of tyrant and showman. As humans we tend to mix both in our behaviour. The rival gangs of Capulet and Montagu in *Romeo and Juliet* display agonic behaviour on the streets but more hedonic behaviour within the group. We use the two systems of power to suit the occasion. In a time of crisis agonic power might be more appropriate, but in managing complex solutions the greatest opportunity we have is to harness the bees-to-a-honeypot power of the hedonic showman.

In order to deal with the paradox of the extremes, Adam Kahane has a model of power that shows how this mix might be successfully achieved, both by a leader and in relationships. Kahane starts by taking the thoughts and words of Martin Luther King, who wrestled with the polarity with which we tend to see the extremes of power and love. King says:

> power without love is reckless and abusive, and love
> without power is sentimental and anaemic[7]

King crucially recognises that love on its own is no practical answer either. Picking up this dilemma, Kahane has a dual model of power and love working together rather than being opposites. Inevitably power comes first. We need power to do anything. Power is, as Kahane says, the drive of everything to realise itself. Love is the drive towards unity of the separated. Kahane cites retired business leader Bill O'Brien's definition of love as simply 'a predisposition towards helping another person to be complete'. As O'Brien says, you don't even have to like someone to show love. Ultimately this is an interest in the welfare of all which links to the highest levels in Maslow's needs model. Together, power and this sort of love make a potent force. This is a direct echo of the choice between the taking Blade and giving Chalice that we saw earlier. Eisler's model suggests that society began with the partnering, giving approach but underwent a drastic transformation into the dominant, taking model. Kahane points to a successful strategy being a mixture of both pure taking power and giving love, and Laloux shows a slow movement away from the violent wolf approach towards a more natural balance.

A graphical summary of this, using the two hands model, is as follows:

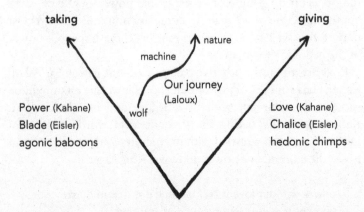

What we are seeing here is the emergence of a giving hand as a balance to the taking hand.

With the polarised view we can see why dominance survives as an option. As Machiavelli puts it in his 16th-century classic, *The Prince*:

> One ought to be both feared and loved, but as it is difficult for the two to go together, it is much safer to be feared than loved.

Shuttling between two poles is an odd compromise. Both struggle on their own for different reasons but dominance at least delivers progress. As a practical aid, Kahane also picks up a model put forward by Charles Hampden-Turner as to how we can reconcile the two forces. In Hampden-Taylor's model we use each force like we use our legs to walk. We can't walk on just one leg nor do we generally hop on both. Instead we move from one to another and find balance between the two dynamically. It is movement through time, place and context that helps us to find an appropriate balance. We tried one extreme, it got replaced by the other. Walking on a balance of both is true bi-pedalism.

Natural spectrums of exchange

Animals find their way in the pecking order. They deal with conflict. They collaborate and they pass on their genes to the next generation. Wildlife fascinates us because we know it holds lessons for us. We have, long ago, seized the power of imagination to differentiate ourselves from animals and yet, are we really clear on how our collaborations differ from theirs? What is the opportunity that our prodigious intelligence and active imagination can blind us to?

Sociologist Richard Sennett, in his book *Together: The Rituals, Pleasures and Politics of Cooperation*, looks at a potential 'Spectrum of Exchange' that exists between the extremes. Sennett divides this area into five main behaviours: from total co-operation at one end of the spectrum, to ultimate, annihilating competition at the other. His five categories are:

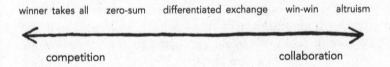

winner takes all   zero-sum   differentiated exchange   win-win   altruism

competition   collaboration

At the far extreme of competitive behaviour is the fight to the death. In 'winner takes all', the loser, the wolf in a fight, the corporate competitor in the market, is destroyed completely. This is simple 'kill or be killed' competition, without any co-operation at all. This is traditional dominant power at work, at the extremes.

'Altruism' is at the other end of the scale. In the animal world it is the insect that surrenders its body to be eaten by others. In our terms it is the option of gift-giving. The difference between the animal and human forms is perhaps the stronger presence of conscious choice. When in modern free society we choose to give a gift, we do so less out of genetically determined instinct than as a conscious will to give for a cause. Such altruism might also fit in a social context where social bonds are strengthened by this behaviour. If we are given to, we tend in turn to be more likely to give. Our language even reflects this: 'I am obliged to you' is a form of 'thank you'.

'Zero-sum' is a fight over the spoils, so called because every gain we make in an equal division of the cake comes directly at the expense of the other. Your gain minus my loss is a zero-sum. Here, all we co-operate about are the rules of the contest. The question of which one of us will win and which will lose and in what proportion is left to the contest. We choose this method because, whatever the odds, we believe that we both have a chance of winning.

If we don't want a competition, we might seek a clear division of territory in the more sophisticated 'differentiated exchange'. Competition between us has asserted itself but we don't wish to fight. Rather we wish to co-operate and agree how we mark out the space between us. You take this and I will take that. Land is divided, a business market is segregated.

Next to altruism on the collaboration end of the scale sits the elusive 'win-win' situation. Here we are aiming to do something together for mutual benefit. Animals might build nests to live in or hunt in packs. We might sign contracts for a joint venture with an agreed business purpose. We find ways of working together that suit our needs. It's a great idea but what does it really mean?

The challenge in the competition vs collaboration model is quite simple in that it is a straight line between two extremes. It doesn't really draw out the size of the opportunity that principled negotiation gives us beyond mere zero-sum gaming: to enlarge the pie rather than just carving it up. If instead we plot this on two hands model, we arrive at a different way of looking at the outcomes of any human negotiation: the 'Power of Soft Negotiation Map'.[8]

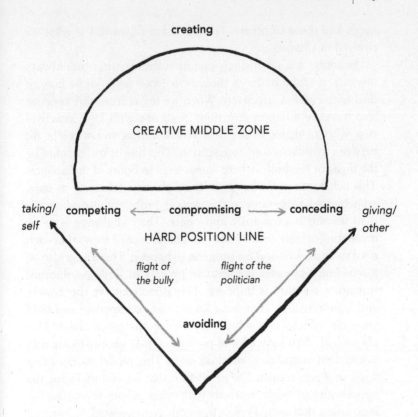

By putting this into two dimensions, we open up two new zones of distinctly human behaviour. First there is a zone of ducking the issue completely, which we call 'Avoiding'. This area is one of neither competing for self nor offering anything to the other; at its extreme it's sitting on one's hands, in complete inaction.

In accepting this inactive behaviour at the bottom we also open up an active area of possibility at the top. This is the Creative Middle Zone, which is where the best solutions, beyond compromise, exist. If real 'win-win' is anywhere, it is here. This the golden zone. Here we don't just split the prize, we work on making it bigger for all. The further we can move into this zone, the better. This is the area we can explore once we separate needs from wants and see our positions as flexible things. To work in this zone we need to find mutual interests and understand our needs and those of others. The groundwork for this is what we covered in Chapter 2.

'Avoiding' is a surprisingly common strategy that isn't always obvious. It is the home of those of us who don't know how to deal with conflict effectively. When we travel from this zone we also travel in different directions. Someone with high assertiveness who struggles to see how collaboration works might flit between avoidance and competition. This line of travel could be the flight of the bully, where fear is used in bouts of dominance. This behaviour will often have fixed position-taking at its core. Someone who operates in this area is probably more insecure than we might outwardly appreciate. Their challenge is to be more comfortable with conflict as a difference of views that each need to be understood for progress to happen. There may also be a reluctance to enter the creative process of finding solutions. Instead, a solution is imposed. This person knows the answer and is immovable. They have knowledge or expertise and hold onto the conclusions which experience has given them. This player will often have a lot of power and may choose to use it in a way that is coercive, or close to it. This model works for a while and gets results. The problem is that we end up losing the opportunity to work creatively with other people. Over time the innovation that would result from this creative work is lost.

Along the collaboration axis there is also another potential direction of travel: between avoidance again and concession. Giving is this person's default setting, particularly in times of stress, but there are risks in the straight from avoidance to giving. If it is giving without respect for the core needs of others, or ourselves it can be problematic. This might be the flight of the weak politician backing the latest vote-winning idea. If it's all about votes, it is too easy to run with either side to the latest scent. Traditionally this was the dual strategy of 'run with the hare and hunt with the hounds': from avoider at one extreme to doormat accommodator at the other. Taking this route is just avoiding the actual work of conflict resolution. In the case of the politician it may result in favouring one faction at the cost of another.

In a personal context, this flight involves a certain loss of the self. If the flight of the bully involves an overassertion of self, here we see an undervaluing of the self. Our needs are going unmet. Accommodation under pressure is one way through but it is unsustainable. To avoid on the one hand and then to compromise our needs to get a deal on the other results in damage. In personal terms this is difficult to achieve in the long term while keeping our self-worth. It's also not entirely respectful of the other as we have not really sought to understand, we have merely conceded. In economic terms we lose money as we continually compromise rather than seeking a working agreement. Either way, we are not standing up for our core needs or challenging anyone else's.

In the middle of the axes and in the centre of the main line there is still the behaviour of compromise. This is essentially 'splitting the difference'; a result in which we get to do a deal that falls in the middle of what we each want. Being able to achieve this is dependent on us each having room to give. It is essentially positional negotiation, where we simply haggle over the thing instead of creating more things. This is a world in which, in order to emerge successful, each of us has to go into negotiations with a bit of 'padding' that we can give away. In an increasingly transparent and competitive world this way of negotiating is still quite common but is coming under more and more pressure. To go beyond it we need to add more things to the mix.

The evolutionary - mutualism

Our most interesting area is the Creative Middle Zone. This is where we want to play. Here we have the opportunity, as evolved humans, to go back to a study of evolutionary biology and discover that the most basic single-celled life-form, the amoeba, can help us out. In 1966 microbiologist Kwang Jeon was studying amoeba when his sample batch was attacked by a plague of tiny bacteria. These cells, which Jeon called x-bacteria, managed to achieve the extreme result of squeezing themselves inside the amoebas. The amoebas fought the invasion and became sick as a result. Many failed to survive but some did survive the plague and when Jeon looked back some months later he was surprised to find that the survivors were healthy, and not because they had got rid of the x-bacteria but because they had learnt to live with their invaders. When Jeon tried to kill the bacteria using antibiotics he was surprised that he almost killed the amoebas too. He worked out that the relationship between the amoebas and the bacteria had changed. The amoebas benefitted from a protein that the bacteria produced. What had started as attack and defence had turned into co-operation.

In evolutionary biology, symbiosis has three types. Parasitism is where one organism benefits at the expense of another, such as ivy growing up a tree. On our diagram that is an extreme of giving or taking depending on our perspective. Commensalism is where one organism takes a leg-up and benefits without helping or harming the other. A bird feeding on insects stirred up by cattle grazing is a good example of this. Mutualism is a symbiosis where both organisms benefit, from pollinating bees to the bacteria living in our guts. This process of productive collaboration is all around us and is ultimately responsible for all life on earth. It is something nature does well even if it is something that we, in our commercial and relational dealings, struggle. When, in the early evolution of life on earth, two single-celled organisms by unique chance merged successfully, the resultant marriage was the ultimate symbiotic reaction: the first eukaryotic cell. These cells are what now make up the human body. This practice of leg-up mutualism is the collaborative and creative balance at the quiet foundation of our being. At its heart, this is how nature works and grows.

Oddly of all the species to help us, it is the simple amoeba that most simply and completely demonstrates the trick of beneficial co-operation. In an extended 'win-win' situation the objective is to collaborate in such a way that we increase the size of what is available to both of us. In order to create we need to operate in a creative role more than a competitive one. This is an important change in the way we think about what we are doing.

In Chapters 5 onwards we will look at the tools that are needed to explore this area more fully. To get into this creative zone there is a shift required away from a competitive, positional and hurried way of thinking. The creativity we seek needs to allow more ideas to emerge and give time for these ideas to be developed. The environment we do this in has to be more respectful of our needs, more forgiving, more human and more open to the possibility of failure. Out of that openness and experimentation often comes the idea that leads us forward to a better set of options and a solution.

The challenge is that this zone is quite uncertain, a place more readily embraced by creative people, such as artists and poets. In 1817 this was famously captured by John Keats who wrote in criticism of fellow poet, Samuel Coleridge. Keats believed Coleridge sought knowledge at the expense of beauty. For Keats, beauty holds the ultimate possibility. He termed the ability to travel happily in this space as 'negative capability' and described it as a quality possessed 'when a man is capable of being in mysteries, uncertainties, doubts, without any irritable reaching after fact and reason'. This is a classic paradox: success and ultimately strength come from being able to exist comfortably in an area of uncertainty. This uncertainty is something from which we naturally recoil. Leaving this stable anchor point in favour of a wild sea of possibility is something that stirs fear in our hearts. Yet it is this very fluidity that fuels our ability to find better solutions.

Strong core is a means to recover this stability, to be able to enter this zone on a more assured basis and also be open to the discovery of the myriad of possibilities there. By holding our certainty and stability more at the core we can be more flexible at the front and be less fearful of the wild winds we will face for a time. This is the Power of Soft: through the storm we can call on our core strength to hold us upright and to keep us moving, through the dark wood we can feel more and be open to what we experience because we are more confident of who we really are. We know that we will emerge from this zone of uncertainty with more of an insight into what we need. Keats's point to

Coleridge is that we need to have the confidence to go into uncertainty in order to become more knowledgeable. Ultimately the paradox is met by anchoring ourselves at core. The next chapter is about how we build that anchor.

CHAPTER 4

STRONG
CORE

If there is anything that we wish to change in the child,
we should first examine it and see whether it is not
something that could better be changed in ourselves.
　Carl Jung

Our structural and habitual preferences declare themselves early.
Habits and customs set in, whether in the corporation or the
individual. I was reminded of this when a young boy, maybe
four or five years old, sat opposite me on the Tube. His mother
took a seat the other side of him and his father stood facing over
him. There was lots of comfort and assurance there for the boy.
Outwardly, he was like a celebrity, with a posse to look after
him. What was different from the celebrity grouping was the
energy. The boy, though the centre of attention, was not the centre of direction. His influence on anything was limited; instead,
everything was there around him, a cocoon of reassurance and
adult direction was being provided for him.

I couldn't help but notice how his mother and father worked
together in a buttress of support for the boy. 'Not long now',
'Nearly home', 'Two stops and then we'll get off'. His potential
fears were named and their solutions followed up in a continual
flow. Who were they really talking to? I wondered as the boy
looked around, taking in the big world. This parent–child situation is not unusual, but as an observer I was shocked by how
little choice the boy was being given and how much his life was
controlled for him by two parents working in tandem. But it also
occurred to me that maybe I, as a parent, would have done the
same.

At their stop the couple moved to get off. The boy, eyes still ablaze in wonder, moved last. 'You want to go home,' came the command. 'No, I don't,' I felt some part of the boy respond. Once the first essential but reluctant barrier of getting off the train had been crossed, the boy stopped on the platform in full view of the still open doors. He looked up and down the platform, his wonder evident, wanting to take everything in. He was still looking around when his mother picked him up and walked away with him.

It is easy to miss the effect that losing touch with our needs in childhood can have on us as adults. How do we know what we want if others tell us all the time? If we say what we want and then we get told that that is wrong, we may stop trusting ourselves. As adults it can become very difficult for us to say how we feel about something. Because we do not tune into the feelings we have we can easily misunderstand our underlying needs and arrive at a result that is rationally justified but not true to what we need. Reason can cover up our underlying sense of what is right for us.

The realisation of how deep this runs became shockingly clear to me while talking one day with a senior lawyer. The matter we were discussing was very private but what I heard initially was a clear expression of her instinctive feeling. She knew what she needed to do about a situation. The problem was that no sooner had she had said this, she proceeded to rationalise her way around it. When I reflected this back to her at the end she had no recollection of her initial gut instinct. I had heard it but she hadn't. I got the sense that she was very used to riding rough-shod over her real feelings. In a way it was no surprise to me that she had become a lawyer: she was good at building rational arguments to support decisions, both hers and, I must presume, other people's. It's a great skill but if it covers over what we really feel it's also dangerous.

Boundaries

This is the first challenge in building a strong core. As a society we tend not to respect boundaries between people. We are too ready to tell others what they should do. We overstep the boundary and then are surprised that others don't respect our own. On the Tube, the young boy was connecting to questions and thoughts about what he was interested in and where he really wanted to go. The value of these inspirations was denied to him in a way that stripped him of some of his vital élan and self-belief. In *The Prophet*, Kahlil Gibran touches on this when he talks about how we encourage children.

> You may give them your love but not your thoughts,
> For they have their own thoughts.

There is, of course, an opposing view. To indulge every child or person in their wishes is liable to conflict with other boundaries. We are tired, after all, of people exerting their 'rights'. This is true, but it is largely a matter of how we see the difference between needs and wants. This is not about someone necessarily getting what they want, but about giving them the opportunity to see their needs, have them understood and to achieve a balance with others. When someone wants to go in a different direction to us, we can take the view that because we already know the answer and time is short, direction or coercion is the right option. Viewed from a position of knowing that we are right, time spent doing anything else can look like an indulgent waste of time. This is a huge assumption that needs addressing. The time spent acknowledging someone properly and getting to the bottom of a problem can pale against days, months and years of continuing disagreement and resultant failure of trust.

There is also a subtle but significant shift in focus here. If we are truly to respect the other in terms of wants and as an individual, it shifts from:

The polarised conflict of:		The mediation of:
What I want for myself	to	What I want for myself
and		and
What **You** want for you		My wanting for **You** what **You** want for yourself

The real win here is that suddenly both parts are held within us. If we do care about the other person and want to deal with them, we want their interests to be respected. Our role changes to one where we are more curious about the other person's wants. In this model it becomes clear that the drawing out of conflicting points of view is a positive thing. We may not like 'conflict' because we associate it with war, anger and people imposing their point of view on us. Once we become curious about another's point of view we open ourselves to the possibility of change and resolution. We are also expecting this in return. What we give to others we expect for ourselves. This ability to see and respect people's boundaries is the foundation of our strong core.

Differentiation

> Fill each other's cup, but drink not from one cup
> Give one another of your bread,
>   but eat not from the same loaf,
> Sing and dance together and be joyous,
>   but let each one of you be alone.

Marriage is perhaps the best example of a relationship where little is written down in the beginning and yet where we see, in the most successful marriages, two people working together to achieve greater things than they would have been able to achieve alone. In this quotation from Gibran's *The Prophet*, marriage works best not by borrowing from the other in a co-dependent way but rather by allowing each to be themselves within the union.

David Schnarch is an expert in the subject of passion in marriage and has written a number of books on the topic.[1] He is a great believer in the importance of 'differentiation'. In order to explain the concept fully Schnarch harks back to the work of Helmuth Kaiser, a little-known psychiatrist from the 1940s. Kaiser once found himself at an ice rink watching a pair of twins perform. He noticed that what stirred the crowd again and again was the fantasy of the two individual performers coming together in a form of unison. This unity of choreographed movement gave the impression of the skaters being controlled by one mind. Kaiser called this 'fusion fantasy'. What Schnarch realised was that much of his work with married couples was driven by a similar fantasy of oneness that is impossible to make work in reality. Time and again, couples believed that they should achieve emotional fusion in order to make a happy marriage. Schnarch's work led him to realise that this was not so. In such a situation people lose the ability to direct themselves and get swept up in the feelings of others. Connection without individuality risks co-dependency. Fusion and dependency are breakers of boundaries and are the opposite of building a strong core.

There is a huge difference between building a ship and building a raft. A ship is built over a period of time with a purpose in mind. A ship is secure when at sea but able to come into port when needed. It requires a depth of water which means we need to navigate the coast and other obstacles with care. Like the seabed, the hull of the ship has clear shape and definition. It displaces water to float. The ship needs a depth of water to float and boundaries between it and the land have to be clearly thought about. The beached ship, like the beached whale, is an unappealing prospect. We thus plot a course on charts of available information and make sure we have that depth available. A communication system is needed, both with shore and other ships. The ship has its own, reliable propulsion system. Changeable weather information is taken in regularly to make detailed on-going decisions. As a result of this care, the ship can ride a rough sea and we can enjoy a clear sunset over calm seas.

By contrast, a raft is built quickly out of materials that happen to be available for the purpose of survival. On the raft, land is our escape route and we get nervous out of sight of shore. We can push the raft off a beach with our feet and never know the depth of the water beneath us. The collection of parts of the raft is flimsy and each wave moves the collection of pieces and stresses the layered ropes holding it together. Our communications are a haphazard collection of shouts to shore, waved flags and, if we are desperate, maybe a fire using part of the structure. If we're lucky, we have a paddle and a small sail. While we wish for a bit of wind to get us moving, any more and we'd be at the mercy of a strong sea or foul weather.

The confidence with which we can put to sea when we need to is a ready analogy for our ability to differentiate from others. This is a skill that builds on having an effective sense of boundaries. It is healthy to be both confident up close, in port, but just as confident alone, at sea. The sort of rugged individualism that only finds happiness in solitude is not good differentiation. It is the ability to be comfortable both up close or far apart that marks the well differentiated. It is about being able to preserve our sense of who we are in the face of difficult interactions. This is why we need to build a core that is more like the well-differentiated ship. The vessel in port retains its identity and does not merge with the shore. We might take in stores and the ship's crew might sing in the local bar on shore leave but our ability to put to sea in the morning remains intact. The raft, built in panic on the beach, is not the vessel we need to be well differentiated. For that we should have the structure of the secure vessel at our core. This requires proper building.

I talked once to a young woman who was struggling in her first year at agricultural college. The other girls didn't like her, she told me. As we talked I learnt she had decided to get in with a group of young women from better-off, privately educated backgrounds. That is what she wanted to be. I realised what the problem was. She wasn't connecting because she wasn't being herself. Everything she was trying to be was borrowed from elsewhere. Everyone could see that and it was easy to knock her down. As I heard more of her story I could see more and more of a gap between where she was and what she wanted to be. I also saw that where she was had a truth and thus a power of its own. She had her own rich experiences to build on. All she needed to do was to see that and believe in it. We talked about privilege and what that idea really meant. I saw her as someone who was privileged in a genuine sense; in her life she had ridden horses and had built up not only experience but a huge variety of relationships from all parts of society; the very wealthy but also those who were passionate and resourceful without having much money. This experience had given her something, a privilege, that the others didn't have. She could connect with people from all walks of life and had a vision others didn't. She didn't have to have a private education and money. She already had enough. I encouraged her to be more confident in herself and to work with what she had instead of reaching elsewhere. In time, everything else she wanted could come to her. This allowed her more confidence and the ability to build relationships based on who she was, not on what she felt she wanted to be.

The idea of differentiation takes us back to the single cell and its development. Cells come from the same material but develop their own distinct properties. As humans we are highly biologically differentiated compared to the amoeba. Many different parts of our complex bodies perform different and highly interrelated functions. The liver needs no kicking out of bed in the morning and the bowel generally needs no reminder to quietly get on with its work. The complexity and differentiation of the human body is what we need in our external world also. Schnarch sees differentiation as a key challenge in families and notes how common it is for children to move away from their parents to succeed in truly becoming themselves. Some move away and some stay close. The challenge of parenting is allowing the next generation to develop more independently without needing physical separation to achieve it. Looking at the life partners we choose through the lens of differentiation is an interesting test. Schnarch notes that we often choose a partner who has achieved a similar level of differentiation, albeit perhaps by different means. This match makes us comfortable and underlines the importance of differentiation in our relationships.

Boundaries also need constant maintenance. It's a complicated thing to get right. We want to show unconditional love for our children yet they can behave in ways that we know are wrong. In order to maintain the boundary we have to be clear and consistent about the principle at the core. If the teenager is rude, the rudeness is the issue. What we have to avoid is damaging the relationship itself. We are hard on the behaviour and soft on the person. A friend once told me about a customer of his who had taught him this lesson in style. After a meeting the customer took my friend into another building down some very long corridors and up many stairs. My friend was utterly confused about where he was. He was eventually shown into a small room and made to sit down in a chair. The customer then proceeded to tell him what his firm had done wrong and why it should never happen again. The feedback the customer gave that day was important but just as important, was the way it was delivered. The room overlooked the Olympic Beach volleyball court on Horse Guards Parade and an important match was in progress. There was an underlying message here, that whilst the feedback needed to be given, the relationship was as important and as strong as ever. We can be hard on the issue and at the same time soft in our relationship. Getting this balance right is the trick.

'All men mean well'

Anne Katherine has written extensively about boundaries and cites a situation between a couple which shows just how subtle but important these can be.[2] On a rushed afternoon of pick-ups and children's appointments, Jerry reaches out to his partner Ellen who is in a bit of a flap and simply says to her, 'I love you.' Ellen is too busy with what she needs to achieve and simply responds, 'I have to pick up the kids.' Jerry feels slighted and storms off to the garage where he is mending the car. At Jerry's departure, Ellen feels coldness and starts to wonder why she is always doing everything around the house, supporting the family on her own. The couple have become distanced and unable to work together effectively.

Anne Katherine then replays this with good boundaries. The key, easily discernable difference is that Jerry doesn't storm off. When Jerry is not heard he has the confidence to ask whether Ellen hears what he has said. She hasn't and he repeats that he loves her and wants her to pause for a moment to take that in. Ellen responds and shares the fact that she feels pressured to get the kids, do the shopping and a dozen other tasks. Jerry in turn hears her and suggests a compromise, reminding her that things don't have to be perfect. As a result Ellen agrees to change her priorities and Jerry agrees to do some of the shopping. The knowledge that both Jerry and Ellen have of each other's good intent makes a difference. This is a question not only of respecting other's boundaries but also respecting our own. Jerry sees Ellen's comments for what they are, not an assault on him that he is subject to but rather something that he can see, observe objectively and deal with appropriately.

Strong Front	Strong Core
Jerry:	
Feeling for Ellen is conditional	Feeling for Ellen is constant
Storming off	Staying, getting the message clear
Instinctively subject to	Objectively observing
Ellen:	
Feeling for Jerry is conditional	Shares her challenge
Must do everything she has planned	Able to hear love

In the second example it is Jerry's confidence in himself and in the underlying nature of the relationship that saves the situation. He is able to see Ellen's good intent separate from the behaviour of that moment. With less dependency on the moment and less immediate reactivity to it, he can more easily pause and rebalance the situation by returning to the ground that he and Ellen share before exploring and then suggesting different solutions to the stresses they face.

The question of good intent is something that it is wise for us all to return to at times. In a heated negotiation between organisations some of the behaviour we see can lead us to question the motives of the other party. The deal we both want to do brings us together in a shared intent; it is just that we choose a different route. We do this partly because we have different priorities. Understanding these different priorities alongside a binder of shared intent helps to make this clearer. George Bernard Shaw did indeed write that 'Hell is paved with good intentions, not with bad ones', but he continued, 'All men mean well.'

Being able to see the good in a person we don't like is a critical skill, particularly in a negotiator. The great Oxford scholar and thinker Theodore Zeldin usefully divides those he doesn't like or can't get on with into two categories: devils and horned devils.[3] Horned devils are those who refuse to listen, enjoy being cruel and are intent on causing harm to those around them. In my experience there are very few horned devils. Most devils are not horned; they are aggressive because they are insecure and appear cruel because they are actually afraid. The difficult thing for us is seeing the fear or the insecurity. This is usually because it is hidden behind a strong front which accentuates the devil. We see devilish behaviour and imagine horns. The person we see as a devil is simply hiding behind protective surface behaviour, which often prevents them from dealing truthfully with how they really feel. They are afraid of something and are as trapped by the shield as we are deceived by it. The trick then is to work behind the shield through ethos and pathos, trust and empathy, rather than simply fighting against it in the realm of logic only. Then the devilish mask can drop and we can see that the horns were never really there.

The writer and aviator Antoine de Saint-Exupéry wrote many wonderful things, including *The Little Prince*, but one of his less well known but equally remarkable writings is a small book, called in English *Letter to a Hostage*, telling the tale of his capture by anarchist militia in Lisbon during the Spanish civil war. Saint-Exupéry negotiated his release by connecting with his captors through the simple enlightening medium of a smile which led to a shared cigarette. This single spark of a smile found a connection between men that the great writer describes as 'beyond languages, classes and parties'. He summarises by saying:

> I can criticise the proceedings of his reason. The proceedings of reason are uncertain. But I must respect that man on the spiritual level, if he toils towards the same star.

This idea of sharing a star to which we are toiling, however we differ on our chosen tracks, is a useful anchor to remember in those dark moments of despair with our fellows. It is rare that we cannot find a shared star that we toil towards. However, if we do differ in our star gazing, our problems are much deeper. Without some degree of shared intent we are wasting our time since our problems cannot be solved by negotiation of a shared solution. If that is so, we are best to bring the real issue to the surface and find a solution to that. If one of us is not ready to negotiate, then walking away from the table is the obvious choice.

In drastic cases it may be that allowing the other party to walk away or, more likely, to do their chosen bidding is not possible. In the extremes of having to protect ourselves or another, coercion by appropriate means into a forced solution might become necessary. This failure to agree intent is one area where negotiation doesn't work. Ultimately we have to respect that we are separate and people have freedom of choice. Asking these questions about intent helps to clarify who is fundamentally different from us and who is just seeing a different track to essentially the same place.

'Control the controllables'

We are separate vessels and not everything is in our control. If we are able to see clearly the differences between the vessel we are and the forces that are external to it, then we are better able to prioritise. Key to this process is having a clear sense of what is within our control and what is not. In competitive sport, any team can go through a bad patch. Perhaps the referee has decided against us, or the decision may even have been wrong. What good does it do for our star player to hurl abuse at the referee? After the fracas, do we want our focus to be on the incident or on the rest of the game? Managing the way the team feels after the incident becomes a priority. It is all too easy for us to feel wronged and for that to affect our play. The counsel from the expert sports coach at this point is to 'control the controllables'. This is also a universal truth. Instead of worrying about what we do not control and cannot change, we are so much more powerful if we accept the logical merit of focusing purely on what we do control: our play from this point onwards. If we accept that we are not the referee, our game becomes a lot easier.

This is the same fate that can befall any of us watching the TV news. Sitting there, we all know what is wrong. It's obvious, if only they did this or that. We wave our opinions and arms in despair at what we see happening in the world. The problem is that the waving sucks up our energy. This behaviour is disempowering. We feel engaged but in reality we are not. Our concern is focused on what we can't control. This is exhausting and diverts energy away from the things we can influence. How often do we tell people what should be done rather than just holding that truth to ourselves and getting on with it? If you suffer from this issue, the best thing to do is to join a voluntary committee. That's the best place to learn that you should only suggest things that you are prepared to do yourself.

Stephen Covey came up with a pictorial way of looking at this. First, Covey looks at all the things that concern us and suggests capturing these in a 'Circle of Concern'. Then there is the question as to how much of that we really can control. At this point Covey draws the 'Circle of Influence' inside the Circle of Concern. It is generally a smaller subset.

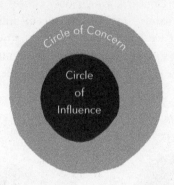

Covey's point, in discussing Proactivity, the first of his 'Seven Habits of Highly Effective People', is that proactive people focus their concerns in their inner Circle of Influence. Reactive people focus their efforts on the Circle of Concern. Reactive people's focus will often be on the weaknesses of other people, problems around them and so on. It's a blaming approach in which they or others become the victim. It's an easy habit to fall into. The trick is to be aware when we, or the team we are working with, start to concern ourselves with things that we cannot realistically influence. At that point a focus back to the things we can influence will usually give the impetus needed. We smile as best we can and leave be the things we cannot influence. In the words of the Serenity Prayer, adopted by Alcoholics Anonymous:

> Give me the courage to change the things that can
>   and ought to be changed,
> The serenity to accept the things that cannot be changed,
> And the wisdom to know the difference.

Sometimes it is empowering just to remember that the choice to leave alone the things we cannot influence is itself within our control. This can remove quite a lot from our list of worries.

Following the general law that what you focus on tends to

expand, by focusing on our Circle of Influence our influence expands. This markedly contrasts with the strategy of focusing on our Circle of Concern, which only causes our concerns to expand. At the same time, our Circle of Influence, actually shrinks. So, what we have is two opposing strategies based on where we choose to focus. This is a useful reminder not to mess too much in other people's business; again a question of respecting boundaries.

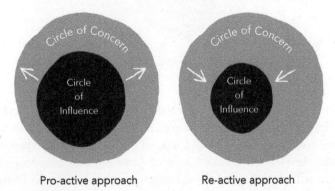

Pro-active approach   Re-active approach

King Timahoe

We need to be aware that what we feed with our energy tends to grow and what we ignore or don't feed tends to wither. Called positive re-inforcement, this method is more effective than we often realise. Many parents practise this with their kids; they ignore bad behaviour and only comment, positively, on good behaviour. It tends to work, particularly with children who only really want attention. If you doubt the ease of the method, 'Dolphins' is an easy game to play. A group decides on something that it wants a person to do. That person is then brought in and rewarded by claps as they move towards the agreed area, object or behaviour. Even complex choices, such as 'to give up', are usually found relatively quickly. Positive re-inforcement works.

But not all re-inforcement is positive. An old tale I often tell involves former US President Nixon and Henry Kissinger who were apparently sitting in the Oval Office discussing policy. King Timahoe, Nixon's Irish Setter, began chewing on the rug beneath the President's desk. Nixon, it is reported, commanded the dog to stop. King Timahoe kept right on chewing. The President commanded again. The dog ignored him. In exasperation, Nixon opened his desk drawer, took out a dog biscuit and gave it to King Timahoe, who retired from the rug to chew the biscuit. 'Mr President,' asked Kissinger, 'do you know what you have done?' 'Yes,' replied Nixon, 'I am stopping King Timahoe from chewing the rug.' 'No, Mr President,' Kissinger replied, 'you have taught that dog to chew the rug.'

We need to ask ourselves how often it is that what we do unwittingly encourages the continuance by others of actions that we actually want to stop. Surprisingly often we are complicit. Changing our behaviour and forcing ourselves to deal with the consequent loss is often the first step to changing a situation. Ask yourself of any undesirous situation: how complicit are you in furthering and unwittingly supporting its continuance?

Attachment and commitment

There is a paradox here that is worth looking at, between the commitment we need to show and attachment. We all know that the most difficult person to negotiate with is someone who doesn't need anything.[4] Nothing is likely to persuade us if we no longer want what the other person is offering. You may be an oil state but if my vehicles and industry no longer consume oil, there is a different balance of power. Power is dependent on attachment. This is the principle at the heart of Buddhism which sees wanting as the direct cause of suffering. In order to end the suffering we can simply detach; thus attachment to anything is the real issue. The point here is not to suggest a strategy of detaching from all needs as a solution but rather to see it as part of a negotiation. On one extreme, if we are attached to an outcome we can't negotiate easily. Low attachment gives us options. How attached am I to any particular outcome and how can I be more detached?

Often good negotiators struggle to negotiate things in their own. The worst situation to be in is to decide one has to have something and for it to be in limited supply. If we decide that we want a particular car, then we are victims of our own attachment. Until we decide that we can use another dealer or buy another type of car we remain attached and the smart seller can discern it in our behaviour. We do the best deals when we can detach from the outcome of the transaction. This is why using a third party, or even better a professional negotiator, will usually result in a better deal.

Attachment is also one of the reasons why creating options is such a powerful strategy. By showing that we are open to different ways of solving the problem we lessen our attachment to any one in particular. Creating a variety of options can also be what tells others we are near agreement. We have to be creative because we can no longer simply give things. On top of strength at core, allowing enough looseness for the other party to make decisions also reinforces the impression of base solidity. This is exactly how Czech intellectuals responded when the US allowed the then controversial film *Twelve Angry Men* to be shown abroad. The film was critical of US institutions yet its director Miloš Forman commented that the US 'must have a pride and an inner strength, and must be strong enough and must be free'.[5] Being prepared to let others take a swipe at us can have the converse effect of showing us to be confident.

However, without commitment at core we flounder. Paul Roseby, chief executive and artistic director of the National Youth Theatre, tells a wonderful story about commitment that he learnt in his youth selling clothes door to door in London. He cites this experience as the best education anyone can have simply because it taught him to knock on every single door. As Paul says, 'the moment you felt weak or challenged by your own fear and I would miss a door, I wouldn't sell a thing the rest of the day'. The swagger and belief goes and everyone knows it. Even if you hate the product, having commitment and belief is key. Again, core and front is the key difference. We have to be committed at core but remain as unattached as possible out front. It doesn't matter which item of clothing Roseby sells, what matters is that he has confidence that the customer should want to talk to him first. From that critical point of contact we can later work out what each potential customer might need or be interested in.

In order to be able to be more like the ship and able to remain offshore when necessary, there is something here also about the ability to exist without dependency. It's like cooking a family meal. I might go to great lengths to cook a fantastic meal which we can sit round the table and enjoy. Hopefully everyone appreciates this and they might even say something to that effect. It's not the same, though, if I need everyone to say thank you and to tell me how great it was. I say this because I remember one particular occasion when I'd worked in the kitchen for hours to prepare a large Sunday roast and no one said anything. I couldn't help feeling a bit annoyed. Then I thought about it. There is a difference between cooking because I love cooking and cooking because I want your approval. I knew it was a great meal and that everyone had enjoyed it, so why should I care? To get something back would be nice but I realised I was actually lessening the experience for myself if I didn't approach it as something I wanted to do and enjoyed doing. If I couldn't see the joy in the task, what really was the point of it?

The walk-away

The biggest turning point I ever saw in a negotiation was literally a walk-away. Hugh, who was leading the client relationship, just got to his feet and started to put his coat on. We'd been in the meeting for only about half an hour but Hugh had clearly had enough. We had a team of consultants busy building a billing solution for one of the big regional electricity companies. It was quite a big team. The client was refusing to pay us and insisting on changing some key contract terms. At the moment when Hugh slowly and measuredly got to his feet, the mood in the meeting changed. We all knew he was serious. He had been calm and matter of fact as he spelled out the options. If we had no agreement, the team would be assigned to other work on Monday. It was Thursday afternoon. The client hadn't really listened to that point, though. It needed the physical change for the seriousness to register. We were done talking and potentially done negotiating. The clear movement and the coat had done it. The client's IT director asked Hugh to sit down. Hugh spent the rest of the meeting wearing his coat. It didn't matter, because it didn't take long after that. Hugh got pretty much exactly what he wanted and by Friday lunchtime we got paid by urgent wire transfer. From this point the relationship changed from one where the client did exactly what they wanted to one where we got a relatively balanced deal. Suddenly their lawyer was on the phone to us rather than ignoring us. It still wasn't easy but over the next six months we renegotiated the deal and successfully delivered a system that allowed the client to comply with a series of structural changes to the electricity market. If we hadn't been prepared to walk away, we would never have successfully delivered the deal. In the long run it was in everyone's interests that we stuck up for ourselves in a way we hadn't done previously.

This incident sticks in my mind as the best example I have ever seen of the walk-away. Mostly because it was a genuine walk-away, including a coat, but also because it came across as truly meant. Hugh was absolutely prepared to withdraw the team if he had to. This would cost us a lot but Hugh knew that working without getting paid was not only a bad option but almost certainly a worse option. There was also a principle here that we needed to respect. Hugh had the firm's backing for taking this line if he needed to. The client could read those signals and knew the situation was serious. Creating this understanding, of a line being drawn, is important. If we don't draw it clearly for people, how will they know where it is?

One of the terms that is used to talk about this walk-away situation is BATNA – Best Alternative To a Negotiated Agreement.[6] What we ask ourselves is 'What would happen if I can't do this deal?' If we can't walk away, our negotiating power is limited. If our power is limited, we need to create other options. Being a buyer with only one option is dangerous. Even if you know that you want to do a deal with someone, your power is limited. Any professional would counsel you to spend time creating other options and increasing your knowledge of what is offered elsewhere. Ideally these options are real and are ones you could exercise. Threats of having another buyer, for example, can work but it's always better if the option is real. An experienced negotiator listens to language and listens to their instinct. They can often spot a made-up story.

The crucial thing is that we ask the walk-away question not just of ourselves, but also of the other person or organisation. Doing that might throw up some surprises. A building contractor I worked with was not happy with his margins, so we tracked this to a situation he was having repeatedly with his clients. One in particular kept coming back, well into the contract performance, and asking for small but subtle changes. Each change by itself was something achievable but together they mounted up. This client was important to the builder and it was far easier to do what he wanted than to risk confrontation. With his requests there was always a small threat, usually around payment. 'Do this or I won't pay your [overdue] bill.' Conceding the changes was becoming a bigger and bigger problem. The builder was costing projects like this at a decent margin, but when I questioned him he admitted that over the course of the build his margin for most projects went down to an unacceptable level.

Once we looked at the situation from the point of view of each other's walk-away things became clearer. It was obvious that his client had no real walk-away option. We were most of the way through a major building project and to change contractors would have been very difficult. Without a good reason it was not a realistic option. The reason the client was making the small threats also became clear. He knew he was on weak ground. From his position he could see that his options were limited. Our conclusion was not that the builder could cruelly take advantage of this but that he had every reason to be sensitively and politely robust. Failing to maintain his project margin was not in his best interests, nor arguably his clients. He could see what he needed to do. The challenge for him now was that he needed to find a way to have a conversation with his client that, without upsetting the situation completely, changed a behaviour that had become a habit for him and an expectation for his client.

Other ways to think through what might happen are the WATNA and the WONA. The Worst Alternative To a Negotiated Agreement (WATNA) flips the BATNA around and asks what might go wrong with your nice safe alternative. This can be useful in interrogating the person I am negotiating with. Their other option may be to use an alternative contractor. Have they really thought through all the issues that might bring? What can help them take off their rose-tinted spectacles and start to worry about how good that option really is? By asking some well-timed questions about things that you know are sensitive issues you may be able to dent their confidence in their alternatives and thereby up your power. This is something you should do delicately as it can backfire.

WATNA analysis also works in limited amounts. How will you know that your alternative will really work? It's a double-edged sword. We want to carry out such an analysis to make us feel confident in our backstop but over-investigating it can be dangerous. Getting someone to think about the worst case alternative as well as the best case is a good way to impose a reality check on them. As a mediator I tend to do this when people are wildly overestimating their case. Finding out the grim reality of the other options available can bring that person more willingly to the negotiating table.

WONA looks at what might happen if you do agree but agree the wrong things. The Worst Outcome of a Negotiated Agreement is what you get if you are not careful and give too much. It asks the question 'If we gave that, what would it be like?' This can be a good way of strengthening our resolve against something we might want to concede. We remind ourselves what living with a bad agreement might look like. Suddenly not having anything or something else, the walk-away, might be better than that.

Scarcity

As a buyer in a business context, the easiest way to raise your power is to expand the market and the competition in it by increasing the number of options you have. As we've seen, if there is only one possible seller then your options are limited. With one option, your walk-away position is restricted; it's either them or nothing. Scarcity of supply works in the seller's favour and raises their power, lowering yours. This does seem obvious but finding oneself in this situation is surprisingly common. We can tend to get locked in because we like a particular product. This is bonanza time for the seller and it's why we have competition laws to prevent dominant suppliers from abusing the market. Where a seller succeeds in dominating the market, either through control of scarce resources or by differentiating their product successfully from others, this has a direct effect on their power and their ability to charge a higher margin.

For maximum power the buyer ideally wants to treat the product they are buying as a commodity, available in many places. Procurement departments work hard to achieve this. Large organisations have a way of doing this which is called 'Category Management'. Category Management seeks to set up a range of competitive suppliers for a particular category of goods. By separating the immediate demand from the negotiation they both increase their power and reduce the amount of deal by deal negotiation. Technical buyers who have a particular need often find it more attractive to simply buy a particular thing from a particular person. That singular, bespoke approach makes it difficult for a procurement expert to negotiate the best deal. In practice a balance can often be achieved between preferred selection and optimum negotiation.

Even if our favoured seller is the preferred supplier, it's usually sufficient just to create another option to allow the process of competition to work, even if it is thought unlikely at that stage that the alternative will be chosen. What is important is what the sellers think, not what the situation actually is. Sometimes the alternative option does end up being the preferred option after all; perhaps the preferred supplier has started to lose their way. By opening up the competition we can see this more clearly. Ideally, this power is used sensitively. Some sellers can be encouraged to stay market competitive more easily than others. Increasingly, in a sophisticated but more transparent market the benefits of collaborating with a particular supplier may outweigh the benefits of open competition. There is a balance to be struck here between the benefits of collaboration and depth of singular relationship on the one hand and accessing the plurality, diversity and width of the market on the other. In an ideal situation, we design a way of capturing the best of both.

From the sellers' perspective, scarcity of supply works in their favour. We all know the panic that sets in when supplies are limited. Creating this impression, sometimes playing on the fear of scarcity, holding supplies back, can work in the seller's favour. A trick such as the expiring offer often ensures a rush in sales, although it can backfire if used too often. Sometimes scarcity can also be created through the course of a relationship by the parties agreeing an increasingly bespoke offer. As a buyer, the more we have contributed to the creation of the solution, the more we feel invested in it. If as a buyer we feel we have participated in the design and it meets our needs in a particular way, then our ability to buy it elsewhere has just become much more limited. Where else would we now go to get the design that we now want, whatever our original need really was?

Knowing and using our expertise well is also a way of limiting the market and increasing our power. Often the biggest mistake we can make is to underestimate the value our skills and expertise have for this particular customer. Asking questions that give us an insight about what others value in us is not just self-serving. They give insight into a different perspective. It is that perspective that we need to work from. Our power lies in the eyes of the person we are dealing with as much as it lies with us. Real power is not what we feel, it is what is felt by others.

One of the most common errors is to negotiate with oneself. This is where we talk ourselves into lowering our price. If the customer has told us that this is what we need to do and we believe them, then that is one thing. Often, however, we end up reducing our price without any stimulus from the other person but out of a feeling that we might be too expensive. Telling teams to stop negotiating with themselves is the thing I find myself doing most often. If we are talking about changing our price, the question has to be asked 'What has led us to do this?' More often than not it is one of the team who has raised the question. This has more to do with a lack of confidence than anything else. If it is a really serious issue we should do something about it, but if it is caused by a lack of confidence it is the confidence in ourselves that we need to address.

Information

It is said that knowledge is power. It's certainly a key component. We can gain information from any number of places. Knowing things socially and attending to simple logistics around the edges of what we are doing can itself create an impression of value. This is something that the secret agent 007 does well. Confidence and knowledge ideally displayed with the right amount of show, not too much or too little, helps. An impression of power in these elements can translate easily from the general to the specific.

We know from looking at the walk-away that our position relative to the other options is critical. Knowing that we have a competitor and then having information about them, their offer and position with the customer allows us to react accordingly. Investing in that knowledge might be a critical part of our strategy. Sometimes it might come fortuitously or be readily available if we ask. On a deal of mine the whole bid team was immeasurably buoyed up when one of the team had seen a member of a competitors' bid team hastily putting together a presentation of their solution for the bid documents on the train that morning. Through this information we found out that our competitor was relying on a known subcontractor for a key piece of expertise and that that subcontractor was reusing an approach from an old and slightly tired deal we knew well. At a stroke we knew our fresher solution was some way ahead of our competitor's. We also instinctively knew that their bid team was operating substantially more on the back foot than we were. As much as anything else, this slightly illicitly but openly acquired information told us we could be more confident that our stronger solution gave us negotiating power.

Information is never more valuable than when it concerns the detail of the deal itself. You can negotiate as hard as you like for a good deal on a diamond on Oxford Street, but if you know the trade pricing for particular sizes and qualities of stones in Hatton Garden, you can save your effort. Who sets the price and what is good value after all? Investing effort in getting 30 per cent off one price is pointless if the starting price is inflated. Moving from Oxford Street to Hatton Garden or taking the advice of a friend who is a regular buyer could be the move that makes the real difference.

A friend who works in the fashion business knows exactly how much it costs to make various types of garments anywhere in the world. This information makes it easy for her to spot which supplier is pulling the wool over her eyes and what she needs to have to negotiate a good deal. As a supplier, having this level of knowledge allows you to know where you stand in the market and to price accordingly. Not having that information makes you vulnerable, both to underpricing and also overpricing yourself. Many organisations have made the mistake of outsourcing key skills. That can work well for commodity services and products, but if your supplier is the only one who now understands how to provide a product or service then you may have lost vital information that is critical to your buying power or your future product development.

Information could also be about the competition or the political relationships within the market or the other party. In large corporate sales we would commonly construct a 'power map' to understand who was talking to whom, who supported the deal and who was likely to be against it. The danger in a complex sale is that you can end up talking to the people who are for the transaction and ignoring key people who have good reason to undermine it. The reasons people choose not to buy can be more useful to know than why others do. It is the wise inventor who instead of looking for praise for his new creation asks how it might be improved.

For leaders there is a challenge here. To maintain traditional dominant power we tend to default to a model where we ascend metaphorically, hierarchically or practically. Power is associated with going up. We go to a platform to take visual height and we command from that point. The hierarchical model requires this, whether this is on the military parade ground or the institutional organisation chart. In this model, power comes from above. The problem is that through overreliance on it we can easily disconnect with where our power really comes from. In this model our information and references come not from our grass roots but from other leaders. Studies have even shown that the most powerful are measurably less likely to take on the perspectives of others. Instead of acquiring more power, what we can end up doing at this point is to develop hubris: excessive pride or self-confidence. We all know that pride comes before a fall. This is often the error of political leaders who, over time, lose the connection to where their power originally arose. Margaret Thatcher and Tony Blair and their exits from power are both studies in the dangers of hubris.[7]

Emergent co-optive power is different. We have to be prepared to descend to a vantage point which allows us to connect and understand. The emergent leader embraces what has become known in extremity as 'servant leadership', where the leader acts as servant of the people. The job of leader is now the job that Martin Luther King so elegantly achieved with his 'I have a dream' speech, to inspire through a connected vision. What gives a leader real emergent power is having the support of a strong crowd.

In Act 4 of Shakespeare's *Henry V*, in the 'dark night of the soul' that occurs before the great battle of Agincourt, this is the choice that Henry has.[8] He talks to his brother who tries to persuade him to meet with the other lords. Instead, Henry takes off his crown, asks for his brother's cloak and with the words

'I and my bosom must debate awhile' goes off in disguise into the night. Henry takes time out by himself but what he does crucially is to wander, without position or hierarchy, through the camp meeting the troops where he starts to understand things from their perspective. With this perspective he is able to reconnect, check that his values are still aligned with those of his troops and prepare his great speech before the battle. His speech brilliantly imagines a future for them beyond the fight, which he knows they will connect with.

This approach to power is thus a 'J Curve'. In order to get the uptick at the end of the 'J' first one has to be prepared to descend, to connect. This is more than just an exercise because real power arises out of this connection. It is personal at first because it is a test of one's own values and beliefs. Are they congruent with leadership of this group? It is then also a listening exercise; to hear stories and to find a way of connecting to the people who are telling them. Does my leadership vision connect? How are these people best led?

This 'J' uptick also depends on a preparedness to accept that you might no longer be the right leader for the group. Emergent leadership is contextual and, like Churchill, you might be the leader for wartime but not for the peace that follows. If we descend to the crowd and take this test, our leadership has just been revitalised and our mandate renewed. Maintaining it then depends on continuing this practice. In the J Curve approach to power, connectedness matters. This is the approach to information that also works when we negotiate; getting to the bottom of everything can matter more than getting to the top.

Time

Power isn't always consistent over time. It can change during the course of a relationship. It can also change by a significant amount. We can start as the anchor tenant, the star of the production, and by the time the development is up and running or the production finishing its first performances, power has shifted away from us. A secure contract written early on might then be wise. We might also be the beneficiary of this power shift over time, the rising star, gaining power as things develop. Leaving our options open might then pay. Making the most of our power is also about using it at a good time for us, relative to others.

One situation I was involved in contained stark reminders of the benefits of timing. A group of companies had got together to bid for a series of large projects. At the beginning all four of the parties were fairly equal. One had a big name but all of the parties had specialist skills and were known and respected for that expertise by their customers. The consortium members had all signed an agreement which set out the terms on which we would bid for individual deals. One of the partners would take the lead and the others would contribute. A project share was to be agreed. The legal agreement was fairly loose and co-operational. This type of arrangement is common.

Over time one project came to dominate. We all put a lot of money into it but one company took the lead. We got to a crunch point before the final bids to the customer went in. The deal pricing suddenly became very tight, and we realised that if we didn't secure a fully agreed contract with them we were at risk of being negotiated out once they won. The lead bidder didn't want to lose our support before their bid so, at that point, we still had power. We wanted to be strong but time and the sales process were against us. We buckled under pressure and let the other company submit without agreeing a cast iron deal. They then won the deal and all our predictions came true. We were quickly negotiated out when they decided they could do the work themselves at lower cost. I took the rap for our decision to let them go ahead. Taking a long view of the situation, we saw how our power had had its peaks and troughs but towards the latter stage had simply dwindled away. We are best knowing when our power is at its peak and using it at the right time for us.

Size

Size and scale are important also. If you are a small organisation dealing with a large established player, this can be intimidating. The trick to managing this dynamic is to play to your strengths not your weaknesses. As Malcolm Gladwell points out in his bestseller on the subject, David didn't beat Goliath by a freak of nature, he beat him by refusing to play by Goliath's rules.[9] Goliath would have beaten a lesser giant who chose to be armoured and equipped with a spear as Goliath was. David, by using his size (he could run) and his advanced technology (his sling-shot), was able to hit Goliath with a hard projectile that had a similar impact to a modern handgun. This finished off the giant. If you are in any doubt about this, Gladwell produces research on war between large and small countries which shows that in just under one third of cases, the weaker side wins. The reason for this is exposed in a further statistic. If we look solely at the smart David players, those who change the tactics, the percentage changes from winning 28.5 per cent of the time to 63.6 per cent of the time. In other words, if you are small *and* change the tactics, you are more likely to win than to lose due to your smaller size.

In this situation tactics that verge on trickery can also work. It is not, after all, your impression of the situation that matters but that of the other person. This is an important difference that we easily overlook. Think Brer Rabbit or the Tortoise and Hare. If you are stuck, think about the Commander of Hochosterwitz Castle who solved the problem brilliantly in 1334. The castle was being besieged by enemy forces led by the rather unlucky Margarete, the last Countess of Tyrol. After an extended lock-in, the besieged forces were getting to the point where they had almost run out of food save for an ox and some corn. Meanwhile the Countess's troops had become unruly and she was growing impatient. The Commander decided to slaughter and gut the ox, stuff it with the corn and throw it at the attackers. Everyone thought wasting their last food source in this way was mad and watched in despair as the animal disappeared into their enemy's hands. However, a short time later the Countess's attacking army withdrew and gave up. They had decided that if the besieged forces could afford to waste valuable food in this way, the siege was going to take longer than they could afford. The strategy made no sense looked at from the point of view of the occupants of the castle but it made absolute sense once seen through the Countess's perspective. Time and again this type of approach works: thinking in their terms not ours might save the situation.

Thinking through what you can make happen may also help. A favourite story of mine concerns an old Italian man in New Jersey, his son Vinnie and some tomatoes. The old man needs some help to dig over a difficult patch of land in which he wants to plant tomatoes. Vinnie would usually do this but he is in prison. The old man writes to his son lamenting the fact that he cannot help his father. Vinnie simply writes back: 'Dear Papa, don't dig up that garden, that is where the bodies are buried, Love Vinnie.' Early the next morning the FBI arrive and dig up the garden. They find no bodies. The next day the old man receives another letter from his son: 'Dear Papa, go ahead and plant the tomatoes now. That is the best I could do under the circumstances. Love you, Vinnie.'

Social influence

We copy others far more than we'd readily like to admit.[10] You only have to watch the way a dancefloor fills or a crowd builds around an event to observe how we do this. It's a logical strategy that allows us to outsource some of our decision-making to the crowd around us as well as to achieve social approval for our choices. We can also use it to give us more power in negotiating. If a particular person is influential or known for their wisdom, they can bring many supporters with them. We can use this as part of our strategy to increase our own power.

Status

One of the most humbling and awe-inspiring things I ever watched was footage from the BBC's *Frozen Planet* programme in which a bison and a wolf fight to the death. The wolf was starving and needed the bison for food or it would die. This was a battle with no mediation possible. The winner won and the loser lost. Many times I thought that the wolf had been so battered and bloodied by the far bigger bison that it must have lost. However, the wolf kept coming back, until eventually it won.

In the light of this ultimate battle for dominance, a natural hierarchy makes a lot of sense. The 'law of the jungle' allows any species to make more efficient decisions about who gets what. When we meet it's handy to know this. If we have to fight at all, whether it's a short fight or to the death, it's very expensive in resources and ultimately inefficient. Efficiency is something that is important in long-term genetic survival and development of the species. As Charles Darwin said, 'those who learned to collaborate and improvise most efficiently have prevailed'. Being able to recognise status is an important skill from our past and remains a vital social and thus dramatic tool today.

When theatre director and educator Keith Johnstone started working at the Royal Court Theatre in the 1960s he had a revelation.[11] Keith couldn't find real life in the scenes he was seeing his students act on stage. So he went in search of the missing ingredient. Eventually Keith found that ingredient and became a master of it. His instruction to his students was to try to get their 'status' a little above or below that of their partners. The result transformed what happened on the stage. It came alive. Keith also realised how everything we do in life is informed by small, usually unseen, status transactions. As Keith puts it, 'every inflection and movement implies a status ... no action is due to chance, or really "motiveless"'.

What Keith is noticing is that when we meet someone we subconsciously display signals that transmit status information. This suggests we are obsessively interested and invested in status, even if we don't consciously think about it. We have available to us a human equivalent of showing others the size of our horns. It's also subtly different from the pure front of puffing ourselves up. This is not an egoic front but rather a set of subtle signals that emanate from the core.

The signals that say 'Don't come near me, I bite' or 'Don't bite me, I am not worth the trouble' are still essential to us. Perhaps more important are all the micro status signals between the extremes that decide relative status and are the lifeblood of social interaction. This form of status is different from any over-all social status. This is what we play in a particular situation to ease or exacerbate the transaction. Thus a tramp, like Charlie Chaplin's character, may act high status to those around him which lowers their status to great comedic effect.

The easiest way to understand and start to use status is to watch for it in social and public situations or in drama and then to practise it, to an observer or an audience. Frankly, it doesn't work so well on the page or in the imagination. The third party view is important because we don't always know what signals we are really giving to others. Because it is relative, it seems to work with a see-saw effect; one person lowering their status pushes the other up and vice versa. The following are good indications of high or low status:

High	Low
Not blinking	Blinking a lot
Holding eye contact	Looking away submissively
Looking away first and confidently	Looking away and then back
Keeping the head still	Frequent head movements
Feet at 10 to 10	Inward pointing feet
Slow speech	Talking quickly
Being still	Moving about
Touching other person	Touching own face

You may well immediately think of people who habitually play low or high status well. A continually moving head with lots of movement and unsure fast talking contrasts sharply with the steady head and gaze of the confident slow talker.

We also play status to space and objects. When we enter a room our attitude to the environment and furniture matters. An apologetic shuffling of a chair is very different to an assertive placing of the chair in an appropriate position. A good actor can, with a gesture of the hand, project a body far larger than his own physical frame. Sitting with our feet on the table is very high status and potentially risky. In essence the more space we occupy, the stronger the signals we send.

Status doesn't always have to be a zero-sum game. Although there is a simple see-saw effect to basic transactions, it is possible for two characters to work together to raise each other's status, to enlarge the sum of the parts. They either create more status for themselves as two friends by upping each other in turn or they simply take it from other sources, by raising their status as a pair relative to others. This is harder to do than simply robbing it from the other person present, but acting creatively can allow us to break out of the immediate zero-sum presumption. When two animals meet, finding more status from elsewhere to raise each other isn't necessary or even possible. Humans can be more creative and appreciative of each other. Context might make this challenging, but finding a solution that delivers more for both is always something worth exploring.

Keith Johnstone tells a story of different teachers he experienced at school. The first was much liked but couldn't keep discipline and eventually left. The second was generally disliked and exerted ruthless discipline; so much so that he never actually had to punish anyone. A third teacher was very much loved and kept excellent discipline while remaining entirely human. The experience of these teachers affected Johnstone a great deal although he could not work out why. Years later, having done his work on status, he realised that the first teacher had been stuck in low status while the second had been a compulsively high status player. While these first two were fixed in status, the third was a status expert, able to easily raise and lower his status as he needed to. He was able to joke with the class and then impose a mysterious stillness simply by being sufficiently self-aware to change his status as he needed. The ability to play status, even if he didn't consciously realise it, is what set the teacher apart. He wasn't trapped by one position, but could prompt a relative lowering or raising of his status at will to great effect on the class.

These three teachers tell an important lesson. Being able to match and vary status is a critical skill. The soft skills can only get you so far. Being liked opens the door but just as it won't get you respect with a class of children, it often won't get you the deal. What works is to be able to be both liked and to play the harder skills well. Matching status to a high status player gains you critical respect. Your power gets a lift and you get taken seriously. Being able to play status is at the core but status alone is not enough. It results in worried children. High status combined with great soft skills is the potent combination. Bill Clinton is often talked about as someone who does this very well. Clinton is reportedly able to talk to people with complete focus, making them feel comfortable. For the moment that he is with someone he lets them feel that they have his complete attention, yet he still plays high status. This powerful, high status in the core with soft, open attention at the front is the ideal mix for maximum effectiveness.

Status is important partly because it transmits an underlying message of confidence. Just like the castle siege, the power that you have is not what you feel; it is what the other person feels you have. By playing high status you can confer a quiet advantage of upping the other person's subconscious estimate of your own power.

Finding the end

In the film *The Usual Suspects* the story revolves around the mythical character Keyser Söze, the ultimate gang chief. Söze is involved in a gang war with rivals but now holds a mystical power over everyone derived from the story of his extreme reaction to a terrible situation. On discovering the rival gang in his house have raped his wife and attacked his family, he proceeds to kill not only the gunmen but also his own wife and family. When I watched this I was stunned. The idea that anyone would eliminate his own family in order, presumably, to have more power over his enemy by the strength of myth and they less over him by way of leverage was shocking in the extreme. Söze then proceeds to track down anyone connected to the gang and kill them also. His power lies in the myth. He has 'the will to do what the other guy won't'. The power of the Söze myth, which is a fabrication created by Kevin Spacey's character Verbal, is that you don't negotiate with it, you just do what you are told or end up dead. This is a use of dominant power which is deeply animalistic: Söze will simply go further than anyone else and therefore will win.

Keyser Söze is an unusual person to have to deal with. Most people, even so-called villains, are more reasonable. If you are taken hostage, the person to really fear is the Keyser Söze character who takes no prisoners. Most hostage takers do keep talking because they want something. This has parallels with the corporate buyer who says that my price is too high and yet keeps talking to me. My bet is that this is just a ploy. In *Goldfinger*, James Bond is in one of the worst fixes seen in any film, strapped to a table with a laser travelling towards his crotch. He looks incredulously at Goldfinger and says, 'Do you expect me to talk?' to which Goldfinger responds with the classic line, 'No, Mr Bond, I expect you to die'. Bond lives because, whatever he says, Goldfinger has not actually left the room never to come back. He is still talking. It may not appear to be so but someone who is still talking or available to hear is still negotiating. Sometimes it is not just the words that we need to listen to, it is also the behaviour. Negotiation only stops when someone leaves, never to return. In the film Bond possesses a piece of information about one of Goldfinger's schemes that he dangles in front of Goldfinger who in turn initially bats it away. Bond then nonchalantly adds, 'Can you afford to take that chance?' and Goldfinger is hooked.

People are reluctant to close a situation completely. In the movies, like life, the situation is mostly left open to negotiation; the hostage is captured and through cunning can break free. We have to contrast the words with the actions. Goldfinger says, 'No, I expect you to die' but he has not actually killed Bond. Bond is right. There is still talking to be done to rescue the situation. This is also the case in most hostage situations. Hostages are taken for a reason and the situation is a negotiation until the door is shut never to be reopened. Often it doesn't matter what the talking is about. As Dee Hock, the founder of Visa, said:

> Until someone has repeatedly said 'no' and adamantly refuses another word on the subject they are in the process of saying yes and don't know it.[12]

Knowing that through the false 'no's' we are in still in a process of getting to 'yes' is the final part of building our Strong Core approach.

CHAPTER 5

TOWARDS

People watching is a great sport. Sometimes we choose to watch and sometimes the watching chooses us. It was the latter case this time. My wife and I were in a busy modern pub restaurant in Sussex, seated by the bar, waiting for our table. This was a popular place, it was Friday night and packed. The old, low door opened and a man walked in with his partner and came up to the bar. The manager, who we'd been watching for some time, was an energetic young man who put his heart and soul into everything he did to keep the proverbial plates spinning. The potential customer asked the manager if he could get a table for dinner. 'No, I am afraid we are booked out,' came the simple answer. Reluctantly the man left.

Not five minutes later another man came in. This man's approach was different. He said hello to the manager, acknowledged that the pub was very busy and that he should have booked before finally asking, very gently, if there was any possibility of a table for him and his wife. The mood was completely different. The manager whom we had seen rushed off his feet paused and said if the man would wait a moment he would have a look. After five minutes of searching and checking the bookings and the situation around the pub, he came back. There was a table available and this man, if he would just wait a moment for it to be made up, could have it.

Time and time again, this situation is played out all around us. Not always are the results quite so starkly displayed. I've watched it happen in railway ticket offices where people in a hurry to get to work treat the ticket vendor as if they are no more than a machine. In that case there is no obvious advantage to us to treat the situation in more human terms, but I am left with a distinct feeling that there is a definite but less tangible disadvantage to all of us in failing to do so. We are all under pressure to get on. This need in turn exerts a pressure to treat more and more of our interactions as mere transactions to be accomplished as quickly as possible. But what gentle human oil are we losing if we give in to that pressure?

This was displayed most strikingly during the London Olympics and Paralympics in 2012. Something very special happened during those few weeks that quickly swept the country. The volunteer 'Games Makers' did something exceptional. They treated everybody as a person. This made everyone feel very different. The Games Makers focused on each of us as individuals not as part of a machine. Nowhere was this contrast more apparent than in the security screening stations. The process of going through a security screening is something we are all familiar with at airports, where we have to disentangle ourselves from our bags and jackets and pass our boxed-up belongings through a machine watched by suspicious operatives while we walk through a security portal. We are generally made to feel like little irksome cogs in a vast machine. Not complying with one element of the process can result in us being told off like a child. At the Olympic venues the experience was completely different. We were greeted by people who smiled at us and were happy to help with every aspect of the process. They asked us how we were and helped us along. Some might find this annoying but most people emerged with a sense of shared joy, reinforced by the Games Makers and their continual upbeat presence. I can be slightly cynical about the commerciality of such events but the 2012 Olympics were very different. That day I even bought a cute Olympic cushion in the shop.

In the early days of my career I left a promising job at a big London law firm to start my own business. Everybody said I was mad. They were right. What I and they didn't realise was just how many lessons I was going to learn from the experience. One of the big ones was how to find the person I needed for a job. I was designing jewellery and I knew next to nothing about it. Instinctively I knew that searching through the trade telephone directory was not going to get me to the person I needed.

However, as a novice at manufacturing and design, that is all I could do. I got on the phone. What I learnt from speaking to many people and going to see some of them was that if I persisted they always knew someone who was better placed to help me. It might be someone in the same company or it might be someone in a different country. I discovered that pretty much all of them knew much more than I did about the subject. Along the way I also learnt various technical terms, like the fact that the clip-like parts that attach jewellery to clothes are called 'findings'. It meant that when I phoned the people who knew about findings I could not only locate them by looking for them in the right place in directories but I also knew some of the language and appeared more of an insider. These contacts connected me to, and helped me have a better conversation with the next person. In hindsight it was obvious that the only thing that led these people to help me was the fact that they cared. They only cared because I cared about them and showed it. Few could actually directly help but I still always asked for their advice and most gave it, in one way or another. Slowly I built a network of people who I trusted, who trusted me and ultimately could help me. The best contacts I made were always recommendations. Often the reason for calling someone wasn't clear. I learnt that this was almost the most valuable part. By loosening my hold on the purpose I had that day, I would learn more.

In the rush to get things done in our busy lives it's easy to forget that we are human beings first. We are 'human beings' not 'human doings' for a reason. Being human is the vital opening through which so much depth and width around our transactions in the world is possible. If we like people, we tend to help them, and people help us because we have made a connection. If our transactions have humanity in them, our lives are enriched. Yet, in our hectic lives this key aspect can easily get lost. All too easily we convince ourselves that the higher functions of the brain are in charge. The intellect is master, with the emotions, instinct and body as its faithful servant. If we believe this, we are making a fundamental mistake about human beings, for we operate best when the intellect is in service to the whole. This chapter is about putting the people-related aspects that are crucial to successful negotiation back into balance. It is about recovering the non-mechanical, less purely transactional softer part that represents relationships and the person. We all know this instinctively and yet it is so easy to allow it to slip. We will also look at why this slippage happens.

Tied up in this question are the systems and structures we use to ease our progress though life. The car is a classic example. We do things while in our cars that we would never do if we shed the shell of power and transaction that the metalled body gives us. A way to see this more clearly is to adopt a more human mode of transport and note the difference. Walking is one way but, as a first step, taking to a bicycle is enough to change the dynamic. In 2013–14 photographer Tim Fisher spent the best part of a year cycling through Britain. This has radically altered Tim's perspective. A person on a bike connects differently with people. In turn, people also greet and relate to you very differently. At the extremes this is obvious. In the city an opportunist cyclist might be just another nuisance to walker or driver alike and gets short shrift. In the Highlands of Scotland and the wilds of the North Devon coast, cyclists are rarer. Tim talked to me about a perceptible line that he kept experiencing. On one side of this invisible line people generally greeted him and returned his greeting. On the other side of this line the greeting simply disappeared. Nobody draws the line. It's just there. As Tim cycled away from a centre of population and towards the remote, he felt it. As he cycled back from the country to the city, he experienced it again. It became a zone of experiment. We know the extremes but what Tim started to play with was the curious border place where one changes to another, where he never knew what the answer to a wave would be. Here a wave from the cyclist might or might not be returned. Incumbent on the cyclist was the will to try.

In the city we know that we are not going to greet everyone. It can become a place of rushed transit through zones that we need to get through quickly. These zones, this haste, this transactional quality is perfectly justified in context. The problem is that the behaviour tends to seep into things around the edges. We are short with the ticket seller at one end of the journey; then it becomes easy to become short with the receptionist at the other end. Before we know it we are doing the same in the office as we race through our transactional day. In a crowd a person who falls gets lost. We tend to assume that someone else will take care of the situation. As people become more objectified, our conversations become transactions about the thing we want to achieve rather than a human interaction within which a request is wrapped.

The challenge is to keep asking ourselves what the people we are dealing with mean to us. If we get to a point where a person becomes either an obstacle, a vehicle or an irrelevance, then we are in danger of objectifying them.[1] Treating people as mere objects is our modern disease. We rightly worry about the way women are objectified in the media but this is a very visible example of a much wider phenomenon. The more we act from reason alone, wanting things from people, the stronger the urge is to treat them as a mere vehicle in that transaction. This is the same challenge we have when we bury our heads in the pillow urging our partners to get up in the night to attend to a crying child. In blocking out the needs of the others and giving primacy to what we want, we take subtle or explicit power over the other person and create a story about why that action is necessary. In the night, we find ourselves coercing a reluctant partner while at the same time telling ourselves that we are busy, have an important job to do and need our sleep. In the process the other's needs, however close they are to us, can easily be forgotten. As we objectify we also label. People become groups or types rather than individuals with needs just like us. In Shakespeare's *The Merchant of Venice*, Shylock's cry is that he is no less a human than anyone else: 'If you prick us, do we not bleed?' When did we stop treating other people as people?

A typical morning in a French office is instructional here. As workers arrive, they shake hands with their colleagues, say 'Bonjour' and perhaps inquire after their health. This approach is far from transactional. At times it can feel like niceties get in the way but this care and these relationships are the key to better negotiations. Taking the time irks the transactional approach yet it builds a basic zone of human connection. This relational wrapper of our lives sustains us and is the key to the door of the rest of our negotiations. The problem is that something intervenes. I was once called into a negotiation in Zurich where we were just about to be thrown out of the negotiations by our customer. My assessment was that we had two problems. We were asking for too much but we were also not attending to the relationship between the key players in the room. Trust had slipped away. We raised points the customer did not appreciate but we raised them in a manner that sought to undermine the trust we wanted to have for each other, as potential customer and supplier. They had stopped liking us and thus stopped listening to us. What we needed to do first and foremost was to improve the relationship in the room and, in concert, focus on the real issues. We made a few changes and, within a week or so, had rebuilt that trust. We treated the people we were facing as people, not just as mouthpieces. We listened and we took on board their concerns even if we didn't always agree with them. We spent more time with the characters round the table to find out who they were and what motivated them. Relations rapidly improved. At the end of the following week we ended up in a bar with the customer's negotiating team where they started to tell us what we really needed to know and to do in order to win, because they now liked us. As a result we brought in an expert who further impressed them with a layer of functional knowledge that our competitor didn't have. We started moving ahead and before long we agreed the contract terms.

What we are doing in the best situations is building a base layer of trust between people that underpins everything. Ideally we create this first. Over this foundation we can build empathetic understanding and then, ultimately, reasoning. The ancient Greeks had words that help to describe these layers.[2]

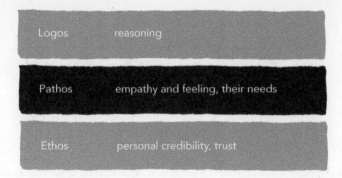

What we don't do is start at the top with logic and reason. The structure doesn't hold if the base layers are not put in place first. If we don't build these base layers, things tend to fall apart.

Taxi drivers and poets

It's a common joke that there are two ways of shopping, often expressed as a difference between men and women. A man needs a new shirt so he goes to a shirt shop. He buys a shirt. Maybe he might buy more than one. After all, once you have a shirt you like, why not get a few of them? The point is he wants a shirt, he buys a shirt, the task is done. The other way of shopping, which my wife and daughter enjoy but my son and I don't, is to just go shopping and see what turns up. They might have ideas on a shirt but they are just as likely to return with shoes, a bag or even a new phone. This can be likened to the way we walk down the street. We either have a destination in mind which, head down, we make our way rapidly towards or we meander, seeing things, perhaps talking to people. Each has its virtues but one is more doing-focused and one is more relationship-focused. We can map it like this:

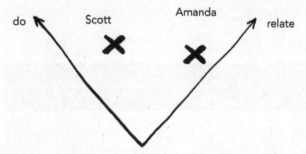

This graph is probably the simplest and maybe also the most important psychological instrument available to us.[3] We can plot any one person's behaviour onto this simple graph. Are they more focused on people or on the task? Do they get a balance of both? The person who is task-focused and is not interested in talking to people, let's call him Scott, would come out high on the do axis and low on the relate axis. Scott is following the example set by the first customer in the pub. He just wants a table. Amanda has a different approach. Completion of the task is relatively unimportant to her but her relationship with people is important. If we set Scott and Amanda down in a high street to complete the weekend shopping, we would probably be safe in betting that Scott would get the task done first. However, what possibilities would Amanda uncover in her conversations on the way? Who would be more likely to find out about the happy hour at the town's beer festival that evening? Perhaps most importantly, who is more likely to have the relationships they need when the water pipe in their house bursts later that evening? Task-focused Scott may be innately more resourceful but Amanda is more likely to know who to call and what favours to call in to get the matter fixed.

Neither extreme of behaviour is, of course, the answer. Once again, a combination is most powerful. In a game of football we don't just pass the ball to players we like or have a relationship with. If we know that they are not very good with the ball, that is likely to have a bearing on our decision also. Part of trust comes from liking and part comes from competence. Loyalty and reliability work together to produce the strongest combination. Thus in the do/relate graph the most successful track is likely to be a zig zag, similar to that followed by a sailing boat tacking into the wind or a goat moving up a steep mountain.

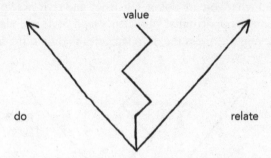

In a commercial relationship, if we are to create value, we need to get to know our customer. We also need to deliver what we promise. That means we need to spend time understanding our customer and their context. In the long term this is critical because as their needs develop, so do our offers. A balance of doing and relating gets us to the highest vale. In business, that is good account development.

If we are over-focused on delivery, our danger is that we become a commodity supplier and lose the relationship. On the other hand, being good at what we do is critically important. Like the football player, we also need to ensure that we prove ourselves by delivery and learn by doing. Therefore most successful people and organisations navigate between these two at appropriate times. As individuals Scott and Amanda are a step ahead if they are aware of their strengths and weaknesses in this regard. If they realise that doing and relating respectively are their strengths, they have a choice of strategies. They could combine their skills with Amanda focusing on account development and Scott picking up delivery, or alternatively each could decide to develop their strengths in the area they tend to focus on less.

This balance has a wider importance. We manage our lives through mediating this difficult dance successfully. Getting into

a taxi and being greeted with the sudden 'Where to, guv?',
I am reminded of this particular directional focus we often
need. As David Allen, the world's expert on 'Getting Things
Done' (GTD) so eloquently puts it, 'If you know where you are
going and what you are doing, efficiency and style are your only
improvement opportunity.'[4] Efficiency and Style are also these
axes. We might express the do/relate axes slightly differently:

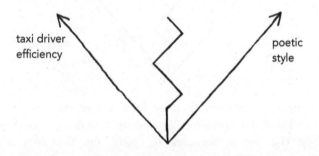

The opposite characteristic from the directionally focused
efficient 'taxi driver' is the poetic, contemplative style. The word
'poet' originates from the Greek 'Poietes' meaning to create. This
axis is also creative and contains what we find in the creative
arts. If life can too often be a 'Where to, guv?' taxi ride of do do
do, brute action and efficiency, this other axis offers a safe way
to explore a more aware, poetic, creative, thoughtful approach
that, with practice, can be accessed at any time. I see these two
not as exclusive extremes that never speak, like the suited business person and cash-strapped artist, but as two opposing axes
where the ideal journey plucks out the best bits of each type of
thinking to create a richly creative but also focused journey.

William is a funeral director in a seaside town on the south
coast of England. Like anyone with lots to get done, he gets
stressed. William has customers to see, arrangements to make
and then something gets in the way or goes wrong. What was
planned for the day starts to go haywire. The stress levels rise
and suddenly there isn't enough time to do everything. The

pressure is on to go faster, to do more and to break through the blocks. At this point we can lose our sense of humour and start being short with people. William's business is different, though. At certain times in the day he has to attend a funeral. When he is in a service he can't check his messages or send texts. To place his attention visibly elsewhere would be the height of disrespect. William told me about one day in particular when his stress levels were sky high. On that day he needed to attend the funeral of a war veteran and found himself in a chapel surrounded by mourners listening to eulogies for the dead man. What William heard moved him. He heard a story of a man who had been a prisoner of war and who lost his hearing when he was beaten up in interrogation. This man had struggled through life, losing his wife but making the best of what he had. As his daughter summed up she said how remarkable her father had been, in particular how grateful he had been for his life and how happy he was. William's entire attitude towards the stresses in his life shifted fundamentally at that point. He got back his perspective on his situation. He realised that there was always someone in a more difficult position than he was. He realised that his business issues were actually pretty minor but he also crucially realised the value, at times of stress, of stopping for a moment to regain this perspective. In his old age he knows he will not be telling the younger generation of his regret at not having stayed later in the office that night to sort through his emails. Oddly, he noted, the solution to the problem of having too much to do was not to do more of the same but rather to stop. It is only when we stop, that we begin to see things for what they are. William's rescue was to take time to listen and talk to others, to appreciate the wider world and to put his situation back into context for what it was: a simple set of problems that could be faced but only if he put them in a wider sense of who he was and how he connected with the world around him. This realisation and the appreciation of a moment of stillness and reflection is now something he comes back to in times of stress. As the Austrian writer and poet Rainer Maria Rilke warns us:

> If your daily life seems poor, do not blame it; blame yourself,
> tell yourself you are not poet enough to call forth its riches.

The danger is that on the taxi driver axis we tend to get stuck in
a panic where the only answer seems to be more speed or more
time. Efficiency can become everything. This is, however, a delu-
sional answer. Life also has a creative, relational and connective
axis that operates largely serendipitously. If, like William, we
stop for a moment and move along the poetic, relational axis,
the answers become clearer and our stresses tend to fall away.

There is also a stark warning here for all of us busy taxi
drivers of the consequences for us of the excesses of doing. I
once got into conversation with a man on a train en route to
Madrid. Bob, it turned out, was an old-time engineer of trucks.
I'd say mechanic but this wouldn't do justice to Bob's clear
philosophical calling as a wizard of all things mechanical. His
phone kept ringing with enquiries from haulage depots all over
Europe who had problems with a truck that no one else could
solve. Bob's answer often seemed to be a simple tweak to a
certain part of the engine. In his opinion, the problem with
trucks today is that we have made them too powerful and too
complex. The problem apparently lay with hills. We used to
accept that a truck slowed down to climb a hill. It took time. But
because nowadays we are focused on driver hours it no longer
makes sense to allow time to climb hills. The truck needs to be
more powerful to make the best use of the driver's time.

What is interesting is what this increase in power has created.
In the first place it has led to engines that drivers can no longer
fix themselves. Bob's drivers used to be paid a lot more and were
more self-reliant. In the days before mobile phones, satnav and
tracking, a driver doing a delivery to Southern Europe was away
for a week, largely on his own. If a problem emerged, he had to
sort it out. Drivers knew how to deal with challenges that inevitably faced them. When they phoned in, you knew there was a
real problem. Today, Bob explained, drivers are less self-reliant,
more dependent on technology and as a result are paid less and
enjoy the job less. The focus on efficiency has disempowered

them and effectively moved them away from the relational axis. This is a salutary lesson in a shifting efficient world. We might cling to our position as a truck driver but if the context around us is shifting to efficiency, if we do not change and find broader relational skills, we will suffer the same fate. If all we care about is efficiency, we will end up diminishing and dismissing our greatest human assets.

There is also a danger here in a concentration of power. In negotiations, relationship tends to be the counter to raw power. Whenever power is high, less emphasis tends to be put on the relationship. The two again work together.

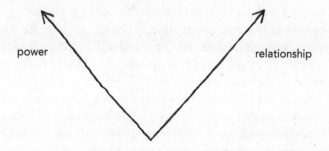

power   relationship

If you are a dominant player, say in the supply of oil, why should you care about the relationship? If you can bomb your way through, why talk? Conversely, where there is little power far more emphasis has to be put on the relationship. We are left with little choice. As a small organisation facing a dominant market we have to call out the favours we can. We network furiously. Creativity thrives in this situation. When we have too much power creativity tends to suffer.

Power against relationship is the main axis that we can all easily play or suffer from when we have a lack of one or the other. As well as feeling this and acting on it when we have little power, it's worth bearing in mind when we have more power. As we have seen, power is at its very best when it embraces the relational axis fully as well. Truly great power combines both.

In striking a daily balance we might also ask ourselves which is more important to us – doing or relating? If you still think that the answer might be 'if in doubt, do', there's one more thing to think about. Getting going early is not the recommendation coming out of research carried out by Michael Bar-Eli and his team at Ben Gurion University into goalkeeping in football. Bar-Eli's team watched many hours' footage of penalties. What they learnt was that goalkeepers save almost three times as many penalties when they stay in the centre of the goal as opposed to when they dive left or right. What is most surprising is that in over 90 per cent of the time in this study, goalkeepers dive when a penalty is taken. Logic would not support this. The reason for the goalie's dive seems to be the social pressure the keeper feels under to be seen to do something. Staying still and waiting is tough. This bias towards action results in the goalie saving fewer penalties. The conclusion from the study is clear: the average goalkeeper acts before they have enough information to decide which way to go. A better goalkeeper would stay in the middle and wait for more information.

Again, it's the balance between the two that actually matters. I once managed to sink a boat while out racing. We had been tacking through the wind but were now stationary. A huge gust hit us and in that moment, mainly because we had very little forward movement, we were sitting ducks. We were knocked flat, the open boat filled up with water and with a lead keel and no internal buoyancy we sank quickly. One of the many lessons was that a boat without movement through the water has no steerage. If I had been able to keep sufficient forward movement through the water, I would have simply steered into the gust and the balance of our keel would have helped to bring us upright. Movement is the sailor's friend. Sitting still in life is not necessarily the answer either. Often the right answer is to 'Start before you are ready'; getting going is what you need to do to get feedback and learn. These two behaviours are therefore genuine partners that are best explored as two legs in our power walk. If we naturally have a goalkeeper bias towards action, the trick is not to hop continually on that leg. If we do, eventually it will break.

Bird brain

As I look outside, there is a blackbird on the front lawn. I am drawn to watch it through the window, wondering if the bird can sense me. Instead of just noticing it, I start to observe what it is doing. It moves in nervous hops. Every so often the blackbird pokes at the ground. The balance between its watchfulness and its search for food strikes me. In between watching out for next door's cat and any other predators it doesn't seem to have much time left to find worms.

What I slowly realise is that this balance makes sense for the blackbird. Should the cat be stalking it from the ground or a bird of prey be circling it from on high, it would be very easy for the blackbird, at any moment, to lose its precious life. On the other hand, the gaining of the worm cannot have such a high and immediate impact on the healthy blackbird. It needs food but the importance of breakfast is far outweighed by the biological necessity of staying alive. Survival and protection are nearly everything.

What the bird feels as we watch it gives us a clue to something far more important for us now. That is the idea of being prey, prey or victim to a bigger force. This is something we no longer feel consciously but it seems deeply ingrained in our mind's core make-up and in our behaviour. The journalist and writer Barbara Ehrenreich set out in the 1990s to try to understand why man has such a predilection to conflict and war. Her conclusion was that we are not naturally quite the hunter or farmer we think we are. Much of our brain probably developed at a time when we were prey for big cats and other animals that roamed the open savannah. At that time, we were far smaller in height and far more likely to be preyed on.

The brain has not changed much in size in the past 100,000 years. That is a long time contrasted against the few thousand years of recorded history. If a great deal of the brain's core development occurred at a time when we were preyed upon, it is not surprising that we still react subconsciously as prey and that fear, in particular fear of loss, can play such a large part of our motivation. It also explains the infant need for attachment and the importance of secure base. If we are not confident of our protection in infancy, then the subconscious feeling of being easy prey throughout our lives may well be stronger in us. The prey theory would also explain many other group behaviours, even the 'rubber-necking' we see on a motorway after an accident. If we were, at this time, lower down in the pecking order, big cats used to hunt us and other animals for food. Once one of us, most probably the slowest or least wily, or another animal was caught, the lion was sated. The rest of us were suddenly safe to gather round and watch the gruesome spectacle of the catch being eaten.

Having an underlying default of being preyed on explains why we can be such aggressive hunters. We easily default to seeing our options as a simple choice of hunter or prey. We might seek the hunter position and in order to be safe, look for someone or something to take our place as prey. As soon as we can, we have a tendency to assume the position of the big cat and adopt the predator behaviour in an 'eat or be eaten' reaction. We know that experience of being bullied can turn us into bullies ourselves. In a curious reverse adoption process, the lion and the eagle and other prey animals have even become our symbols of nationhood. This is true of corporates also. The company I worked for when I made my realisation at the start of this book about my own style of negotiation proudly displayed an eagle as its corporate symbol outside its major offices.

The extent to which this predilection to thinking of ourselves as prey varies according to other factors in our upbringing and lives. My suspicion is that it will have some effect in all but the most self-aware and mindful of us. Knowing that we can so easily default to a prey position helps us deal with situations where it occurs. As an example, I once worked with a consultant who was having difficulties with a project. He described to me a meeting with two women who had suddenly become, in his view, unreasonably resistant to a change in branding strategy. I outlined the idea of prey predilection to him and asked him whether thinking of himself as a lion threatening their very existence explained the problem. Is it possible, I asked, that they see you as an aggressive threat and thus are now simply acting defensively out of pure self-protection? This provided the answer for him and for the rest of the meeting he referred to them as 'the antelope'. Once they had come under the influence of fear of being prey, their willingness to engage in any logical discussion had disappeared. His first action was to stop behaving in a way that would remind the antelope of the presence of a lion.

This reaction and its imbalance between a powerful away instinct (from loss) and towards (to gain) is what sits at our instinctual core. Beneath our intellectual reasoning and emotional feeling sits a basic, bodily held, motion-based instinct.

This instinct works deeply in us at all times, and because it is working at a relatively deep unconscious level it is challenging to work with once it kicks in.

The relationship in strength between the two forces is hard to compare empirically and will vary depending on the situation. However, there are rough estimates of the order of magnitude which put it at something like 1:10 – we walk tentatively towards but we run away. Nowadays, we also tend to point a finger as we do so.

Self-conspiracy and blame

If we know where the away instinct comes from, it is hardly surprising that it has a guilty secret, acquired in its past. When a hunter is cornered by a lion, the hunter's instinct tends to be self-preservation. So it is also with the away instinct. In times of stress our instinct naturally leads us to give self higher priority. We can easily default to a model where we put self very much at the centre of things.

This one necessary part of our instinctual drive lies at the heart of so many of our challenges. In improvised drama we see it clearly when we learn to perform. Something goes wrong on the stage and the first thing we want to do is to rescue ourselves by coming up with a funny line or doing something clever. At worst we can freeze with stage fright. We go away into ourselves. This is an unhelpful journey. In extreme circumstances it can lead to suicide. In such a situation what rescues us is reaching out towards others. The solution is relational. In theatre, experienced stage performers know to overcome this instinct, embrace the difficulty and ask fellow performers for help. To survive and prosper we go towards, not away. The same is true when we face difficulty in our lives. Retreating within can be the worst thing to do. It feels right but the mature answer will usually lie in ignoring the instinct and instead asking for help. We have to see the away instinct for what it is, an instinct.

One of the things I see a lot in conflict situations is how readily we externalise the problem. This can take a number of forms but the same thing probably drives it. In the hunter and lion situation, seeking separation between ourselves and the lion as the problem is a smart move. We are not likely to move towards the lion or look upon it favourably. In a modern context, seeking the same separation works differently. Distancing ourselves from the problem can easily work against us. It means that we look for reasons to avoid taking responsibility. If something has gone wrong, therefore, a finger pointed at an external cause is an easy reaction. How easy is it to huddle around the water cooler telling tales about the lions in our lives? What saved us with the lion seems to be what we are fighting still in the workplace and at home; we externalise, we blame and we move away into self.

It gets worse, though. What we also run away from is often a bit of ourselves that we don't like. Why do we get so annoyed when our partner leaves a mess in the kitchen? If we care about them and we really are the tidier half of the relationship, wouldn't we just clean up? Often the things that most annoy us are projections of ourselves. We tend to get more annoyed by the mess if we tend to be messy ourselves. We see our own failings and move away from them. This often comes up in coaching situations where a client cannot understand their anger over a simple act: the open fridge door, the unwashed cup. Why do I get so annoyed? It's not rational. Are you good at being tidy? I ask. The answer often stalls us. Actually no, I'm just as bad, is the reflective answer. If we are genuinely coming from a position of being without blame ourselves, then excusing our partner or colleague is easy; they clearly forgot and we have a chance to help out. The problem is when it goes deeper. We don't want to empty the bin ourselves. We get annoyed by the bin overflowing because the failure, the tendency to stuff that little bit more in, is actually a bit of us.

> Why do you look at the speck that is in your brother's eye,
> but do not notice the log that is in your own eye?
>   Matthew 7:3

One of the things I always try to observe particularly is what each of us say about others. This perhaps harks back to the question of 'the bigger the front the bigger the back'. So often what we see in others and dislike, we end up naming. In truth it's ourselves we are shaming. If someone annoys us because they talk too much, we should perhaps ask ourselves first whether that annoyance tells us something about what we don't like in ourselves. A common question I ask of people is what angers them. In their answer usually lies a clue as to the deepest issues they face. Anger is our insight to the deepest questions.

Our anger can so easily get misplaced. The ferocity with which we get angry at, say, another driver often cannot be entirely attributed to the situation itself. When we get cut up on the road it is perhaps our need for control and autonomy that so upsets us. If we have had a bad day and been pushed around by a difficult client or boss, is it more or less likely that we will also be annoyed by the way we are treated by the traffic? It can be easier to externalise the anger we feel onto these external situations that trigger it. When a customer doesn't give us what we need we feel cheated. Yet that is their right. What really upsets us might be our underlying sense of insecurity with our job, which is itself rooted in our desperate need to belong. Where we see these reactions in ourselves we would do well to take time to be more aware of them, to sit with them a little longer, and to ask ourselves where they might really come from. The closer we can bring the real cause to ourselves and our own need, ironically the more we gain.

The thing to remember when we get angry is that by externalising the cause we also give up control. If what was making us angry was a deeper cause held within us, we actually have more control over it if we take it back. If we realise this, we can do something about the need we have: we can own it. To know this is great news.

> I was angry with my friend
> I told my wrath, my wrath did end.
> I was angry with my foe,
> I told it not,
> My wrath did grow.
>> William Blake, 'A Poison Tree'
>> from *Songs of Experience*

People have always been surprised that I like nothing more in a corporate setting than an expression of anger. This is because when someone is angry I feel that we have two things. First, we have expression, which is better than no expression. Behind that expression lies a need that we can find out about and potentially meet. Second, the anger shows a lack of real power. We get angry because that is all we can do. The powerful tend not to voice their disquiet. They have a means to act. If someone is angry in a corporate context, it is usually because they are in a desperate position. It's good to know that.

Loss

The bird's away instinct leads it to value what it has, its life, much more highly than the value of the gain, the worm. Loss is therefore part of the strong protective away instinct. When we are trying to convince people of something we will often focus on what they will get from the change, the gain. Thinking like this is logical, a function of our developed thinking. We may notice, though, that people will struggle to accept a change. Either they act convinced by rational argument and then don't follow up or maybe something just keeps them from accepting what seems like a perfectly logical argument. What may be stopping the change being accepted is not a lack of belief in the gain, but an underlying sense of loss. The loss subconsciously swamps the gain. This sense of loss can have the effect of making us fixed and positional to what we have rather than fluid and open to possibility of what we might gain.

the non-obvious loss   overwhelms the small gain

This effect is often called the 'loss heuristic' or 'endowment effect'. In short this is the inbuilt preference we have to avoid a loss rather than experience a similar gain. On an expenditure of £100, a £10 discount to £100 from £110 is nice but a £10 surcharge from £90 is immediately unattractive. The surcharge triggers a different reaction. We want to avoid it at all costs. It is a loss of £10. Same money, different feeling. This effect also means that we tend to value what we have at more than the actual cost of replacing it. In one experiment testers managed to get people who had been given a mug to put a value on their mug.[5] The testers also offered the same mug to others to buy. On average the losers valued the mug at $7.12 and the gainers at $2.87.

So, in many situations loss sits below the surface. What we see on top is reluctance or lack of movement. Maybe the valid proposal you are making is not landing as it should or the work team are struggling to make a necessary change. If we dig we can often bring to the surface the loss that lies beneath. Asking a question like 'What have you got today that you won't have with …' can help surface the potential loss. Like Blake's wrath, once named it can shrink. Once talked about and made real the loss often goes away or becomes easier to deal with. The blockage is now named so that it can be included in discussions rather than remaining as a block. The challenge is to prompt a process to enable this to happen.

Models

Nowadays we accept far more readily than ever that people have different motivations and ways of seeing things and that we each have different strengths. There are many models for understanding different types of people. In my experience a few key ones really help. The first that really made an impact on me was the Social Styles Model. When I joined Andersen Consulting in the 1990s it is one of the things we used in practice. It's a simple two by two that divides people into four essential types.

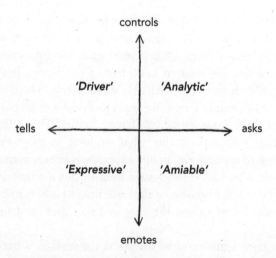

What interests me most about this model now are the axes themselves, which we will come back to later. What we focused on at the time, however, were the types. Anyone who wanted to be successful in the firm at that time needed to be a Driver. The firm was very much an organisation that liked and traded on control. We had quite a few Analytics; but it was best if they were in support or technical roles. Drivers are decisive, action-oriented people. Their downside is that they tend to dominate and not listen. Our legal and accounting folk tended to be Analytics. They are thinkers who do the detail and tend to be more considered and risk averse. A good sales or marketing person might be Expressive: imaginative and enthusiastic but also prone to the occasional fantasy. Finally, the Amiables are endearing, supportive and easy-going but prone to dithering. I was, at that point, moving from Expressive in a mostly Amiable direction and often felt slightly out of place as a result.

What was crucially important to us was to see these styles in our clients. To an Expressive IT director we listened, indulged and then sold a solution to meet the grand vision. To the Analytic we presented a detailed plan to be pored over, answering every possible question. Using the wrong strategy with the wrong person caused fireworks. In time, everyone learnt that. This model has proved its use in sales situations and is now quite widely used by many organisations in different forms.

Nowadays I tend to see leaders through a slightly different practical lens that is perhaps simpler. This is the Visionary, Operator, Processor model – or VOP – which was developed by experienced business operator Les McKeown.[6] What Les noticed is that most people in business tended to fit into one of three major behavioural types. To start a business we need a Visionary, someone who sees into the art of the possible; an imaginative soul who gets excited about what could be. The problem is that the Visionary is not easily tied down and flits from one thing to the next. With only visionary skills the job of work itself tends to go undone. What happens is that the successful Visionary teams up with an Operator, someone who likes to get on with things; the master of doing. Together this pair make thing happen. As the business grows these two realise that it cannot survive on their energy and ball-juggling alone. They need more people. More people brings the need for some process. This produces a requirement for the Processor who brings structure, control and compliance. These different types can be summarised as follows:

	Motivation	*Behaviour*	*Perspective*
VISIONARY	Starting	Talk, Think (Solve)	30,000 feet
OPERATOR	Fixing	Do, Decide (Action)	The runway
PROCESSOR	Systematising	Analyse, Align (Control)	Underground

The difference I see in these types is in the way that we use our imagination. The Visionary and the Processor both have fertile imaginations. They are just used in different directions. The Visionary sees the possibilities, the Processor sees the risks; both are useful viewpoints and, like the Analytic and the Expressive types, they need to be sold to differently. The challenge is that if we can't see that these are different viewpoints and see them instead as truths, that can create difficulties in a team. The Visionary and the Processor thus tend to clash if they have to work together. The Operator, on the other hand, is actually more interested in getting things done. If the Operator is not kept busy, you'll know about it soon enough. Others, though, will see the Operator as too simplistically biased towards action, whereas the Processor can be seen as too systemised and the Visionary as overly sweeping. In a team or in a negotiation if you can see that people have these different motivations, behaviours and perspectives, you are better informed about how you relate to them.

It's important to remember that these are all types and this is only a model. It's not the truth. The reality is that people will usually be a bit of one and a bit of another. Rarely is it as clear as the model and sometimes a person starts a business on their own navigating between the two needs of vision and operations. Les also has a fourth type, the Synergist, who is a master of all three and can move about at will. Moving towards the Synergist style is the eventual goal of the wise.

Elements of other models tend to be useful in different circumstances. One of my roles was to take over the leadership of about
thirty people who were not functioning as any sort of team.
There were many elements to this challenge including some very
particular and personal challenges. One of these concerned two
managers who really didn't like each other but needed to work
together from time to time. There was a possibility to split them
up permanently but both had negotiation responsibilities and
I felt they at least should make an effort to understand why
they clashed. By chance, in a review meeting with Alison, the
more senior of the pair, she mentioned her interest in learning
more about the people side of the job. She also said that she'd
done a psychometric test and would like to understand it better.
Given the situation, this proactive interest was music to my ears.
It turned out that she had her Myers Briggs Type Instrument
(MBTI) results. Myers Briggs is now the granddaddy of all
models in this area and was the 1950s brainchild of Isabel Myers
who worked with her mother, Kathryn Briggs. MBTI was
originally invented on the back of Jungian-based psychological
archetypes in order to help people to get back into work after
the war. Everything is easier to understand with something to
push against so I plotted up on a flipchart the MBTI types and
asked Alison to circle her results. We then together plotted what
we thought the results for her antithesis, Michael, would be. I
joined up the circles with two lines that showed the differences
between them. It looked like this:

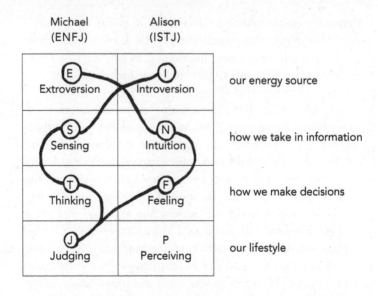

This showed a clash in three key areas. Firstly, Alison was 'introverted' (the I) whereas Michael was very much more 'extroverted' (the E) in both senses: he was loud, outgoing and expressive but he also got his energy from the external world. This explained some of the feedback I was getting about him. Some people just didn't like him. Others could bear his extroversion and respected his underlying ability more. Alison by contrast was reserved, she needed her own space to dwell. Introverts think to talk whereas extroverts talk to think. This was enough of a clash in itself. An extrovert invading an introvert's space can be highly threatening. I'd seen this happening between the pair in the open space area we shared. Michael crowded Alison and she hated it; it exhausted her.

Secondly, Michael was more 'intuitive' (the N) compared to Alison's 'sensing' (S) approach. Michael tended to see his own internal big picture, whereas Alison was focused on the facts, what she could actually see, hear and read. Michael would describe the ocean as big and wide, Alison would say that it was wet and blue. This meant that even when they were in the same room, they picked up things differently.

Thirdly, the way they made decisions was different. Michael was much more of a 'feeler' (the F). Alison was a 'thinker' (the T). She would think things through thoroughly and logically and could be quite tough on people, whereas Michael was friendlier. Although he could be quite loud he would think about the people involved. Ironically, although he came across as brash to some because of his extreme extroversion, emotions and people really mattered for him.

Alison and Michael came together in the 'J' at the bottom. This is no great relief, however, because it stands for Judgement and measures their propensity to rush to conclusion and stick to a fixed schedule. Being the same here, as opposed to a 'P' – a Perceiver – who probes more and enjoys the journey more, can cause as many challenges as it might solve.

The key for Alison lay in the first three levels, with the clash in the second two being very much central to the core of their work. Alison considered this and started to talk about a few situations where she had clashed with Michael. What she now understood was how they each heard and processed information differently. They could listen to what a client said in negotiations but whereas Alison focused on the words themselves, Michael saw the bigger picture through his own mind's-eye. As a thinker, Alison then made logical conclusions whereas for Michael the people and his felt trust in the situation factored more highly. This slightly different way of listening and processing was not only at the heart of their difference but was also a more general lesson for Alison about the limitations of her worldview. Now that she knew others could see more than her, she was more able to see it herself. In future negotiations, Alison reported that she saw more of these different approaches at work and found it easier to accept them and deal with them sensitively.

This is a very quick journey through three models because often it is not the models themselves that are interesting but how we can use them to help understand a situation. Being stuck in a model isn't necessarily helpful. However, the Social Styles Model in particular is built on something quite fundamental. The horizontal axis is essentially a measure of how someone asserts themselves in a group. At one end of the scale we can assert by telling and at the other end of the scale we find out, by asking. In telling, the energy, the information, comes from us; in asking it comes from others. The vertical scale is a measure of responsiveness to emotions and feelings. At the top of the scale, we keep our emotions hidden inside. Either they are not there or we suppress them. What we do is to take control, we reason. At the bottom of the scale we emote freely to others.

This model, then, follows the on-going tension between the intellect and the emotions and picks up self and other along the way. Expressed slightly differently it looks like this:

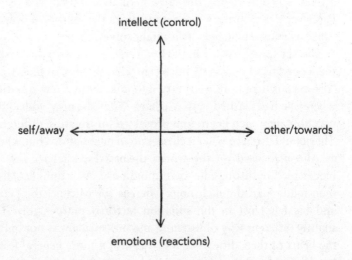

You might notice that this can also be mapped on to our bodies. The head tops the model in the same way as it forms the top part of our body. We don't really know where our emotional centre is located, but somewhere near the heart around the solar plexus at the base of the ribs is a good starting point, although it may well be lower. The emotions sit atop the motion centre in the navel, above the pelvis, which is also roughly where our centre of gravity is and from where they can easily and directly mediate the physical bodily movement that ultimately drives our whole body physically away or towards. A movement to self is simply a pulling back into the body and a movement towards others is simply a move forwards. Our intellect sits in a complex system like a rider on a horse. Too often we believe that the rider is in charge when really the horse of our emotional being is the one ultimately with control, and the legs to prove it.

The reverse, though, being completely ruled by a bucking horse and the primitive urges we have, is not the answer either. Our challenge is the integration of the whole: horse and rider working together. To be truly whole we need to be able to move around freely. To be one or the other is ultimately not to be whole. Cutting ourselves off in our heads from the engine room of our emotions is like cutting off the bridge of the ship from the rest of the vessel. We can live in boxes but the challenge for us is to be able to move fluidly around depending on context and need. This works on the horizontal self/other dynamic also. Each crisis is different. In bereavement our best route to wholeness is probably to reach out to others. In a fire, though, we don't want to explore the community dynamic and ask others. Instead, we need an immediate and clear direction.

Stephen Covey's answer to this challenge is that we look at the word 'responsibility'. That word is worthy of being broken down into parts. Responsibility is the ability to choose our response. It is both Response and Ability to choose. What it accentuates is the potential of the gap between stimulus and response. These two don't have to be directly connected. Attention training and mindfulness is ultimately about expanding the space between stimulus and response in order to create a reflective moment in which we can make choices. In this space lies a huge amount of freedom and power that is available for us to take. If we can feel the stimulus coming in as an emotional flicker then all we need to do is unplug our immediate reaction to it. Into that gap goes our 'response able' freedom to choose. Daniel Siegel sees the process of the stimulus coming in as a 'Wheel of Awareness' with our awareness at the hub in the centre. Using that model we can see things that happen as being separate from us. They are on the outer extremity of the wheel. They are not us and we do not have to be subject to them. We direct our attention along the spokes towards them as separate things. We don't have to be consumed by them but can choose how we respond.

Ultimately, instead of thinking in terms of 'I am ... (happy/sad/an emotion)' we understand that we are simply experiencing the emotion at that time. 'I am angry' becomes 'I am experiencing anger'. There is a subtle but critical difference. It visits our house and passes through. To start to see a physical or time distance between stimulus and reaction also helps. We can therefore step away or leave the room for a moment in extremis. Instead of being given a hand grenade that is just about to go off which panics us, we have instead an explosive on a slow-burning fuse that gives us more time to think. To be able to do this on demand, in a potentially difficult situation, is the ultimate goal. If we can do it whenever we need it, our power grows. We also access the nirvana of remaining calm under pressure.

It is a choice, initially and then later. As wise Nepalese Buddhist and teacher Yongey Mingyur Rinpoche says:

> Ultimately, happiness comes down to choosing between the discomfort of becoming aware of your afflictions and the discomfort of being ruled by them.

The secret of meditation, mindful living and attention training is the ability to build this awareness and our ability to choose a response. The first thing we learn when we try to meditate is how many thoughts we have that come rushing by like trains.[7] We learn that we don't have to get on a train at that point. Meditation is partly the process of waving to the trains but letting them go by. Greater self-awareness allows us to grow and exert choice in this space between, stimulus and response. In the same way we learn to manage the thoughts that come rushing in, we also learn to manage the emotional impulses. The power of this process is that, like any fitness training, it builds and tones our mental muscles.

Albert Einstein famously said:

> The intuitive mind is a sacred gift and the rational mind is a faithful servant. We have created a society that honours the servant and has forgotten the gift.

In our rationally focussed world, we do need a reminder of the gift but perhaps we are partly in this bind because we know that the intuitive, more emotional part of the mind can also be a bad master. Once again, there is a balance to be achieved here. How we achieve this mediation, between head and heart, for ourselves is a very personal thing. Possibly our biggest life challenge is to get this delicate orchestration between emotion and rationality to work and to open up more space to make better choices. Perhaps the trick is to make sure first that our sacred emotional gift is fully heard and then, if our rationality should indeed prevail, it should do so, but only just. Alongside our creativity this in essence is what being human is all about. In order to do that it's first important that we form an accurate understanding of what we perceive with our senses. Forcussing on this process is our next port of call.

CHAPTER 6

AWARENESS

Perspective is the Achilles heel of the mind.
Dee Hock

It's a fine summer evening on the far eastern end of the Chilterns. A group of cyclists are out on the road enjoying the gentle roll of the hills as they flatten out towards Cambridge.[1] I am bringing up the rear, and am enjoying a quiet, relaxed ride. As I reach the crest of the hill, I can see the rest of the group ahead, strung out over quite a distance. They are descending rapidly and the leaders are moving towards the beginning of another hill in the distance.

The pressure in my pedals eases as the wheels reach the summit and I quickly take in the information ahead of me. Within a second, I know from slight clues of colour, shape, style of riding and my own expectations of each rider where all the others are and how long it would take me to catch up to the front of the group if I so wished.

What I don't see at this moment is each rider as they actually are. I don't see that the second rider is wearing a red top with baggy green shorts and cross-correlate that with what I observed John to be wearing earlier, thus building a proposition that John is that second rider. I don't need to go that far or waste that much effort. Instead, I take in just enough simple information to know that John is second and Steve is a distance out ahead.

The power of the human brain is that it doesn't just collect information, as a computer does. We immediately see patterns and connections. These connections tend to be made purposively. My tendency is to look for a distinct purpose, to see where the riders are. Thus, the information I get tends to be filtered towards that purpose. The rub is that this quick processing of information that can be so useful to us can also be our downfall when we negotiate or deal with complex situations. This power to purposively see patterns and make quick suppositions from them can lead us to miss vast swathes of useful information. This chapter aims to help us to understand why so that we can start to choose how, and thus what, we observe. There are at least eight key ways in which our awareness ends up being restricted.

The purposive

As you think, so shall you hear.
Sydney Banks

Our first challenge is to see that very often our vision is limited. Instead of a clear lens we see things selectively. My focused view of the road ahead as I come over the brow of the hill is exactly that, focused. Like a car driver in a hurry, it is too easy to be so focused on the task in hand. Meanwhile other information, either side of our focus, can get missed completely. When we are racing to an appointment the cyclist emerging from the side street can go unnoticed. This phenomenon also works more widely in the way we process information. Our state of mind can influence how we interpret information. A happy man receives challenging news differently from an unhappy one. If we are tired we tend to see things as bigger obstacles than they really are. We say that 'hills look bigger to a tired walker' and they do.

This phenomenon of focus is also known as 'selective attention' and there are plenty of videos on the internet to illustrate the point. The most famous is by Daniel Simons and Christopher Chabris and concerns a group of players passing a basketball. At least that is what we are asked to focus on. If you haven't seen it, I won't spoil your chance to watch it. A modern favourite is Richard Wiseman's Colour Changing Card Trick.[2] An easy test to do on your own right now is to get a paper and pen and then take thirty seconds to look around you and write down everything that is green. If you really want to do this test, do this now or don't read the next paragraph.

Once you've completed the test, close your eyes and make a mental list of everything that is brown. How do the two compare? The tests all work best in pressurised situations. If you are in a classroom situation, perhaps offered a prize, told that you are competing with others or that people of a certain intelligence generally do well at certain aspects of the test, you are more likely to have the focus required to prove the selective attention that the test is aimed at.

On my journey to deal with this problem, what I didn't expect to find was a solution to selective attention through running. The idea I came across arose from a method of training put forward by ultra distance runner Stu Mittleman.[3] Mittleman uses a series of three heart rate zones to run in and has developed a method of working out your heart rate in each zone. What he does is encourage you to notice more about your visual, auditory and kinaesthetic states as you move through the zones. In the base zone you are comfortable and notice a lot about what is going on around you. As you speed up into the most efficient zone this changes. My most interesting finding was that above a heart rate of about 134, as I moved into the top zone, my vision noticeably started to tunnel, I found it more difficult to focus on what was either side of me and tended to have less 'bandwidth' available for particularly visual information. The fact that this happened seemed logical; my body was choosing to conserve resources and focus on what it felt really mattered – the road ahead.

Because I was aware that this was happening, I started to think about the effect in detail and also played with it as I endeavoured to train within the zones. One day I started to experiment with the idea of managing my heart rate through my consciousness rather than accepting it as an output of how fast I ran. This involved opening up my tunnel vision. I found that if I made a conscious effort to open my field of vision, to notice the trees and bushes and to listen for sounds around me, that helped bring my heart rate down. I was conscious it was not the main lever but increasingly I used it as one of the methods to help me manage my state. The tunnelling of vision that started as an effect of exercise and a higher heart rate could also be used as a trigger to reverse control my heart rate.

The experiment didn't stop there. I found that if I was stressed going into a difficult meeting, the technique also worked well then. By making a positive effort to look around and notice things I could feel my stress level coming down. Stress and narrowing of field of vision seemed to be related. The exercise of looking around and noticing more had a wider effect on my state. I also began to start conversations just to help this perceptual widening to happen and learnt that even a pleasant conversation with, say, a receptionist would also help me to relax and take me out of the narrow stressed zone that I might otherwise be in. The idle chitchat that we can so easily strip out of our lives in service of a narrow purpose has itself a broader purpose.

As well as being situational this narrowing of vision can affect our wider lives. The forces that drive us compulsively to achieve and to focus on outcomes can be addictive. As educationalist Ken Robinson points out, this narrowing process starts in school.[4] Then, as we go through life, these pressures can funnel us towards more and more specialised and limited experience.

Because:

One of the myths of ageing is that we cannot do all the things that we once could. But the actual fact about ageing is that we cease to do all the things that we once did. As our search for a vocation settles into a fixed 'job', as our search for a mate settles into marriage, as our many expectations settle into a finite number of fulfilments, as our aspirations settle into steady certitudes, and as our broad range of potential movements settles into a narrow band of habitual movements, we will inevitably find ourselves looking in fewer directions and moving in fewer direct ion s.

(Somatic practitioner Thomas Hanna's words and my arrangement of them).[5]

If the accepted goal of being 'grown up' is that we obtain more certainty and fixity, creating a funnelling effect towards singular focus, then the marrying up of this with less time to look around is going to result in a massive diversion away from what is there and towards what we expect or want to be there. We all experience this narrowing of our habits and experiences. As a result we are all receiving substantially fewer inputs. Quietly we know that the best things in life, our partners, our friends, the coupling of sperm and egg that made us, are things of random chance arising from a wide range of possibility. The good news is that once we see this perceptual narrowing, we can do something about it. This might mean taking a different route to work so that we lift our heads and notice more or it might mean taking more time simply to look around. Anything we do like this will have an immediate effect on our awareness.

The positional

I was driving and I saw a runner with his dog ahead of me. It was someone familiar, out for a training run on a quiet country lane near where I live. I was in no hurry and steered the car out into the road, away from the runner and, seeing the runner and his dog move out also, moved out fully to avoid what I saw. I'd quickly calculated that what they needed from me was a wide berth.

At that point, the runner stopped running. A runner slowing down to a walk is hardly unusual but something told me that this sudden change required my attention. A moment later, I was alongside and for the first time could see what he had seen: a horse and rider appearing from a bridleway alongside the road. I could now see that the runner's dog was pulling towards the horse. The runner had seen something which I had not.

In order to really understand the runner, I needed to to see things from his perspective, which was different to mine. Effectively there are two levels of seeing. I thought I was aware of the runner and had all the information about the situation. I was already taking evasive action and thought I had things covered. What I still wasn't seeing was the next level, what he was seeing. Ideally, I needed to see him first through my eyes, and then, if I really wanted to understand him properly, to see through his eyes as well. It's too easy to make the mistake that what we see through our eyes, from our position, is what the other person sees, when it isn't.

What we are dealing with here, when we work with others, is a two lens model. Not only do we need to see accurately through our own lens, we also need to recognise that what often matters most is what the other sees through theirs. This is not easy. Seeing through two lenses on a good day introduces at least twice the level of distortion. On a moderate day that factor of complication is probably generous. Two lenses can easily give two squared, i.e. four times, the expected level of distortion. Seeing from someone else's perspective is harder than seeing through your own. Getting rid of distortions and misunderstandings in the signal can take more time than we expect.

The sped-up

Walking across Russell Square in London, I notice a woman on the path in front of me. She holds her phone as a camera pointed in my direction. It's a beautiful autumn morning and as I get to just beyond where she was, I stop and look back. She has moved on but I now see what she saw: the criss-crossing paths, the fountain in the centre, trees in various states of leaf, people walking to work, others with dogs and the café emitting steam in the background. It's a great view to take in. So much depth to tap into, if we choose. This appreciative thought leads me to the contrast between the quick photo I have just seen being taken and the drawing we might have made, had a camera not been available.

What would we do without the 'dark chamber' that we can now carry round us in digital form where light can be processed and saved into an instantly shareable image? We would simply do what people used to do, we would draw the image to share with others using paper and pen. In doing so we would have to accept that the image may not be as accurate as the photo and it would certainly take more time but that time would be used for a purpose. I would need to take this time from my day because I would need to look at each object in view, take it in, in order to reconstruct it on the page. In this way of seeing, the trees would no longer simply be trees that I can now, having briefly looked at the view, no longer accurately recall. I would have to look at the trees well enough to be able to draw them in detail, the shape of their trunks, the texture, then the pattern of their branches and leaves. And that is just the trees. Taking in this view and drawing it would take me all morning.

This photographic approach of 'just enough' is an inevitable function of our busy lives. What happens, then, when we enter the meeting room for that vital conversation? Do we suddenly change perspective and see all the detail? Incessant busyness and focus on the pathway we need to follow can strip colour and context from the edges of our lives. When we first join a motorway from a smaller road, we might notice the speed we are travelling at until after a while that speed seems normal. Our eyes adjust. Instead of focusing on stationary things, we are primarily focused on other traffic, which is moving along with us. If we do look at anything that is still, it will usually be large and thus visible in the distance, like a pylon or a building. To communicate with us on the motorway, huge signs are needed which we can view from a distance. In our sped-up lives on life's highway, the signage doesn't always get enlarged to cater for the speed we are now travelling at.

In the office 'busy' can become the language also. I once watched from a hot desk in a London office as one young man approached another who was sitting adjacent to me. 'Hi, how are you?' he said. 'Busy?' 'Yeah, I'm busy,' his colleague replied, 'busy, busy, always busy. You?' 'Yeah, busy, real busy,' came the response. The conversation went on like this for a bit longer but no useful information was disclosed other than mutual confirmation that both were indeed busy and thus everything was good with them. Like cars on the motorway, no context was shared.

In excess of busyness, our diary, which starts as a tool to serve us in planning, can become the master, cracking the whip over our week. We lose context. Suddenly, it is not we who decide what we are doing next, it is our diary. It doesn't matter that we are not in the mood for a creative planning workshop at 2pm. It is now in our diary so that is what we are doing. In such a focused schedule, things that could be present but seem to exist round the edges end up getting lost to our sight. The human touch, the little contextual clues and the creativity that the meeting really needs to allow it to come alive grow out of the very thing that busyness prevents.

Once, frustrated by a meeting that simply was not happening despite emails going back and forth between PAs, I broke through this haze to get a result. The meeting was about a very sensitive matter where the company I was working for needed to build influence and gain information. I remember pausing and thinking for a moment about what I could do to break the cycle of clashing diaries and priorities. It was suddenly obvious. I turned to the meeting organiser and asked if I could have the other person's mobile phone number. The cat and mouse of diaries and possible meeting locations had to end. I called the client's commercial director on his mobile and he answered. At that point we were into a different, human conversation. We covered the meeting and why each of us wanted it to happen. The breakthrough came when I asked where he travelled into London from. He came into King's Cross and his train stopped at a main station 20 minutes from where I lived. Would he be happy to break his journey one morning? I asked. Yes, came the answer. We found a day when I needed to work from home and set a date. The meeting we had over a coffee in my car in the station car park was one of the most honest and helpful I have ever had. It happened because of the breakthrough we made back into useful personal contextual information. This happened both in the setting up of the meeting but also in the meeting itself. When we met we didn't just discuss what we needed to discuss, we also picked up areas of communality such as the journey into London, the joys and trials of living a long way from work, children, schools and a variety of related matters. This context allowed us to do something far greater. We still had focus to come back to but we were able to put it into context. That context made it easier both to get to the meeting in the first place, and easier to communicate openly and commit to our outcomes once we met.

This contextual loss is highly evident in modern forms of communication. Email, text, instant messaging and all the other short forms of contacting each other have been with us for a very short time. We are only just getting used to them. One of the emerging problems is that they lack context. While an email may be a great way to agree a time to meet it might not be a good way to agree all the other details about that meeting. It certainly isn't a good way to do anything that requires a conversation. The purposes for which these forms of communication now get used is far wider than letters tended to be. If we need input or detail from the other person, a conversation is likely to be a better method. Just because email exists doesn't mean that everything can or should be agreed using it.

Voice communications such as the telephone have been available for much longer than pure data but we are still getting used to the additional difficulty that occurs when we lose visual clues. For many this is not a problem, either because they are more auditory than visual anyway or because, like anyone who loses one sense, we can get used to getting more information from another. This isn't true of all, though. Many people and thus many conversations lose a great deal of information and context as soon as face to face shifts to voice to voice.

We therefore need to take care that in the search for a greater width of experience we do not lose the depth that makes it really work. What point are hundreds of clients and a full diary if we don't know them well? We can lose ourselves in busyness but the danger is that we stretch ourselves too thin. The decision we have is between depth and breadth. As the breadth of our attention grows the depth must suffer. And sometimes it is just more depth in the immediate present, that we urgently need.

The filtered

The 1950s are a long way to go back for some guidance on this topic. In 1953 design gurus Ray and Charles Eames made a classic film for IBM about the basics of communication. 'A Communications Primer' is available online and takes the process back to its very basic components in an unusually straightforward and compelling way. The film introduces a signal transmission system that can apply to any communication, from a simple buy signal between stockbrokers in New York and Los Angeles to complex two-way 'intercourse by words'. The system introduced by the husband and wife team relies on a diagram by mathematician and ex-Second World War code-breaker Claude Shannon, a pioneer of modern digital processing and communications systems. Shannon's diagram of the process is reproduced below:

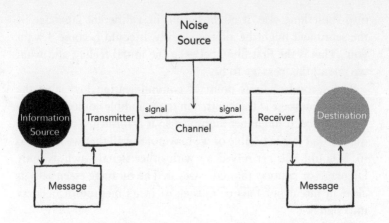

Shannon allows us to separate communication into its component parts. As the message originates, what is striking is the separation of actual source from message creation and transmission. The broker, say, decides to sell but then puts that decision into a 'Sell' message that needs to be transmitted by a transmitter. In the same way, we may have a feeling we want to communicate but that is separate from the transmission we actually make. Origination and final understanding of a message are separate from the process of transmission or receipt. At the other side of the communication, the message needs to distilled out of what has been received via the transmitter. In putting the process like this, Shannon shows there are a number of easy interference points in a complex process of communication. Both parties have multiple filters. In choosing to relay a message there is a filter between feeling or thought to message. Then there is a further filter in transmission. How we say the message can affect it also. On the other side, in receiving, the same two filters in hearing and translation also exist. In addition, there is the opportunity of 'noise' between. That is at least five easy opportunities for the message to get distorted.

If we take a simple piece of desired communication, as the Eames' film does, of a feeling of love, this starts as a feeling in the instigator of the communication. It may be translated by them into a simple message of 'I love you' but it might be translated into something else. It might be put in a different language or the sentiment might be altered slightly. It could become 'I want you'. This is the first filter, between the initial feeling and what we intend the message to be.

The second obvious point of communication loss is as the intended message is transmitted in to an audible communication by the voice. It might get mumbled so it is misheard or made so quietly that it is inaudible or we may not say all that we intended to. It could also get mixed up with other signals such as body language or context that confuses it. The message essentially is clear in intent but fails or falls short in its method of delivery into signal.

The third point of potential signal loss is in the communication channel between transmitter and receiver. The signal could simply be lost through distance or being passed through a confused medium or it could be the victim of interfering noise. Either way, the signal, in the space between, is vulnerable and exposed. In the hands of any receiver the key words of 'I love you' could be accentuated and thus picked up but a message and sentiment of love could be lost. What is actually received could be an unclear 'I xxxx you'.

Finally, there are a set of filters in receipt which mirror those in transmission. Just because the ear hears the words, the filter between ear and felt sense might impose a feeling of something else. Context, perhaps a row or a betrayal, might be in mind, resulting in the actual heard word being translated differently. What is felt is no longer really love but perhaps an appeal or an apology. In other circumstances, perhaps in passion, whispered softly or after a special evening together, the words, even combined with other signals, could be filtered to mean something very different and more powerful.

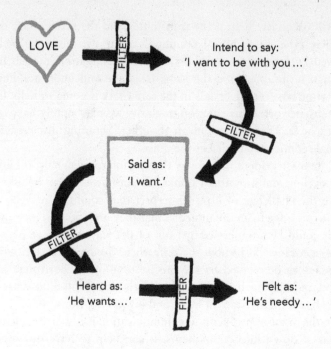

How a message can get distorted
through the various filters

Noise is anything that gets in the way between transmission and receipt. It is the external world getting in the way of what we communicate.

One way of dealing with noise interference is to create redundancy; we create extra signal to deal with it. This could be as simple as shouting or turning the volume up. Sometimes our systems have built in redundancy. The simplicity of the 'Buy' or 'Sell' signal allows a letter or two to be misplaced or the word to be mispronounced. Our brains are also good at allowing redundancy in places, particularly in visual communications:

> we can awlyss mkae smoe ssnee wtih mxniig lrettes up
> as lnog as the fsrit and lsat lrettes and the oedrr of wdors
> are kpet the smae

It will obviously help if the transmitter and the receiver are of similar type. In technical communications we might be well served by having the same or at least a compatible model. In human terms, speaking the same language and understanding the same non-verbal signals in the same way is going to help. In the absence of a clear solution or clarity we may simply have to work at it. That doesn't mean shouting. Shouting just creates signal redundancy to defeat the noise.

Filters are evident in the way that we interpret signals. If I am out cycling and a motorist honks his horn at me from behind I have the challenge of how I interpret that sound. It may be a polite message from the motorist that they are about to pass me or it could be an annoyed 'get out of the way, you piece of...' message. How do I know the difference? To expect a clarity of message to be relayed by the precise tone of the horn may be expecting too much. It is far more likely that I will filter what I hear based on my state of mind and my assumptions.

In the event of problems in communication it is worthwhile to break it down into components. It can help to have our own 'wiring diagram' to refer to, to see the problem more clearly. Often the problem is simply with the filters that are in operation. In that case simply being aware of this and double checking, asking about the message in a slightly different way, helps to achieve clarity. The message can often get distorted early on, in its gestation. What starts as a feeling of love can end up voiced as something else. If that is so, obtaining clarity about the real nature of the feeling, beyond the words used to transmit it, can be the most valuable thing to do. Other times the problem can be in receipt, the message, though heard, simply fails to get through a filter that resists it. Again, to be aware of this and to use other methods to assist the blocked filter can be the thing that saves lives.

The Judgemental

The human brain has a design constraint that is fundamental to the way it works. This constraint is the need for a baby's head to pass through its mother's pelvis.

In our on-going development to be smarter, wiser and bigger brained this problem could be easily solved. However, evolution has already chosen to solve it differently. The boundaries of this 'obstetrical dilemma' were already tested by our decision two million years ago to walk on two legs. That development itself put its own pressures on the balance of possible solutions to the problem. Walking and the need to be able to run once again changed the needs of the human body. The forces of evolution sorted out the dilemma by a radical solution. In order to gain mobility, the human female developed a smaller birth canal which is balanced out in turn by a shorter gestation period and a smaller, and initially softer, brain at birth. Human children are thus born early with the biggest possible head they can have. Yes, it hurts but any bigger and birth would hurt even more or simply not be possible.

The result of this design constraint is that the brain likes to work efficiently. It has to, as it can't afford to get bigger. Thinking, which usually involves the pre-frontal cortex, is actually hard and tiring work. It's like running a resource hungry application on a smartphone. The base operating system would like to get by without it if it can. Use the sophisticated application too much and you will flatten the battery very quickly. As a result we operate cognitively in two gears. If we can answer a question by using our base system we generally will. We might be asked what we think about something but if we can answer the question based on how we feel about the question, we probably will.

A question like 'What is 2 plus 2?' is very different from 'What is 102 divided by 6?' The first we can do easily but the latter stalls us for a moment and requires our concentration. To answer the more complicated question we have to fire up a different part of our brain. We generally don't like to do this. The end result is that a journey into the intellect is like going to consult a smart lawyer. It can be illuminating and sometimes it's essential but it might also be expensive. Thus, if you can keep your propositions simple and instinctually appealing, you are more likely to get them quickly accepted.

Over the past few years there has been a multitude of research, writing and practice on how the brain works. Daniel Kahneman in *Thinking Fast and Slow* describes how our minds work in two systems: System 1 is a lazy controller that makes quick judgements, and System 2 is a slow but busy analytical machine that finds answers and makes up stories to justify our quick judgements. The problem with our lazy judge is that he tends to interfere everywhere. He has a role but it should be limited. Our good judgement is what helps us make decisions when we need to. The judge, however, is a busy soul and is keen to put his time-saving skills to work wherever he can. Our job is to control him. The ability to exercise our judge at our moment of choice is a critical skill.

An analogy is the theatre director who makes notes or 'observations' of what she sees on the stage.[6] They contain no interpretation or judgement but merely record what is seen. This allows the director to talk to her cast about what happened and what she observed and to get feedback on it. 'I noticed that you changed the script after laying the table in Scene 2. How did that work out?' contains no judgement. It's pure observation. Visually it might be seen like this:

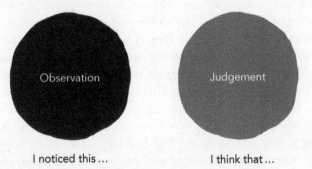

I noticed this ...   I think that ...

Consider what often happens when we give feedback to others. Perhaps this is in a formal review setting where the other person is highly sensitive to what we think about them. The danger there is that observation and judgement can too easily get mixed together.

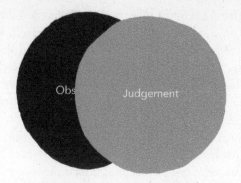

It is too easy for the judge, once active, to take over. The effect of this on the other person is often to produce a defensive response. What is being shared is not observable facts but judgement on them; one person's interpretation. The other person will likely defend to protect a different positional interpretation. First, they may see different facts anyway, positionally or otherwise. Second, they may have selected a different part of what happened. Thirdly, their view of the facts may well be different, a different judgement. Lastly, they may well hold a different position about themselves and their role in the situation anyway. Going to judgement without ascertaining these initial questions exposes you to a potentially large gap, which can quickly open up. Often this gap in observation, judgement and worldview will result in the other person, in a stress response, actually ceasing to listen. As long as the gap is open, it is that gap that needs attention. Defence will take priority, their pulse may well be higher and the opportunity for pure observation is likely lost for some time.

Giving feedback can be a stressful time for employees and employers alike. A coaching client of mine, Liz, was preparing for a session with one of her direct reports that she was particularly concerned about. Alan's performance was generally good but he was being especially hard on his team and potentially abusive at times with his demands for work to be done overnight and at weekends. One employee, Nigel, a talented young lawyer and diligent father, was at particular risk of leaving because of the excessive demands. Alan had high standards and expected them of others. Liz and I rehearsed the discussion she knew she needed to have with Alan. First, Liz played herself. She started well. She talked about the process of review and the work we were doing. After a short while she started to say what she thought about the situation. She implied that I, as Alan, was responsible for Nigel's stress and that I was pushing him too hard.

What surprised me, playing Alan, was that from that point I stopped really listening to Liz. From the moment I felt judged, all my focus went onto defending myself, my inner Alan. Even playing the role, my stress level was up and the conversation fundamentally changed. Even when Liz came back to more factual matters, the level of trust had dropped. I didn't mention this to Liz and we then changed roles. I then noticed that when I shifted from pure factual observation to judgement, Liz reacted in the same way. Afterwards she reported the same finding back to me. We both experienced that the closer we could stay to the clear observable facts or to inferences, judgements and conclusions made by the other, the easier the conversation was. This is not to say that hard messages cannot be given but just that thinking about the effect that the different kinds of information can have on a conversation may help you get more out of it. One of Liz's conclusions was not only to run the session with Alan slightly differently but also to collect more observational input from others that she could use. Ideally this would be factually biased information but she realised that even having some judgement from others would help her to adopt a more independent stance in the feedback conversation.

This observation and judgement distinction is the creation of a gap between what 'is' and what 'ought' to be.[7] As babies and then children we are full of wonder, as we find out what 'is' as we learn about the world. The tearing of paper, the movement of a set of keys brings fascination and mirth. The essential discovery of what 'is' ties us back to this curious, open state that is particularly strong in early childhood. As we grow older and assimilate into a rather fixed state of the world, another dimension starts to intrude. This is the question of 'ought'. It's the birth of judgement. As a child, when we cry someone usually comes. The next time they ought to come again. When I smile at you, you ought to smile back at me. We also learn the 'ought' of authority, first from parents and then from school and other figures of authority. The parental 'ought' is what we need to do to avoid being told off. This external instruction may well be different from what we internally want to do. We thus start to feel the tension between these two directions; your judgement is different from mine. Judgement leads to separation between what 'is' and the various 'oughts'. The difference between your judgement and mine might be painful. This is the same stress that we had as a naughty or conflicted child and which we carry forward into our adult lives. Understanding and mediating this balance between what 'is' and the variety of 'oughts' is a key skill of the mature adult.

The emergence of 'ought' in our lives brings a divergence in views. My 'ought' is not necessarily yours. Social norms and rules may help us here in that there may be a consistent way of doing things. On a country lane we are in the habit of thanking the other driver as one or both of us pulls over to let the other through the narrow road. If we pull over and a driver ignores us, most of our passengers would take a consistent view of that behaviour. In the city, however, our expectation of a thank you may be very different. Other matters on the road are more a matter of law. When we see another driver visibly using their mobile phone while driving we know that is a breach of the law and they ought not do it. The phone call that we might take while in the car is, of course, altogether more of an allowable emergency. In a behaviour known as 'fundamental attribution error' we tend to judge other's behaviour differently from our own. I have a clear reason for my misbehaviour, anyone else who makes the same mistake may well be an idiot.

In Germany the law is called 'des Recht'. 'Rechts' is the word for 'right' as in right-hand side, 'richtig' means 'correct' and 'rechtens' means 'lawful'. Judges and lawyers are 'richter' and 'rechtsanwälte' respectively. Here, rightness is written into expectations of the law and lawyers. In many places this works perfectly. After all, the smooth running of society and business depends on there being a clear and certain way to, say, set up a corporation or to get married. Unfortunately we know that in many daily situations there is often no single answer as to what is actually right. Anyone who has ever commissioned a lawyer to tell them what is the right answer in a dispute knows this. The truth is that very little in life is 'right'. The closest thing to a right answer is in clear man-made constructs such as mathematical sums that we understand with our reason. 4 is the right answer to 2 + 2. Ideas and things that we observe with our senses or imagination tend not have a 'right' answer.

> If I am weak on the law, I bang on about the facts. If I am
> weak on the facts, I bang on about the law. If I am weak
> on the facts and on the law, I bang away on the table.
> Attributed to an anonymous insurance claims manager

In negotiation one of the earliest lessons I wrote myself was that 'logic is not persuasive'. This principle was important for me to remember as it ran completely counter to the way I had been operating up to that point. As a result of the training I had had and the law firm I had worked in, logic was highly prized. When I negotiated, I used logic because I thought there was a right answer. I became increasingly frustrated in negotiations because it didn't really get me anywhere. I remember one particular turning point in negotiating a profit sharing arrangement with an electricity company who was a potential new client. Following a meeting about the principles, our client had written up their version of how the scheme would work. In our view they had completely misunderstood what we had proposed and agreed, so I suggested some major changes to the draft to make things clear. I particularly remember the frustrated sales director asking me whether we could just accept the client's version, rather than simply suggesting our much better, draft wording. How much did it really matter? At first this looked to me like a crazy thing to do. It was unclear and incomplete. I took the challenge, however, and worked to understand what the client had done and what the differences really were. This took much longer and the output of the exercise was far less visible but I realised that the client had just understood the profit share differently and thus expressed it in a very different way. After much deliberation I concluded that we could, after all, accept the draft with one easy to agree tweak. This change also made the client's logic much clearer in a way that they subsequently appreciated. I realised that not only was the client's mechanism different from ours, we had all misunderstood it because of a few words that could be changed. We then managed to agree the mechanism quickly and had a happy client. This happened because as a team we had moved from a position of two opposing and irreconcilable rights, to one where we sought to accept the client's way of seeing things. Neither was actually right, both were possible, but we did have to choose one. We chose to go to where they were and, once we were there, found a way to make that work.

We all make mistakes and if I ask you how being wrong feels you might answer 'bad'. The thing is that being wrong itself feels no different from being right. It is knowing that you are wrong that feels different. Kathryn Schulz has written a book on being wrong and in her TED talk on the subject brilliantly demonstrates this with the Looney Tunes cartoon characters of Roadrunner and Wile E. Coyote.[8] Roadrunner runs very fast on mountain roads. Coyote is always chasing Roadrunner whose trick is to carry straight on as the road bears left or right. This is fine because Roadrunner is a bird. Coyote, on the other hand, has no wings. As a result he is often left in mid-air, legs furiously spinning. We wait for the inevitable drop. Coyote still thinks he is on the road. The realisation that he isn't comes a moment later when he looks down and sees where he is. It's the same with being wrong. It is not being wrong that feels different. It's realising that we are wrong. If you think you are right you feel the same, whatever the truth really is. As Shakespeare tells us in *Hamlet*, 'there is nothing either good or bad, but thinking makes it so'.

Being wrong is something we are taught to avoid. We get the approval of our parents, our teachers and the organisations we work for by being right. We then tend to defend this fixed position once we acquire it. It is far easier if our judgement of what 'ought' to be concords with that of others. We then tend to seek the clubiness of that concord. This can lead to a trap in which we either reconcile the difference or we don't. If we see something different in another's judgement, the first thing we ought to do is to check whether there is a factual difference in what we see.[9] We might question the observable 'is'. It's after all possible that we might simply see different things. The way out of the trap at this level is to check the facts: do you see what I see? I see three molehills. Aha, you say, you see four. Where are the four you see? At this level we can escape by resolving the factual difference. If we cannot resolve the question at the factual level, we tend go to judgement. This is now more about the interpretation you make from the facts. Why is your 'ought' different from mine? If we can't agree, we can easily come to the conclusion that the other person is either ignorant, stupid or both. What other explanation could there be after all? Well, there is another way out and this goes back to the question of intent. If ignorance doesn't explain it, maybe evil intent will. If all else fails, it's perfectly possible to explain the other's different conclusion by the fact that they possess malevolent intent towards me or my organisation. If they are a supplier perhaps they just want to rip us off? If we are not careful it is easy to start with a simple difference of views and end up thinking of someone as either ignorant, stupid or evil. Stopping this escalation is the work that we need to do by anchoring ourselves first in the observable facts and then working from there.

The power of judgement occurs when we reserve it to its rightful place: to help us to make our own decisions at the appropriate time. Without our own judgement on our own matters, we would be in trouble. From one perspective, we need to preciously protect our judgement. In a world full of social constructs that tell us what to do and when, we need to allow it to guide us. The green man at a pedestrian crossing helps us to cross the road, but ought we to trust it at all times? If we don't look at the base information, we may find ourselves crossing a road into a speeding car that failed to stop at the red light. That shouldn't have happened, but is blaming the system or the driver likely to help us if we are run over? Being able to harness the power of our own judgement to guide our own decisions is where its power lies. On the other hand being able to control its intrusion into everything we do and, in particular, to control its journeying beyond our own boundaries into the affairs of others becomes a critical skill.

The patterned

We tend to see patterns everywhere. We might see human faces in nature or look for familiar shapes in the presentations of information.

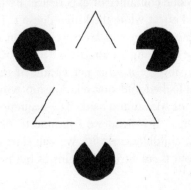

This is a 'Kanizsa Triangle'. We see triangles in the pattern but there are none there. We also see the white triangle on top of the lined triangle but again, there are no triangles. We see what is not there but we think we see it because it follows a pattern. We favour patterns over what is actually there. Sometimes what we see might be following a natural pattern but not always. Like a detective with a hunch, it might be a good hunch but it might also prevent us from seeing what is really happening.

This tendency to see patterns can happen with people. Sometimes we meet someone and have a clear initial reaction to them, often a negative one. This can happen because we instinctively see in them elements of someone in our past, particularly our childhood. Without being consciously aware of it, we tend to transfer our experiences of the person we know to the person we have just met. This instinctive, protective strategy was first described by Freud and developed by Jung, and is commonly called 'Transference'. Sometimes it can be of great help as a warning system but if we understand what is happening we can also see it for what it really is.

It is inevitable that our minds become a container of shapes into which things fit. The container into which new experiences are poured is crafted by the sum of experience up to that point. Our reason benefits from seeing patterns of causation that help to build this container. A kitten simply chases a ball of wool in play, whereas we look around the corner for the cause to add pattern to our container of experience. By that method we learn cause and effect while the kitten doesn't. The downside is that we build a container which can restrict our thinking. There is a danger that in seeing a butterfly we just label it as such and cease to really observe it. Our perception of the butterfly can effectively be blocked and our relationship with it objectified. As St Clement of Alexandria said, 'The beginning of truth is to wonder at things.' If instead we continue to observe our own butterflies with childlike curiosity, we will start to might notice new things about them. Structure helps us but not if we become restricted by it.

The imaginative

> The power of things we fear lies solely in our opinion of them.
> Dee Hock

One of the things that really sets us apart as humans is our imagination. There is a downside to this wonderful faculty, however. The same tool that brings us the ability to imagine the possibility of different futures and thus to make choices can also conspire with fear. That is the ability to imagine monsters; literal monsters but also bad stuff of all descriptions. Because we can imagine, we can imagine what might happen.

Given that there is so much information available to us it is odd that we aren't always in the present moment at all times. Instead we often tend to find ourselves in our imaginations, either in the past or in the future. Some of us are more affected by this than others. Having a more fertile imagination is great for some things but leaves us open to a drift away from reality when we least want it. Either way, we are not always totally in this current moment, taking it in and making the most of every aspect of it.

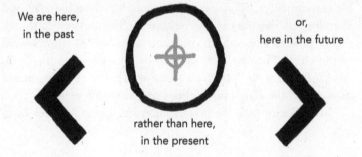

We are here, in the past

or, here in the future

rather than here, in the present

An immediate and fair reaction to this is that we inevitably have to spend some time thinking about what happened in the past in order to learn from it. Second, some degree of planning of the future is necessary. Both these points are, of course, correct but do we overuse these excuses and spend too much time reflecting and planning?

Eckhart Tolle uses the term 'clock time': our ability to move into the past or future at will, in service of the present.[10] Contrasted with this is 'psychological time': thinking about the past or future and simply dwelling on it. We all do this, but what is the point? Doing or planning to do something as a result of our experiences may be a good use of our time. But if nothing happens as a result, it is, at best, a waste of our time and, at worst, it reinforces our negative judgement of ourselves. Either way, it is time taken out of the present moment, potentially cutting down our observation of what just actually happened.

The same is true when we look into the future. If we are going to spend valuable time doing this, shouldn't we make sure it's because we are actually, at that moment, making real plans for the future? Sitting in bed thinking about the writing I am going to do is pointless. Once I have the idea, going downstairs and actually writing will serve me far better. How can spending time simply dwelling on the future really be more valuable than being in the present moment more fully?

This is the crisis that we so often find ourselves in. Whether we are late for an appointment or a disaster has occurred that appears to upset our plans, we end up thinking about the possible consequences. While we do this, we leave the moment and abandon all the possibilities within it. The answer is to ask ourselves what precisely the problem is that exists right now, in this moment. Then we have to focus on what we can actually do now and deal with that. If we focus on what might happen, we miss out on the actual possibilities that currently exist.

The difficulty with the present moment is that it forces us to act.

Instead of going into the past   or the future...

we have a hard choice in the present. We either accept it, do something to change it, or remove ourselves from it.

I once heard a beautiful story on the radio from an elderly gentleman who had become well known for his happy demeanour and community spirit. Brian was a widower struggling to get over the loss of his dear wife, and initially he spent time alone looking at old photos, remembering his times with her and reflecting, as things happened in his life, how he would like her back with him to enjoy the moment. After a while he realised how crazy this was, so he decided to get out, meet new people and enjoy what he still had. The result was an incredible transformation. Brian lit up the airwaves that morning with his positive attitude and love of life.

Even the memories we do have are selective. In recalling the past, the mind is perhaps not really interested in the truth. Instead it selects and manipulates. The best metaphor I have ever heard for the memory is that it is not an ordered filing cabinet but is more like a compost heap. Layers of reality are stacked on top of each other, which start after a while to break down and blend into a mass that is no longer the actual truth but a version of it. That version serves a purpose but also blends to that purpose. The past thus becomes not the true past but a selective and perhaps putrefied version of it, where the strongest smell wins through. If that is the case it may also be that the human memory does not exist to serve the truth but rather to inform experience. Perhaps all that matters is that we remember the parts that will serve us well, particularly the lessons that will protect us. If a hot flame burns us, the memory carries that experience accurately even if the detail of who lit the fire and when the fire was is lost or distorted. After all, we know that emotionally charged events create much more vivid memories those with no emotion attached.

When it comes to the future we would do well to temper our imagination with a degree of reality. The best strategy perhaps is that of the Stoics, who recognised anxiety as a virulent growth that flourishes in the gap that opens up between what we hope might happen and what we fear could happen. As our imaginations play havoc with what might be, this gap can grow ever more threatening to our overall mood. The Stoics said that rather than comforting ourselves with the joy of the best outcome we are better served by coming to terms with the very worst. Once we can see and accept the worst outcome, we can start to see how we might cope with it and learn from it. This is not to accept failure but rather a strategy of our awareness. We still hold onto our commitment, belief and confidence at core but accept at front, out in the world, the possibility of the worst possible position we might achieve. By accepting the worst it becomes easier to stop worrying about it and to build confidence to achieve our best.

The assumptive

Being halfway up a tree can give you a great view. That is where I'm sitting as I write this. What is perhaps more odd is that I'm sitting on a seat that is more often occupied by our local butcher. He has added a ladder structure to the tree with a seat at the top to allow him to have a comfortable view over the field. I walked past here the other day with my daughter and we decided it would be a great place to write. We are not, however, going to cull the wild deer from here, as the butcher does.

The ladder serves as a way of thinking about the assumptions we make. So often, we find it difficult to stay in contact with the ground, connected to the directly observable facts. The ladder we climb all the time is in our imaginations. We imagine what might be rather than sticking with what we know. We climb the ladder and, before we know it, we are several feet above grounded reality. Instead of seeing clearly over the field like we do on this ladder, we climb into an imaginative cloud that starts to distort the way we see the facts of a situation.

It's entirely normal to make this mistake. I was talking through a situation recently with a friend when I realised I'd been caught. A meeting I had booked with Stephen, an old colleague, had now been cancelled three times. It really didn't seem worth bothering to try to set the meeting up again. As far as I was concerned Stephen didn't want the meeting, as was clear from his cancellations, being difficult to get hold of and quite brusque on the phone and in emails. Stephen was now a very important chap and, I told myself, had more important things on his mind. That was the easy solution and one I was, until that point, in the process of taking. I'd told myself a story, Stephen didn't actually want to meet me.

My friend's question to me was quite simple. He asked me how Stephen had been when I last spoke to him. The answer completely changed the way I was looking at the situation. It brought me back off the ladder and back down to the ground. When we had last spoken Stephen had talked at length about a problem he was experiencing with his team and had been quite clear that he wanted to talk about it further. My friend asked whether I'd had any real indication of any change in that desire from Stephen. I hadn't. I realised that until Stephen made it clear that things had moved on or that he didn't want to have the conversation any more, I had every right to follow up. I was reading far too much into the simple logistics of setting up the meeting.

So, the next day, I decided to test the facts. I sent a follow-up email to Stephen to check his real interest. He responded immediately confirming the desire to talk and copying his PA. I had my confirmation that this was no mere politeness. In the end, we had a fruitful meeting and Stephen, without any prompt from me, apologised for his ridiculously busy schedule and his less than fully organised PA. I had experienced another great reminder of the perils of assumptive thinking.

The ladder looks like this:

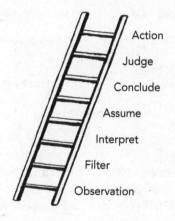

What happens on this ladder is that all our weaknesses in awareness combine together to produce pretty disastrous results. Not only do we filter information, we also filter in interpretation against our beliefs. So, if we are having a bad day we might interpret using our beliefs about the person, the situation or ourselves at that moment. We also make imaginative assumptions and draw conclusions.

This can also happen if two people start making assumptions

about each other at the same time. Take two colleagues, Joe and Helen, who are normally on reasonable terms with each other but have agreed to meet for a coffee at 3pm to talk about a new project on which Helen might be working as part of Joe's team. Helen is late because her boss kept her on after another meeting with an urgent request.

We start at the bottom with the facts, the time on the clock, and end up, at the top of the ladder, in a very different place for both.

Joe thinks:	Helen thinks:
I'll demand a daily update	I'm not working with him
She needs managing	He's always in my face
I can't trust her	I can't stand his OCD!
She's never really cared	He's always so aggressive
I'm not important to her	He's annoyed with me
(Checking his watch) She's late	He's been waiting

It's 3.15pm

Joe and Helen both make assumptions and end up in a very different place from the facts of the initial lateness. At any point, preferably before they get too high, either one of them could have seen what was happening and jumped, with the other's help, off the ladder.

There is a classic situation in *Annie Hall* where Woody Allen shows part of this process to great comic effect. Alvie, Woody's character, and Annie, Diane Keaton's character, are both on separate therapists' couches talking about their life together and how they don't have a good time any more. Each has a different view of why their relationship has turned bad. As each therapist allows Alvie and Annie to unfold their perspective, the question is then asked separately as to how often they actually sleep together. It cuts from Alvie's response of 'Hardly ever...' to Annie's of 'Constantly...'. The punch line is that Alvie goes on to say '... maybe three times a week'. Annie echoes Alvie's words with her own: 'I'd say three times a week'. Alvie and Annie at least agree on the facts but their view of them is somewhat different.

We've all been in the situation of noticing that someone is staring at us. We may think we have the answer: 'I'm looking awful today'; 'It's that hat I'm wearing'; 'He thinks I'm an idiot'. Whatever the possible explanation is, it's likely to be wrong. Many times I have looked at someone in the street in admiration of what they are wearing or simply because they just look interesting. Over time I've realised they don't necessarily know this. The joy of being human is that the imagination intervenes, but this can be destructive also. My eyes are focusing on their wonderful hat but their eyes, in noticing my attention, send a message that is too easily influenced by their heart. What is felt responds more to our sense of self-belief. That can so easily destroy the message. 'Great hat' can so easily become 'God, I must look a prat'.

Seeing things differently is what makes us human. We all see different things. To be aware of this trap is half the game here. Once we can see that there are many possible interpretations of what is, things get a lot easier. As F. Scott Fitzgerald wrote:

> The test of a first-rate intelligence is the ability to hold two opposing ideas in mind at the same time and still retain the ability to function.

One of my failings in negotiations was that I took many years to realise that the capacity to see things from different points of view varies from person to person and situation to situation. Perhaps we are too stressed about the outcome or too single-minded about the process. This struck home after a big first meeting with a new and important client. A team of six or seven of us left the client's building after a day of meetings and sat in a local bar for a group debrief over a few bottles of wine. For me, as the commercial lead for the deal, the day had been full of important and contradictory messages. This wasn't what the sales lead had heard, however. I was shocked to hear that he had a good impression of the day. In hindsight I realised that I should not have been surprised. He had heard essentially what he wanted to hear: the client liked us and our solution. A few tweaks were necessary but we were on the right track. In contrast, I had heard subtle but clear messages, that the client team didn't understand the value of our partnering strategy and the focus of our sales proposition. We were pushing wholesale change and innovation but the client was telling us that some of the things that we felt made us distinctive were not what would win the bid. I was confused why what I saw was not seen by our sales lead. Perhaps the team needed an upbeat message but we also needed to hear clearly what had been said to us. Having spoken up about what I heard, I left the meeting with my tail slightly between my legs wondering if I had just been mistaken. Some eight months later we lost the bid for a number of reasons including price. The reasons for our loss included some of the things that had been mentioned to us on that day. I realised that what I could have done was to expect and understand the different perspective that the sales lead had. If I had presented more detailed factual information of what I had heard and worked from that instead of my judgement of it, I might have had a better chance to reconcile our different perspectives. If I had myself worked from a place of observation and had asked the rest of the team to do so also, then I'd have stood a better chance of making my point.

This particular client also taught me a big lesson later. In their team they had one person who took thorough notes of what was said. When they debriefed, this person went first. They built their conclusions about the day rigorously from the facts. This makes it far easier to see the assumptions, filters and differences in judgement that we all subsequently seek to make.

So, given these eight ways in which our awareness limits us, how do we improve our ability to make the most of what is really there?

The San Scan

Conscious of this quest, I asked an executive producer of natural history programmes what most struck her about the power of awareness that animals have in the wild. Her answer, given instinctively and out of a formal interview, surprised me. From all she had experienced, everything from the frozen through the forested to the desiccated ends of the planet, the thing that had impressed her most was the extraordinary focus shown by the San people of the Kalahari desert. Her answer was not after all animal, but human. The San have, however, exceptional powers of awareness of the natural world and can detect tracks of people and animals where we would see nothing. In particular, the San still practise an ancient form of hunting called the persistence hunt. At the end of the hunt, the single tribesman who makes the kill enters a hypnotic state to focus on the single kudu, a kind of antelope, that he kills. This state is such that he notices little else that is going on around him; effectively he is locked in his own focus for that time. The tribesman performs a deeply respectful ceremony to return the spirit of the animal to the desert sands, giving thanks for the life he has taken, and can remain in this state for a period of days as he recovers from his own physical and mental exhaustion.

The hunt does not start like this. The BBC programme *The Life of Mammals* shows the San's hunt for the kudu in full. At the beginning the San hunters scan the desert in silence. They listen for distant sounds, feel for the rhythm of the moving herd and look for the faintest of marks that might show the whereabouts of the kudu. The San see and feel clues everywhere. They can read a footprint or a sound like we would read a book. At a certain point the San make hand signals to show they have picked up a signal which they start to track. The hunt enters a new stage as the kudu have been found. The group now works together and communication is vital. Suddenly the kudu take fright and break cover and the hunt enters its next stage. The focus shifts to finding the single bull kudu who is vulnerable to the chase as he carries a heavy set of horns and will tire more quickly. The tribe's task now is to split the bull from the pack so they can track him alone. This can take hours but at a certain point a huge stick is thrown in the air as a signal that the final stage has started. In this stage, one man, the runner, runs down the single kudu. This part of the chase works because the man on two feet who sweats through his skin and can carry water in his hands is ultimately more efficient than the four-legged furry animal. At times he loses the kudu as it goes for cover. The runner then enters the mind of the animal and deduces the direction that he feels it would go in. Soon enough the antelope is found, exhausted. Then, with the greatest of respect, the runner, utterly focused on the kudu, kills it with his spear and performs the ceremony of returning its spirit to the desert.

Our challenge, as we have seen, is that too many things pull our awareness away from what is really there. The San start with an advantage over us in that their powers of observation are exceptional. Nevertheless we can still learn from their model and apply it. The way the San instinctively solve this is by having at least four separate levels of awareness each signalled clearly as the stage starts. One solution therefore is that we arrange our strengths in awareness in a series of levels. In that model we can, like the hunters, align our skills to what we need at each stage. This will depend on the task at hand but key here is that we save some of our skills for later stages and then use them sparingly for the task in hand. Here we might need to practise the skill of the 'busy bartender' who is able to achieve a balance of focus on a particular customer and an awareness of the overall picture across the bar. This duality of operation can help us move around from phase to phase and back where necessary.

An outline model would look like this:

Stage	Description	Emerging Capability
Scan	The default stage, taking in all available information, asking questions	Observation, Curiosity
Connect	Busy Bartender – multiplicity	Imagination, Pattern
Select	Decide	Judge
Execute	Absolute focus, execute agreed plan	Purposive

If we did this, our focus in negotiations would be mainly in the first two levels: Scan and Connect. Only towards closure would we dip into Select and Execute where we would allow an appropriate level of judgement and selectively purposive behaviour. Spending our time mostly in Scan and Connect is our soft front.

CHAPTER 7

TOUCH AND FEEL

If we throw a stone into a pond but see no ripple how do we feel?

In the mid 1970s illustrator Jack Kent wrote a story for children called *There's No Such Thing as a Dragon*. Billy Bixbee is a small boy who, in traditional fairytale style, wakes up one morning to find a kitten-sized dragon sitting on the end of his bed. Fortunately this is a happy dragon and when little Billy pats its cute head it wags its rather lethal-looking tail contentedly.

The problems start when Billy goes downstairs to tell his mother. 'There is no such thing as a dragon,' she says firmly. So Billy goes upstairs to dress. If there is no such thing as some-thing, Billy thinks, then it would be silly to pat the dragon on the head. Billy therefore ignores the playful and expectant dragon and goes down to breakfast. The dragon notices this and responds; it starts to grow. The now dog-sized dragon sits on the breakfast table and eats most of Billy's breakfast. Sitting on the table is not normally permitted. However, because there is no dragon, telling the dragon to get off the table is not an option.

The more it is ignored, the bigger the dragon gets. As it starts to take over the house, Billy's mother has to go from room to room by way of the windows in order to get about, while still denying the dragon's existence. Things reach a point where there is no area of the house that doesn't have some part of the dragon in it. Finally, the dragon gets hungry and takes off after a passing bread van, taking the house with it.

Mr Bixbee comes home but his house has gone. When he finds the house he wants to know what has happened. Given that the house is now sitting on a rather large dragon, Billy's mother's assertion that there is no dragon falls away. 'There IS a dragon … a very BIG dragon,' Billy insists as he pats it on the head once again. Immediately the dragon wags its tail happily and starts shrinking. The story concludes with the family petting the by now kitten-sized dragon. As to why the dragon ever got so big, Billy concludes, 'I think it just wanted to be noticed.'

This story was told to me in the context of work with families and children. The message is that our dragons need to be acknowledged and talked about. There's a danger that if we can't talk about bad things that happen, the problem just grows. By sharing the experience with someone else and being heard, the problem tends to become more manageable. If we talk about, say, someone's violence towards a child we will hopefully realise that the perpetrator is the one with the problem, not the child. Being open about the problem allows us to see it in context and to avoid the possibility of the child thinking that they are at fault.

Teach us to sit still

Lack of hearing is a problem that happens at the core of our being. At its deepest, we can all fail to listen to ourselves. It is all too easy to live in our heads, separated in feeling from the rest of our bodies. Like Mr Duffy, the cut-off bank-cashier in James Joyce's *Dubliners* who 'lived a short distance from his body', we can be at disease with our physical selves. One of life's many challenges is that we can tend to get tied up by our thinking process and not hear what our body is trying to tell us. Our high-level brain functioning can take control and the rest of our body can become a mere transport system for our heads. In contrast to those who are in touch with their body messages directly, we can become increasingly insensitive. In extreme, we are like the marathon runner who simply ignores the pain.

At some point our bodies, if they are not heard at all, tend to rebel. The dragon makes itself known. Tim Parks wrote about this in *Teach Us to Sit Still*. Tim had a growing problem with extreme pelvic pain, which his doctors diagnosed as an enlarged prostate. He was faced with quite a serious operation that itself had repercussions and a worryingly uncertain outcome. As a result of his lack of belief that this was right for him, he embarked on a journey of discovery into alternative ways to deal with the problem. His eventual salvation came though meditation, the ultimate deconstruction of all drama. By this method he was able to release the dragon, reconcile the pain and manage it.

Tim Parks came to this conclusion:

> Texting, mailing, chatting, blogging, our modern minds devour our flesh ... We have become cerebral vampires preying on our own life blood. Even in the gym, or out running, our lives are all in the head, at the expense of our bodies.

Getting back into communication with his body, hearing the pain and working with it enabled Tim to avoid an operation that some urologists estimate as being unsuccessful in up to half the patients who undergo surgery. Tim talks of the joint conspiracy that it is possible for our thinking minds to have with our doctors. What we generally demand is a cure that doesn't touch the deeper question of our life as a whole. In turn the doctor doesn't prescribe something holistic like meditation because it is not part of their normal professional toolkit. The doctor is an expert, but the only person who can really hear the myriad messages our body has for us is us.

Being heard

Hospitals are a key place in our lives. The ward makes good drama because extreme emotions are felt there. One cycle of life starts and another one ends. In between, emergencies happen. In the Maternity Ward, women become mothers and men suddenly wake up to being fathers. There is an emotional charge everywhere. There is also searing pain. When I first became a father, I experienced a form of hearing, presence and listening that I had never experienced before. For a while my role was to hear, be shouted at and to assist where I could. As my wife went through rather rapid dilation, she threw up. Begging for serious pain relief didn't help as it was 'already too late'. Yet today she describes this as 'forgotten pain' because it was expressed. The pain got voiced and heard. In Montaigne's words:

> If the body find itself relieved by complaining let it complain: if agitation ease it, let it tumble and toss at pleasure; if it seem to find the disease evaporate (as some physicians hold that it helps women in delivery) in making loud outcries, or if this do but divert its torments, let it roar as it will.

In this roaring the truth comes out. Often it is not the first cries that are the true release. The layers below, which come out once the process is in flow, are the critical things that really need to be said. If we sing we first get used to how the voice sounds. With confidence the voice reaches its zenith of expression just as the nadir of pain is passed through and truly felt. As an active listener our role is to curate a space where this expression is able to start, build, flow and complete.

Being heard is so much more important than being right. In our daily lives and in our negotiations we can easily make the mistake that this is all about getting to the right answer. First, as we have discussed, there is rarely such an answer, and secondly, even if there was, arguing with someone is not the way to prove it anyway.

If we look at basic human needs, more point to the importance of being heard than the need to be right. If you need convincing, here is a list:

Appreciation

Fairness

Understanding

Trust

Respect   *outweigh*   Being right

Consideration

Nurture

Inclusion

Acknowledgement

The dragon has a simple strategy for not being acknowledged. He just grows until he is seen. If we did the same when we are not heard, things would be very different. Everyone would definitely get to make a contribution in every meeting; their dragon would demand it. Unfortunately the dragon is only a metaphor for the thing that is not surfaced. The dragon isn't us or our behaviour. If anything, when we are not heard, we get smaller, losing confidence, as the dragon gets bigger.

We all experience contexts where we struggle to get a word in edgeways. Part of this may be contextual but part may also be possible for us to change. It is quite easy to contribute unwittingly to not being heard if we give off signals that we are used to it. The message has suddenly and quietly been passed round the room that we are to be ignored. So how does this happen?

If we grew up in a family where we struggled to be heard, we may have developed a strategy to try to deal with this. We may have talked fast or loudly or we may have grabbed at every silence whether or not it was a good time to make our point. We may then have carried this strategy through into our education and into our social and working lives. If we talk like someone who is used to being interrupted, we will signal that and duly get interrupted. In order to be heard, we need to act as if we are used to being heard. To do this we need to first become aware of anything we do that undermines us. Then we need to consciously shift that behaviour, so that it helps rather than hinders us.

A common strategy is talking fast. We tend to talk fast in order to stop people interrupting us, to get our point in before others grab the space. But as soon as there is a space for others to get a word in, the fast talker tends to get interrupted. When we talk fast we display less self-assurance and lower status. Voice transmits status as a series of messages, which are read subconsciously. Artist Marcus Coates has even shown that the human voice slowed down enough resembles a lion's roar, a high status animal.[1] Conversely the call of the lar gibbon speeded up 5.2 times sounds like a canary, a much lower status operator. By following this speed strategy we undermine ourselves. It's the slower-voiced lion that gets most attention, and as humans we know that instinctively. We listen much less to the canary. If you want to be heard, first slow down. It's hard but ultimately it's the solution.

Anyone for tennis?

A conversation can be a bit like a tennis match. One player has the ball, the opportunity to speak, and hits it by speaking. The other player responds by hitting the ball back, by speaking in turn. After a while it's a routine. It's a game where there can almost be an unwritten rule that each of us speaks a roughly equal amount. There may be the odd volley, the surprise interruption, but the match proceeds as we pass the responsibility for speaking backwards and forwards. How much we speak is an easy thing for us to keep tabs on. So much so that we can feel guilty if we judge we have spoken significantly more than the other person.

If we apply this model to a matter over which we disagree, we tend to get a very competitive type of tennis match. Each argues for their own point of view with their own logic. Shots are made, felt to land and inevitably parried back. Thesis meets antithesis. It can feel like we are making progress because we state our case with a volley of words that are propelled by the force of logic. Any progress depends on a belief that a synthesis of the opposing arguments will somehow emerge. In practice this is rarely the case. Each of us are more likely to become solid in our positions as a result of this process. Worse still, if we each have advisers or supporters, this group-think effect can help to make our belief in our logic even stronger. This type of 'dialectic' exchange has historical support going as far back as the Socratic dialogues and gets a regular shot in the arm in movies and public life, whether this is Rhett Butler in *Gone with the Wind* with a 'Frankly, my dear, I don't give a damn' style of interaction or today's confrontational Prime Minister's Question Time.

The flaw is to think of this as mostly a question of speaking. If, like a tennis match, there were some rules that surrounded the exchange, that decided points, then that might work. A good shot could win a point. In a debate, it is the audience we are trying to convince, not the person we are debating with. If this behaviour makes us appeal to the audience or win the point under the rules of the match, then maybe it is a wise strategy. The dialectic exchange works in such a system because a winner is decided or chosen. However, if we are trying to convince the other person or marshal a common approach over the short term or persuade a wiser audience, then the strategy is rarely successful because the person on the other side has not yet been heard or their perspective understood.

Theodore Zeldin captures nicely the difference that makes a productive conversation: it should start with a willingness to emerge from it as a 'slightly different person'.[2] As Zeldin puts it, good conversation shouldn't just result in a reshuffling of the cards but rather the creation of new ones. It is a creative act and creativity has its own requirements in order to flourish, not least the preparedness to take risks, to allow time, to trust and to show confidence.

Zeldin's creative point concurs with the great gift we are given by our imagination, which is the ability to think ourselves into places that we are not. Among its advantages is the ability to see things from another's point of view. We can go further than simply feeling their pain, we can imagine what it must be like for them to feel pain. This skill allows us to break the backwards and forwards action of the tennis match. The parrying of the ball backwards and forwards can be compulsive, partly because it helps to define us, giving us positional definition. We do have a choice, however. We can choose to leap across the net to the other half of the court. Our imagination allows us to do this, to start to see things from the other's perspective. In doing so we engage the empowering and creative force of empathy, which goes far beyond sympathy. The sympathetic response would be to give them our better quality racket and to pity their plight. Empathy allows us to think ourselves completely into their place, free from our ego. When it comes to the time for solutions, the ideal, even then, is to see possible solutions from their perspective.

As George Bernard Shaw puts it, the empathetic version of the golden rule is not simply 'Do unto others as you would have them do unto you', but rather 'Do not do unto others as you would have them do unto you – they may have different tastes.'

In achieving this step across the net, the first and most difficult part is moving from our own position and sense of control. In this game, two people cannot successfully pursue different strategies. The ultimate game is where both players are prepared, at times, to move with the other and no control is sought at all.

This method of working from what is there rather than from where we are is the essential skill of negotiation. In London's V&A Museum there is an exhibit that shows the value of sharing this same perspective. This is Ane Christensen's 'Negative Bowl'. In this otherwise simple copper bowl, Christensen has cut away a shape that appears as a three-dimensional box inside the bowl. The brick-like shape only appears when viewed from the front. The artist's perspective can be so easily missed. Once seen, visitors tend to test the angles of sight to the illusion and then, if they are accompanied, ask their companions to try that line of sight also. This is a piece of art that encourages us to line up together and see it from the same perspective. Only then does it fully reveal itself.

The importance of perspective-taking permeates further than we might initially realise. In the 1990s Xerox set up a research team within their Palo Alto Research Centre known as Xerox PARC. In an era when the firm was moving away from just selling copiers to being 'The Document Company', this team, the Work Practices and Technology Group led by Lucy Suchman, looked at the uses to which documents were put and the inter-section of documentation with technology. One of their studies was on a regional airport. The team monitored the activity in the ground operations room, interested in the flow of documents, timetables, luggage tags and so on around the room. This gave them valuable clues about how people really worked in the intersection of documentation, people and technology. Some months into the observation the room was demolished as part of a programme of reconstruction at the airport and the operations room resited. The team continued to observe the operations staff in the new location and noticed that the documentation had changed. They were observing the same people handling the same traffic with unchanged aircraft landing and departing times. The only thing that had changed were the chairs. In the old room the chairs were on castors, people could easily move around and see things from a colleague's perspective on their screen or look through a window to see the airport tarmac. In the new room the chairs were fixed to the ground. Because they could no longer easily see things from other's perspective, new safety procedures, more documentation, had had to be introduced. The lack of ability to take relevant perspective from others had added process to the system. Removal of soft had necessarily led to an increase in hard systemic measures.

In practice much depends on the context. Many couples remark that their best conversations happen when they sit along-side each other in a car or sitting up in bed in the morning. Facing the same way helps. If the view is changing, as in a car or on a walk, this may help also; we are already moving the same way together. Physical things in the surroundings might also help. Before we agree on more abstract matters we might find agreement in the timing of our stride, our enjoyment of the weather or the beauty of the view. This can also differ slightly between men and women. Women are often more comfortable facing each other than men are. One explanation for this may be historic, rooted in men's traditional role as hunters, together but alongside each other, focused on prey, compared to an ancient female role based more around a closer shared activity or a fire.

Furniture and setting become important in encouraging a listening conversation. A big formal room with a large angular table makes the situation challenging. Tables themselves act as a prop. To come around a table to share a meal is one thing but to come round a table to negotiate can mean a tabling of positions that we struggle to share. At a table we face each other but our tools and documents tend to face us. Often we make the error of having our own documents rather than a shared version that is common. Changing this dynamic to a shared version can help with trust. Creating a shared list or picture on a flipchart or whiteboard counts for far more than a previously prepared presentation. Everyone has a tendency to refer to shared artefacts, particularly a good picture. As soon as someone gets up and draws a diagram people tend to focus on and refer to that.

Between two people chairs are best arranged at right angles to each other, the perfect compromise between the need to face each other to talk and the creation of a shared view. It's a coaching position. A low table on which things can be seen and shared is the perfect accompaniment to two chairs, half driving together and half facing. Ideally warm rather than cold drinks accentuate the mood by temperature. This sort of position isn't always possible, but if we watch two co-workers in a flexible situation moving together on chairs on wheels this is the position they will often adopt out of choice. This is what we emulate if we want success in the more formal setting.

One wise chairman of the judging panel for a prestigious award told me that a forced change of perspective is the tool he uses to corral the disparate views of his judges. Instead of letting them argue for the candidate they favour, he forces a shift by getting them to argue the case for the candidate they least favour. If they do this systematically, they hear what others have to say about that candidate and process it fully rather than dismissing it. This gives them a completely different perspective.

To test students' skills in negotiation, George Loewenstein and his team at Carnegie Mellon University constructed a study using the facts of a real legal claim arising from a motorcycle accident. The subjects were asked to negotiate a settlement to the claim with one acting for the claimant and one for the respondent. Some pairs were told who they were acting for before reading and considering the facts and some weren't. The subjects were given money to negotiate with and told that a failure to reach settlement would result in a deduction being made as 'court costs', so they had a real incentive to settle. The outcome was that the people who knew who they were representing beforehand failed to settle in a quarter of all cases. When the pairs found out who they were representing later only 6 per cent remained unsettled. If seeing things from both perspectives has such an effect on our ability to solve things, why is it that we do it so rarely?

Inner interrupters

Most of us can listen when we absolutely need to and want to, but something gets in the way and prevents us from paying full attention. These talk terrorists exist within each of us and vary depending on our own mood and psychology. In time we can start to identify and then deal with them. For starters, however, there are some common 'Inner Interrupters' that keep popping up: the Inner Competitor, the Inner Expert, the Inner Creative, the Inner Judge and the Inner Orator.

The Inner Competitor - me too!

The Inner Competitor is in full flow during pub-talk when our friend wants to tell us about his new car, we tell him about ours. When we get told a holiday story, we end up telling the story about the amazing holiday we went on. We are driven to do this because something in us says it's right to do so. We feel that telling our own stories is joining in. Is this true, though? Do people who tell us their stuff, who compete with us, engage us?

The only way to check this is to swap sides. We need to try telling our stories and noticing how we feel when as soon as we have got our story out, we get told one in return. Sometimes this is why we need friends and acquaintances who are as bad as we are. So perhaps just notice this for a bit. Tell a story and see what happens. Notice how you feel about the response, good or bad. In the absence of compliant friends a fairly easy exercise is to try it out explicitly with a partner and to notice how we feel in each case. First, with a 'listener' who just 'ups' our story with their own, and second with a listener who listens to our story by showing real interest and asking us about it. If we find the first situation really annoying, we should also ask ourselves why. Part of the reason may be the recognition that we do it ourselves.

Being competitive is not a bad thing, it's just that setting our goals based on others or certain external factors can be limiting. It's a question of who or what we are competing with and why. We salute Roger Bannister as one of the greatest competitors of all time for breaking the four minute mile. Yet what sets Bannister apart was perhaps more complex than just competitiveness. Bannister's running was not that different from that of John Landy, a close competitor of his. What was different was their attitudes to that challenge. Prior to 6 May 1954 when Bannister broke the four minute barrier, Landy had always been at least 1.5 seconds outside it. Landy described the four minute hurdle as 'a brick wall' and famously said, 'I shall not attempt it again'. Then, 46 days after Bannister broke the barrier with a time of 3 minutes 59.4 seconds, Landy was the second person to do it, in a ratified 3 minutes 58 seconds, significantly quicker than his previous times. Landy held this new record for over three years. What is more, when the two men met in the 'Miracle Mile' at the 1954 Commonwealth Games, Landy lost the race in the final turn of the last lap as he looked over his left shoulder as Bannister passed him on his right. The nature of competitiveness that drove Landy might be seen as a limiting factor. Landy, who many of us have never heard of, looked for a competitor to show the way. Bannister didn't. If we are always looking forward or back to others, that is our Inner Competitor at work.

The Inner Expert – me already!

The Inner Expert is a close relation of the Competitor. Both are fuelled by a need to prove themselves, but while the Competitor is charging to get up the mountain, the Expert aims to talk from the peak. This character has come to define their value by their expertise. At worst, like a learned parent, we start to feel we should have an answer to everything. If we struggle to say 'That's an interesting question, I don't know', we probably have an Inner Expert pushing for recognition. We feel we should know.

Expertise is something we tend to build our careers on. We can do our 10,000 hours of practice at whatever it is we are known for and this can come to define us.[3] I am no longer simply Hilary, I am Hilary the successful lawyer. This expertise becomes our front to the world. Having ability and expertise, like being a great athlete, is a good thing, and to be regarded as an expert is true recognition. The danger only comes when the Inner Expert gets in the way and feels the need to prove this expertise; to have it is one thing, to have to speak of it is another. This can limit our ability to do what we then need to achieve. The Inner Expert can be particularly annoying when what we really need to do is to ask questions, be quiet and listen.

The expert inside us can easily offset what we are really good at. You don't get to be good at what you do in many areas of work without being able to listen. To be a good lawyer you have to be able to learn case law, listen to the facts of situations and take them in. Listening is something that many of us are actually rather good at, it's an essential part of what we do. It's just that something has started to get in the way. A part of the expert helps us but part hinders us.

A friend who regularly trains law firm partners and associates in business development and sales skills gets quite frustrated with this. If he asks a group of lawyers if they are good listeners, they inevitably say yes. Partly that is true. To get the whole truth, he puts them in a situation to try this out. The situation he chooses is a simple first meeting with a new client, say the legal director of a fairly large company. These exchanges often start well, but what mostly happens is that fairly quickly the Inner Expert spots an opportunity to speak: either an area of expertise to pick up on and develop or a chance to prove themselves with battle stories. The conversation very quickly narrows to cover the area of expertise only. If the lawyer is an expert in property, that will probably be what they end up talking about. Even if the 'client' is briefed to talk about a broader range of problems, the lawyer tends to focus on the thing they know. At some point the lawyer might ask if there is anything else to discuss, but by then the person playing the legal director simply does not feel like opening up about the crisis in another area that they might have mentioned. Why should they mention this to someone who is so interested in solving other problems in his property portfolio and whose skills are clearly limited? Asked later whether they asked about other work the lawyer will be able to say that yes they did ask and no there wasn't any. Everyone then acts surprised when another firm gets that work.

If the Inner Expert's first problem is that of narrowing the conversation and thereby losing the thread of opportunity that is ready to be offered, the second Expert problem multiplies the first. This is that even the most secure and confident expert loves telling stories. A good story told succinctly might add credibility, but the problem with a lot of what the expert says is that it can come simply from a place of proving the expert's worth and expertise. Often this can be self-defeating. Either it is not necessary, or an impression of trying or needing to impress or just takes attention from what needs to be talked about. If what we really needed to be talking about was not discussed because of the expert's intervention, then we have all lost out.

A final guilty secret of the expert is that getting to a solution and applying skills is a far more attractive option than shooting the breeze with general problems. Instead of asking more about the pain that is being felt, the expert wants to apply the fixative bandage right away. Failing to acknowledge and understand the pain is a sure killer of a sale. The stronger the pain is felt the greater the desire to fix it eventually becomes. This dynamic is present in negotiation also. When we are in discussion about an issue we can easily focus on the solution too quickly. In sales training we call this the 'solution conspiracy'. Our desire to solve the problem gets in the way of proper deep understanding of the issue and proper recognition of the drive to solve it. To fully support a solution we need to know that we have investigated the need and to feel it badly enough to push hard for an answer to it.

The Inner Creative – distracted

Compared to the other interrupters, the Inner Creative has purer motives. This is the part of us that we cannot control, that simply has ideas. It is our subconscious and our imagination. We are busy listening but something sparks a thought. Before we know it we are thinking about the shopping or whether we fed the dog that morning. More poetically we might notice the view or recall a memory. Before we know it we have missed what has been said; we are not entirely present.

A small part of this interrupter is useful but needs rigorous control. This is the intuition. If something that is said triggers a thought about a particular idea or a story, that might be useful. The trick then is to hold it and interrogate it. 'Is this really for the other person or is it just mine?' Our mirror neurons allow us to sense what others are really feeling. Sometimes therefore we can have an intuitive gem that might be worth sharing. The balance of probability is that this is rare, however. We are far more likely to be listening autobiographically and filtering it through our own experience. We need to be careful about trying to solve others' problems from our perspective. Sharing our story can sometimes help but it is our story not theirs and we are not best placed to make the connections for others. If we seriously interrogate the thought and it survives, then maybe we can test it.

If we do decide to share it, we ideally ask for permission first. Saying 'As you said that, I had a thought, would you like to hear it?' can work better than simply saying our idea. It can also help not to try to interpret the observation. It should be enough to share what we simply felt, to see if it gets any recognition first. The best way to do this is to be clear that we are laying the thought on the table and are completely open to whether the other person picks it up or not. If we show any attachment to it or any desire for them to pick it up, that tends to be unhelpful.

One technique I use if I get a particularly intrusive thought is either to just write it down or, more unobtrusively, quickly 'ball it up' in my mind and throw it at something. So if I have a thought about Mark's new car, I'll simply throw the thought away but at the car, preferably with Mark in it. This way I deal with the thought but also create enough of a memory to bring it back later if it is indeed relevant. I have learnt that it seldom is. Looking back at these potential interruptions later is what helps us see them for what they really are.

Part of our 'Inner Creative' is actually more of an inner to-do list. These are the things that are on our mind that pop up from time to time, either randomly or because there is a connection. To an extent, these are easy to deal with as long as we have a good process for capturing our 'to dos'. Things tend to be on our mind because we are not attending to them. As David Allen, the 'Getting Things Done' expert, says, 'There is usually an inverse relationship between how much something is on your mind and how much it's getting done.'[4] Our minds are for having ideas, not holding onto them. If you have a to-do item that your subconscious knows you have not captured somewhere in a system, it will keep bugging you until you do capture it. You don't have to buy the cat food that keeps popping into your head right now, you just need to write it down on your to-do list so your mind confidently knows it is captured somewhere. That way lies a degree of inner peace and freedom from to-do reminders as you try to listen intently.

Another range of intrusive thoughts are the rest of the stream of things that come to us when we try to switch off our thinking mind. Anyone who has tried meditation will be familiar with this stream of thoughts and the skill that the successful meditator builds over time of being able to notice these thoughts without either judging or following them. Here, the skills learnt in meditation, of choosing where we wish to place our attention, are useful as we focus in listening. The ability to focus is very similar. To listen well we need to deal with these thoughts and to be able to control them. This is something that comes with practice. A regular meditation practice will help do this.

The Inner Judge – ought

Sometimes our Inner Judge is so large that the judge is all we are. Standing at the end of a dance floor thinking about whether we really should give it a go, talking to ourselves after taking a shot in a game of tennis, golf or life, the Inner Judge likes to take over. The judge stops us, tells us what we are, tells us what we might be and tells us what we should or shouldn't have done. The voice we heard growing up, telling us what we should do, has grown up itself and found a home inside us.

Some years ago I came to terms with part of my own Inner Judge. For years a voice had been bothering me when I went sailing. In a race as the helm, steering the boat, I'd invariably screw up some element of tactics; quite often the start. From that point I'd start grumbling to myself about what an idiot I'd been. I later found out that to the others it seemed like I was blaming them. In truth I was invariably just blaming myself. All the way up the first leg of the race I'd be blaming myself and feeling bad for what I'd already done. As a result very little of me was concentrating on what was happening at that moment and what I could do about it now. My performance plummeted again and the judge got what he wanted, a victim. They say in a choice between good and evil the one who wins is the one who gets fed. Well, I was definitely feeding the bad guy.

This came to a head on a course where I ended up looking quite closely at the various parts of myself. I realised this part that I had noticed most on the water was quite a significant part of my life at work and at home. It was getting in the way more than I realised. What we were encouraged to do on the course was to draw the character that was causing us the problem and to give it a name. My Inner Judge was, it turned out, an owl-like creature called Oswald. Oswald just appeared from time to time on my right shoulder and picked me up for what I was doing, had done or was about to do. As I got to know him a bit better I realised what an unhelpful and mean character he really was. He picked me up for stuff all the time, stopped me doing anything adventurous and was a real drag on my self-esteem. With Oswald in tow I was guaranteed to feel bad about myself.

Making Oswald real allowed me to see him. This meant I noticed him when he stepped on my shoulder and I could start to have a conversation with him. Rather than just being ruled by him I could deal with him. Because I could understand him I even drew a picture of him and enjoyed tearing him up. Because I knew where he was physically I could pluck him off my shoulder and stamp on him. This was a huge change and a key part in my ability to have more awareness and dialogue with these competing forces in my head. Once Oswald was quiet I could listen to what was happening on the water and in life once more; suddenly I noticed more and had more confidence about dealing with whatever came up.

The Inner Orator - winning by talking

Passion is a precious thing but sometimes it needs reasoned help to release its full potential. I once worked with a woman who was extremely successful and driven. She was a single mother with a teenage daughter. The pair were continually at loggerheads and their arguments were ruining a precious relationship.

The daughter kept walking out and doing her own rebellious, sometimes dangerous, thing. The mother explained the situation to me and I listened to the words she used. I realised that she was expecting the force of her argument to move her daughter towards her. The opposite was happening. As I listened, the image of a rope between them came to mind. It felt like each was sitting on a chair at either end of the room. She was trying to pull her daughter bodily towards her with the rope of her words. I asked her if this image had any resonance for her. She said that this caught it exactly. I asked her whether she thought pulling her daughter to her point of view was working. She decided that it wasn't and, having now seen it that way, she couldn't now see any reason why it would. We then agreed that a better strategy was to ditch the metaphorical rope. Instead she decided to move her chair and to go and sit alongside her daughter and see things from her perspective for a while. With this physical model in mind the conversation changed itself. Next thing I heard, they were best friends again.

This is the problem that the Inner Orator has. It believes that words will win and that logic is persuasive. It is based on an assumption that the crucial part of making things happen is voicing them; by saying what we want to happen, it will somehow happen. The Orator can also be fuelled by a belief that the outcome will be 'fairly' judged somewhere out in the world. For the Orator the passion goes into the talk and not into the listen. The Orator fails to see that words themselves are just a tool. Instead, the Orator needs to get down off the chair, stop shouting and go and sit next to the other person. We move from seeking to take the stage with our words to giving it to the other person with our simple presence. Our time to be heard comes later.

Sometimes we wonder with children why it's so important to be there for the little moments, whether it's the school play or just the latest piece of homework.[5] It's because it is the presence that matters rather than any sort of comment or praise. Praise has the downside of building conditionality and external judgement. We love them but only if... If a child looks up from a drawing expecting praise and we give it then we build a model where things are done for praise. High praise simply raises the bar of expectation. The better reaction is the generous gift of simply being present, which might mean showing you notice something about the drawing or asking how they feel about it. Asking a child about the colour of the sky in their picture might result in them telling you why they chose that colour or what is about to happen next. It's harder work because it requires engagement beyond the first step of physical presence. Presence shows that we care about the person. It is also what builds trust and allows the real gems to be shared freely. Ultimately, being present to share is more important than any amount of validation of the thing they have just done.

This process often takes longer than we think. This is partly because trust has to be built. It's also because the really important things tend to get hidden. First, there is the obvious, the things that we will say straightaway. We might have something that we have decided we definitely want. We might be annoyed with someone or we might have a different point of view. This is the obvious top layer, where we start. It's often not the truth, however. Because we tend to armour up and take positions there is usually a lot more truth about the situation that needs to come out and will do so if we let it. Now, there are limits to this. You have to be careful sometimes about the breadth and depth of what you get into, but the paradox is that you often have to go a little deeper than you feel you have time for. The truth will often out because you allow it time; then things will resolve themselves into a solution quite quickly. Conversely, not allowing the time often ends in a block, which oddly takes more time. There is a magic in giving space and time. Things are released because we give space showing we are ready to receive. What we are prepared to receive is of course not yet known.

Men do not find that for which they search nor accomplish that which they set out to do. Search and ye shall find Jesus said. He did not say that you would find that for which you

sought. You find something else. That is the paradox of
adventure.

John Stewart Collis

Because there are levels and depth to most things the metaphor I
tend to think of in this process of curious inquiry is digging. You
have to get beyond the surface stuff and ask questions and give
space for the things that lie beneath. The first thing you are told
is often just a clue and the person you are listening to may not
even realise that. It helps to be genuinely curious. For the talker,
the process of talking it through might be revelatory as well. You
might be helping them to think of the issue as a series of layers
for the first time. Because it's buried, they may not see it themselves so you have to let them find it. By your questions, you
allow them to do that. Pointing things out to them doesn't work.
No one really likes to be told straight out that their clothes don't
fit. First, you have to allow them to tell you that they worry
about how they look, then you might have an entrée to ask when
they last went shopping. By this route you might get to the real
answer on their terms.

The digging you do is not an unlimited exploration of the
ground in our backyards, which can take forever. It's more like
clearing out the back of a truck. There are sides to the space and
eventually a floor. Our job is to clean out the truck and not to
leave undiscovered gems. We have to make sure we get all the
big rocks and end with a final sweep of the floor; often the gem
that unlocks things is hidden deep down or in a lump that is
congealed in a far corner. Exploring that far can take time but
is likely to repay all of us. Coach and writer Nancy Kline is a
master in allowing this type of slow exploration of undiscovered
space to take place to the extent that she coaches with the simple
question 'What do you want to Think or Feel or want to Say?'
Nancy teams this with a lot of silence and her absolutely undi-
vided physical, mental, emotional and spiritual attention. She
starts her coaching session with this question and might ask it
several times throughout the session. Later she starts the ques-

tion with 'What more...' but the key words are the same. The thing is, though, that it is not the same question. Each time it is asked the context and interpretation are different. I once watched Nancy coach by this method and experienced the effect that her ability to give her complete attention to someone had on that person. In the safe space that was created, everything that needed to be discussed about an impending career change emerged spontaneously. At a certain point the person Nancy was coaching seemed empty of thought. He was. Somehow he heard or Nancy emphasised 'Feel' in the question rather than 'Think'. Something subtly but substantially shifted and a whole new set of thoughts came out based on feelings. These feelings gave a path to a much more important set of issues in the career change, which were the fears and challenges that needed to be faced and dealt with if any surface strategy was to work. Never have I heard so much come out prompted by so few words. It was the attention and trust that had developed that allowed this to happen.

The Orator has to realise that listening and speaking are two very different things. We tend to think that listening is what we automatically do when we are not talking, but just because we have stopped talking doesn't mean we are now listening. We might just be quiet, at best waiting to speak, at worst, listening for what we want to hear. In practice, we are usually waiting for them to stop so that we can start talking again. If we are already clear what we are going to say next, we won't be listening. Listening involves the other person knowing that they are being heard. If we haven't seen definite signals indicating that we are being heard, we might well assume that we aren't.

In a meeting you can easily tell how well people are listening by how much silence there is. If there is a pause between a person stopping speaking and the other person starting, it is more likely that what has just been said has been considered. This is unusual, however. More usual is that people end up speaking over each other to a greater or lesser extent. If there is no gap between speakers, it's likely that no one has fully considered what has just been said. If what they say is a different point then the fact that they have just been waiting to speak is confirmed. Acknowledging what people say and letting them know they have been heard is the first step. Many corporate meetings are full of Orators. If that happens to you the meeting may well need a leader to help break the pattern. If it is a corporate-wide problem then the challenge is a deeper one.

To really get what listening is we need to address the Orator problem and sever the link with speaking. When we speak we tend to think predominantly about what we say. We focus on the words we use. In the same way, listening well isn't just about the words. Language isn't the feeling, the intent itself, it is merely an expression of it. What another person says may give a highly accurate picture but, as we saw in Chapter 6, because it passes through their filter from a feeling into words, through a signal medium, soundwaves, and back through our filter into our understanding, it can often get distorted. There is also the difficulty that if we listen from our position we hear from our position also; our interpretation is from our perspective, not theirs. Listening well, and understanding what is really meant, through these filters is a real skill.

Instead, we need to defrock the Inner Orator completely and treat silence as our friend. In doing so we properly pass the baton of oration to the other person. If we do an exercise with two people talking where one person occasionally and on purpose resists the temptation to speak after the other has finished, we learn something special. If you have never tried this, you should. It's a powerful thing. If we are listening to someone and they stop talking but we continue listening, a gap of silence emerges. Because we don't pick up the baton, all the expectation remains with them. The silence may continue for what seems like a long time but usually the person who was talking will continue. It might take a while or it might happen quickly, but generally they will continue. If we swap roles and become the talker, the weight of expectation on us becomes strikingly evident. Unless we intentionally pass the baton with a question back to the other person, the natural order of things is for it to remain with us. When you are listening, silence is your biggest tool.

Using it encourages the talker to say more because all the expectations about who will fill the silence rests with them.

With a confident and accomplished listener what starts as simply a weight of expectation can become a gift of silence that has been passed to the talker. A space can be created that allows a far greater flowering of thought to be expressed. If there is no one else grabbing the space, more space becomes available for the baton holder. What previously had to be squeezed into a short burst can be expressed in a relaxed form with the odd confident pause for thought. It can be difficult for the talker to accept this gift outside a professional therapeutic or coaching relationship. Accept it we must, though, for our own sanity. Stilling the Inner Orator becomes our biggest opportunity. After all, if we already know what we know, whatever makes us talk of it so incessantly?

Wisdom isn't an answer. Wisdom is a question

> As far as I am concerned, wisdom isn't a guy on top of a
> mountain with waist length hair. Wisdom isn't an answer.
> Wisdom is a question. I went to see a shrink once. And I was
> so disappointed that the shrink didn't have a big bag of
> answers. I came to be very grateful for it later, that what they
> have is a big bag of questions. You have the answers.
> Billy Connolly[6]

As a listener your main role, alongside listening, is to ask questions. A good question is 'open' – open means it has no direction as to the possible answer whereas a 'closed' question can be answered simply with a 'yes' or 'no'. What we are trying to do is free our question from any load or expectation. If someone mentions their dog we don't ask whether it's a Labrador. We ask them to tell us more about their dog. By doing that we allow them to go in whatever direction they like: breed, colour, nature, where they walk the dog.

A good question often starts with 'What…?'

Most things can be put after a 'what'. It is very empowering and practical.

It forces a focused but still open 'What is stopping you?' from a 'Why aren't you?'.

A good question never starts with 'Why...?'

I've heard 'Why' referred to as psychological terrorism. The more you observe it the more you will see why's ugly accusatory tone. Maybe it's the question that parents most often ask naughty children, but 'why' seems to get more of a push-back and less traction than any other form of question. 'Why' questions can come across as something to be defended rather than the simple manifestation of curiosity. Even if the question seems OK on the surface, you will often find it makes the person a little less comfortable and more guarded, perhaps even subconsciously. 'Why do you think like that?' is much more comfortable expressed as 'What makes you think like that?' This less-threatening question focuses the person on the external cause and the practical answer, which is easier to talk about. The answer should give clues as to the real issue anyway; it is just a less confrontational way to get to the answer.

A good way to practise listening is to listen for words and metaphors.[7] Noticing words is a great thing to do as they can act as a hook. In a social situation this can even help rescue a conversation. All you need to start a conversation is a first question. After that you simply listen for words (and sometimes metaphors) that give a clue to the next question, when and if needed. If you get a succession of words, ideas or themes that seem to matter to the other person, that is fine also. You simply go with the one that makes most sense to follow on with. Making it clear that you are building on what they have said makes the conversation easy. It's rare that there isn't something in what someone says or even how they say it to provide a hook for your next question. The trick is to disengage your inner interrupters and to listen.

The importance of metaphor is easy to underestimate. As well as listening to the words people use we can also listen to the images behind them, which give us clues about the underlying feeling. I once listened to a managing director talk to a sales team of about thirty people. The talk was full of instructions, thoughts and messages about how the organisation should build its sales capability. By noticing the metaphor used by their leader I could see a problem. The metaphor was the common one of war. I noted more than a dozen words which used the image of fighting. This is how the leader illustrated what she wanted the team to be doing. What was clear was that this was not a metaphor favoured by the majority of the sales team. Nobody in the team mentioned or probably thought about the imagery itself but the underlying message still got through. The message was well crafted and engaging in many ways, but expressed as a war metaphor it was difficult for them to build on. This started to explain why the organisation was going backwards in terms of sales. Noticing these metaphors sometimes gives you the insight you need to see the question differently.

So, even before we get to the more pressing 'What...?' questions, here's our list of the top 5 ways to respond to get more:

1. Silence, say nothing. Nothing at all. Just give your utter confidence that there is more they want to say and that you are waiting to hear it.
2. A gentle 'mmm' or a 'yeah' – and nothing else, your attention and nothing else.
3. If you have to use a word, 'and ...' is best – together with maybe a 'then?' or a 'what?' (buts are just that – a butt).
4. Link into a key word you have heard them say but keep the question deliberately load-free. For example, if they have talked about something leaving a hole you might say 'What kind of hole is that [hole]?'.
5. Ask them how the thing they are talking about makes them feel.

So that is a very slow journey into very few words at most:

1. Silence
2. Mmmm.
3. 'and ...'

4. 'What kind of a ...?'
5. 'How do you feel ...?'

Landing our point

When I was little I thought painting was all about paint. The first thing I would do was to reach for the pot of paint and the paint-brush and start painting. Now I know that painting is mostly about preparation. With DIY painting, it still frustrates me that so much time needs to be spent on digging out rotten wood and filling and preparing the surface, but I now reluctantly accept that this is time well spent. The craftsman pays great attention to preparation and takes a great deal of time to check the underly-ing surface is ready for the final coats of protective colour. So it is with negotiation. The majority of our work lies in building understanding. Once trust, empathy and understanding have been achieved, finding a good solution that meets all our needs well tends to come remarkably easily. It's also something that it is difficult to give generic guidance on because it's so contextual. The core skill is to find the point at which to start applying the paint, to build the solution.

The best triggers are when we see something in what we hear on which we can securely build our final layers. Once in a long negotiation with a potential customer we hit a stumbling block over a detailed legal question of liability. The customer was con-cerned that if we defaulted in certain circumstances the notional financial limit set in the contract would operate unfairly against them. In each of our negotiating sessions this point would fail to get resolved. Because it was one of many issues, we didn't spend much time on it. Gradually not being able to answer the point was starting to erode trust. The problem was that we felt we understood the point. We had taken the issue back to our head office team and discussed it and the answer was a clear no.

When we came to this point in our latest negotiating session, we suggested a change of tack. Instead of discussing it in open forum, a room of some ten to twelve people, we put forward the idea of a sub-meeting. This immediately changed the physical dynamics. Three of us went off to a separate room: the customer's lawyer, our lawyer and I. In that session we spent sufficient time to allow the customer's lawyer to explain, from first principles, what the problem was. We encouraged him to get all his dirty washing out and put it on the table for us to see. We didn't put our case at all but merely listened to him and asked questions so that we could see how the issue arose, when it arose, who in his organisation was concerned by it and why. Through this we realised, as we feared, that not solving this one issue would result in our whole bid being unacceptable. However, we also heard what the customer's lawyer said, which was that a number of particular types of default under the contract were actually their real concern. Now that we understood this we could see a way through. His needs, behind his position, were clear. All we had to do was suggest an acceptable way of dealing with these situations. From the understanding that we now had we were able to build a set of conditions into the contract that kept the customer happy. We still had to broker these with our head office and that wasn't easy. Faced with the knowledge that this was a potential deal breaker, we could emphasise the importance of giving this comfort to the customer.

Sometimes we have to lay out our case more fully. Again, preparation is essential but how we build and layer our case is equally important. An example I was given in a workshop was an ambitious young leader, Adam, who was preparing for a discussion with his new boss about a promotion. The underlying issue was that Adam knew the new boss didn't think he was up to the job yet. We decided to work through the situation as a group.

One of the group acted the part of Adam's boss. As she expressed her opinion on his lack of experience, Adam did the usual thing of countering her point with his opinion that he was indeed ready. We stopped for a moment and asked the woman playing his boss how that seemed to her. Her reaction was that she was a bit annoyed by it. Had he really understood her point? We then swapped over and replayed the situation so Adam could try this out. He felt the same thing. Had the point really been taken on board? What boss is going to trust someone who doesn't show that they take on board what they say? Had she listened to his response and taken it seriously, we asked? No, she had not.

We then replayed the situation a number of times but coached Adam to do a few things differently. First, we asked him to dig further into what his boss needed and to bring out her 'pain'. She had a problem and needed a senior leader to fill this role. Adam made sure this pain got exposed. It was a felt gap, which needed a solution. Adam therefore had an expressed need to 'sell' to. Second, when she made her point about Adam not yet being up to the role I got him to imagine himself crossing the tennis court of the conversation to her side of the net. I asked him to imagine himself picking up the ball for her and playing it again, to show that he had heard it and that he wasn't afraid of it. If we do this, instead of responding immediately, the original speaker, the one who asked the question, usually then considers afresh the statement they have just made. Seeing our own shot replayed in front of us will often result in reflection. Was what I said really so fair? Was it even such a good shot?

For Adam, saying 'So, what you are saying is that the sales team are a difficult bunch and you don't think I can deal with them...' was hard, but by saying it he realised he'd shown that he'd heard and that he understood. The person playing his boss confirmed how much better that felt. She also said that she'd already started to question the truth of her own assertion. Things changed because Adam hadn't simply played the defensive game and played the ball back. Contrary to how it might feel, that shows confidence. From this point, things also tend to get easier. I asked Adam to tell the group about some situations where he'd showed his ability to deal with tough situations. One of the stories he told was about how he'd worked with the sales team and they had won an award. This helped Adam to build his own sense of power and confidence in the situation. He was good at his job. Instead of allowing Adam to respond to the assertion, we then got Adam to tell the story where they'd won the award to his boss as an amusing factual anecdote. Stories help because they are observations of facts. A good story allows us to make our own judgement rather than being a judgement itself. This then became a case of Adam diffusing the issue with a story that showed the complete opposite of his boss's concern. He didn't need to state his opinion, the facts of the story did it for him. A little while later I got an email from Adam saying that he'd had the conversation, used the coaching and had got the job. Doing the right preparation matters.

CHAPTER 8

CONNECTING

In 1964 Shel Silverstein published a controversial children's picture book called *The Giving Tree*. The book is controversial because the boy in the story constantly, through his life, makes requests of the tree. The female apple tree is happy to provide. This is a story of a tree offering a solution from its bounty, in response to the boy's wants. First, the child and the tree play. A relationship forms. The boy makes a king's crown with the tree's leaves, eats its apples and sleeps in its shade. The boy is full of playful joy. The boy is said to love the tree very much and the tree is happy. The boy marks his love for the tree with a love-heart and his initials on the trunk.

Later, in adolescence, the boy returns to the tree after a long absence. The boy now doesn't want to play. He has other loves and this is shown by a second loveheart, with a girl's initials, carved above his original expression of love for the tree. The boy's focus has changed. He now wants money to buy things. The tree has no money but suggests the boy picks and sells apples to make him happy, which he duly does. This makes the tree happy. The tree's happiness turns to sadness in the long absences, however. It is their relationship that the tree wants.

On reaching adulthood, the boy returns to the tree again. There is no time for simple play now. The boy is busy building a life and wants a house. The tree duly gives up its branches to make planks to build his house. Later, in middle age, the boy returns to the tree. He says he is too old and sad to play and now wants a boat to take him far away. Again, the tree has no boat but offers a solution, in the form of her trunk, which he accepts. The trunk, bearing the marks of the boy's previous loves, is carried off. Finally, the boy returns in old age. The now wizened old man needs 'a quiet place to sit and rest'. The tree is able to oblige with its remaining stump. The story simply ends with the words 'And the tree was happy'.

Silverstein's story caused controversy because it is, at the extremes, either a story of selfless love from the tree or of reckless abuse by the boy. There is the 'Giving Tree' of the title but there is also a 'Taking Boy'. Imbalance between what is selflessly given and what is ruthlessly taken forms the story's backbone. We see total, unquestioning, unconditional love being given by the tree with very little evidence of thanks from the boy. He simply ages and his demands develop. He seems bereft of reflective wisdom and is referred to as the 'boy' throughout. If the tree's selfless giving had resulted in any significant change in appreciation the story would have had a very different feeling at the end. Silverstein's choice is to focus on the extremities of giving and what that means. He chooses to leave us with a happy, still giving, tree and what seems like a still taking aged boy. The underlying message is that someone is not responding to the other's giving. The tree has enabled a relationship but only by giving everything she has. Something is broken.

The Giving Tree, which is now over fifty years old, provides a reflection on the many extremes of needs and wants, love and power, awareness or lack of it and the abiding anchor of relationship. What really sustains this story is the relationship between the tree and the boy, formed in infancy. The boy's love wanes but the tree's remains. This is a relationship where at least one party is happy to see the other happy, even if that happiness turns to nothing. This is unconditional love that sustains the bond, however imbalanced.

The Giving Tree also stands as a model for our own relationship with the natural world. The flaw in the giving of love and the giving up of power, in the form of apples and wood, is that these are given with no boundaries being established. It is all take. This is largely the economically driven relationship with the natural world that we have placed ourselves in. We do take with little consequence, even though we know that growing up without any boundaries results in spoilt children and puppies that piss on the carpet. There is a clear environmental message here for us as we negotiate our own accommodations with nature. The challenge is that in this negotiation, nature is a largely silent partner and finds it difficult, in the short term, to negotiate terms in return for man's taking. Like the apple tree, nature has a limited ability to communicate its needs to us for a successful relationship. If we fail to establish what these are, the relationship will fail.

The Giving Tree also illustrates the extremes of giving and taking and the perils of each. Without an emerging balance, much is lost. At the extremes of giving this might be a parent giving up everything for a child. In this excess of giving there is very little opportunity for the child to give back. In being so strong and unconditionally giving the tree perhaps seals its own fate. If a balance is to be achieved we need much higher levels of awareness and responsiveness. We each need to appreciate the giving that we receive.

I was fortunate once to watch this need for reciprocation unfold in a group situation. After one of the group had spoken about what he did and the sacrifices he made for his clients, another person made some pertinent observations and paid the speaker a very heartfelt compliment. What happened next was critical. The speaker did not explicitly receive the compliment or thank the person for it. The kindness was left hanging in the space between the pair, as if it had not been said at all. The point of brilliance was that the observer then picked this up. She explained that she had made the comment specifically to see what would happen. Because she understood the problem she saw a potential pattern. She wondered whether there was something wider going on here: the speaker was able to give selflessly to others but not to receive. This comment was entirely consistent with the speaker's selfless devotion to others. She explained that as a giver of a compliment, she felt moderately slighted by the lack of response. She had not really got the sense of being heard. She felt the behaviour of not being able to receive was a block for the speaker.

In the group, we could all see the critical importance of this for the speaker. We can easily find ourselves in a situation personally or professionally where we give to fully accommodate the needs of others. In doing that, what damage do we do to ourselves and the others if we are only able to transmit and are not set up to receive? Part of giving is surely the ability to give space for others to choose to give themselves and to reward that behaviour when it happens to encourage its growth. We need to receive and to respond to the other so that we work in close co-operation, between the extremes of mutual giving by each. Giving has a joy and gets reciprocated, but at the extremes it can struggle to be effective. Once again, the solution is a boundaried balance between gift and response.

In Chapter 3 we plotted giving and taking onto the two hands model. We are now in a position to update this overall model to include some of the other elements. We have seen that the way to approach our negotiations is shaped with trust at its base. Crucially the power balance sits atop this, informing how everyone's relative power in a situation is felt by all. Next, we make sure we understand our needs and then, through observation, questioning and listening, we create a complete picture. Then comes the process of creatively crafting a solution, the creation of options that we can move towards and the necessity of an increased focus on logic to inform our reasoned analysis of these options.

Diagrammatically, and updating the Power of Soft Negotiation Map, this now looks like this:

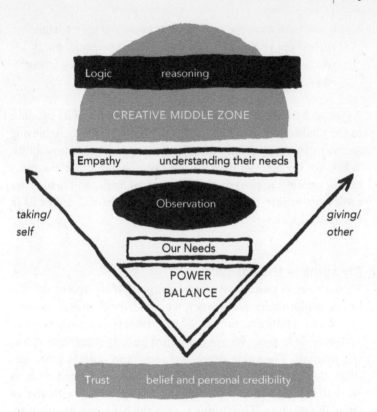

What leads in our external engagement is first our relationship and secondly our observations. We stay mostly at an open soft front, scanning and connecting. If we don't have a relationship already, we need to build one fast. Our approach itself can do that. Our focus is on relationship and observation and is in contrast to any approach that prioritises our judgement, our needs or our position about how our needs might be achieved.

In evolutionary terms achieving this creative reciprocation becomes more and more important as we move away from the world of finite objects into the world of concepts and ideas. This is a place in which we move beyond simple ideas of giving and taking into a zone of co-operative creativity where we have the opportunity to produce a whole that is greater than the sum of the parts. As George Bernard Shaw nicely put it:

> If you have an apple and I have an apple and we exchange
> apples then you and I will still each have one apple. But if
> you have an idea and I have an idea and we exchange those
> ideas, then each of us will have two ideas.

As we go forward from the metaphor of the tree and its produce
to the challenge we all face in our daily negotiations, achieving
access to this multiplicity of ideas becomes our new possibility.
When we do this we need to ask ourselves whether the positional, owning approach that we started with, and which we
took with us into the industrial age of objects, still serves us in
the age of ideas.

My spine is the baseline

Strong Core is more than just a metaphor. If we accept the line
of our evolutionary ascendancy, we also have to accept an early
age of our evolution: the age of invertebrates, animals without
vertebrae or a spine. We are descended directly from these spine-
less animals. The spine developed some 500 million years ago
when the first vertebrates, in the form of fish, appeared. Fish, as
we know from our dinner plates, are very largely a matter of
spine in structure. Their spine is also the fish's engine of movement, core to their body.

Evolution tends to try things out and accepts that some
experiments are dead ends. In evolutionary terms, one option
of development from the vertebrate fish has already been tried.
This was development of the spine without much brain – the
dinosaur experiment.[1] What we now see as an evolutionary
cul-de-sac lasted a few hundred million years and then ended. If
we take a long-lens view of evolution we could easily see that we
are simply in a slightly different, current experiment: one of
spine combined with upright bi-pedal movement and a much
larger brain. Our challenge is perhaps to make this evolutionary
experiment an even more successful and long lasting one than it
already is.

In evolutionary terms, the fish spine precedes both the modern human form and the modern human brain.[2] We could say that the brain has grown out of the spine in a number of key evolutionary steps as we have developed from lizard to primate and then to human. The spine has always been and remains the part of our bodies that connects all our capability together, from our more recently developed reason, at top, to our more deeply held motion and emotion lower down. This is perhaps why the spine is so important. It connects and it is core. Our soul and our consciousness are held more deeply in us.

As we have seen, though, it is too easy for us to live in our heads too much or to become victim to our own instinctive reactions. The first error in listening is not to employ the range of capability we have through the length of our spine, in our daily living. This self-knowledge in turn allows us more perspective in negotiating our relationships. Our full being is there to be heard if we make sure that we listen to it. In particular, if we live through reason only, we tend to take a different, more calculated perspective.

George Bernard Shaw was a religious man but not part of any established church. He was a great believer in the 'Life Force' of evolution which presses through man in the form of consciousness. He believed that for man to evolve it is crucial for this consciousness to evolve. Shaw's comment about reason and reasonableness in *Man and Superman*, which I quote in Chapter 2, is much misunderstood as a prescription for bloody-mindedness. It is not unreasonableness in this form that Shaw is against.[3] The words in full, which appear in a list of 'Maxims for Revolutionists' promoted by his character Jack Tanner and appended to the play under the title 'Reason', are:

> The reasonable man adapts himself to the world: the unreasonable one persists in trying to adapt the world to himself. Therefore all progress depends on the unreasonable man.
> The man who listens to Reason is lost: Reason enslaves all those whose minds are not strong enough to master her.

Shaw's comment is about the danger of reason. His religion

elevates individual conscience above any external ready-made morality. This is about listening to a deeper force within us and being true to that. Superman is available to us, but not if we enslave ourselves to head-based reason. The challenge for us is being alive to that force and being able to connect and listen to it. Progress depends on the unreasonable man because this person follows the true life force through conscience and does not deform himself to conform to what is already there.

The spine, then, is the means of connection between the value that reason brings us and our deeper knowledge and abilities. We have already seen that a simple way of looking at this is to take the ancient Greek ideas of ethos, pathos and logos to build a stack that gives a simple representation of this connection. This can also be thought of as a journey along the spine. Reason, or logic, is at the top, Empathy in the middle and Trust at the base.

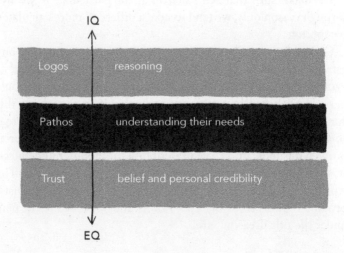

Whatever we do will benefit if we see it as a connection between these three parts mediating our actions. Relying on logic or reason is rarely enough. How many arguments or misunderstandings have grown up or persist because we deal with them in this heady top zone of reason alone? When things are failing, we have to go back to trust and empathy before reason. This is the foundation on which we build.

Reason's role is to be our saviour. Without it we would be savages. We need reason to and modify our emotional reactions to stimulus. Creating the space between the event and our reaction to it gives us the ability to reflect and decide. This is the paradox, for simply running away from the savage is not the answer either. Within this base part of us we hold the benefit of many millions of years of evolution and our connection to that from which we came. To live through reason alone, without the benefit of our evolutionary stem would be to miss out on what makes us humans and not machines.

Run away, walk towards

A great thing about being two-legged humans, and not fish swimming around, is that another dimension of movement, relative to the spine, has opened up; forwards and back. We stand up and raise our heads directly above the seat of our emotion and motion. Because our spine is vertical, a fundamental change occurs. Our spine now takes gravity, compressed through it, along its length. Our opportunity for movement itself now operates perpendicularly, through the spine, rather than along it. Instead of moving headfirst into everything with a spine like an arrow, like a fish or a reptile, our motion is initiated by our hips at the base of the spine. Our spine is located out of and above our centre of movement. Taken out and placed in a chiropractor's window display, we can also see what a large structure the human spine really is. We also notice that at its front the spine has more ability to flex. Its cushioning between vertebrae and its softness all sits here, deep inside the body. The part that is touchable or visible, at our backs, is just the bony rear face of the vertebrae that surround the spinal cord, which is itself deeper inside the body. The spine's softness really does face forward. This bipedal opportunity of joining together the vertical spine and the horizontal towards and away instinct is in essence the diagram we ended Chapter 5 with. With Trust, Empathy and Logic overlaid it looks as follows:

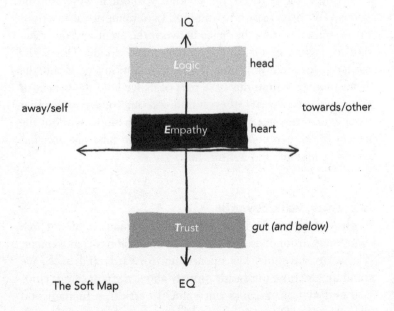

The Soft Map

Into this we can easily co-opt our recurrent theme, the paradox of two alternative extremes, represented by our two hands. This arose in the analysis of power when we saw that love or care towards others, mixed with power, makes all the difference to the exercise of that power. A mix of power with love is potent. We then saw these as a contrast between giving and taking hands. When we looked at the importance of relationships we also saw a poetic plane of relating that exists as a contrast to the activity of doing. Again, the ideal is not an exclusive use of one or the other, doing or relating, but an appropriate mix. Underneath all these comes the basic instinct of 'towards and away', the instinctive driver of our behaviour: to run away from bad things and walk towards good. This principle of towards other and away into self unifies all these other paradoxes. They are essentially versions of the same thing. We also saw how easily we are imbalanced by the far stronger away instinct. The protection of self and the instinct to move away can easily dominate.

It may be that the thing that helped us instinctively run away from threats deep in our historical past may now be our biggest challenge. This same, deep-seated urge to act in preservation of the self in the face of instinctively perceived danger acts against our interests in many modern situations. We see things we fear for ourselves in others and we instinctively recoil, seeing the thing as an external threat and seeking external blame. In crisis situations we can easily shut down and tend towards self-protection. When we feel threatened we reach for a weapon, whether it is actual or metaphorical. The perceived 'surgical precision' of this weapon, seen through our reason, can seem highly attractive, however destructive it is on sober reflection. In our working and private lives we achieve status for the self in the form of expertise and knowledge, then we act in protection of it. Becoming aware of this behaviour, rather than being subject to it, is our major life opportunity.

Dominant power and the evil it causes is a key observation of the soft approach. Many who end up endorsing a kinder approach are people who have seen for themselves the damage the excesses of mankind's power can cause. It is not so much that we don't try it, it is that we do try it and see its limits. In the very first chapter I mentioned Leonard Cheshire who came out of the Royal Air Force at the end of the Second World War to focus on helping people with disabilities. What I didn't mention was that Cheshire made this career change having been the official British observer of the Nagasaki nuclear attack. Seeing the effects of the ultimate bomb is what transformed the ex-bomber. In the American Army, a similar thing happened to John Rawls who observed the aftermath of the Hiroshima attack. Rawls had also had a distinguished war career, having been awarded a Bronze Star for valour. After what he saw at Hiroshima and then suffering a demotion for refusing to carry out an order to discipline another soldier, Rawls became disillusioned with military life and left the service after the war for an academic career in moral philosophy at Princeton.

In 1971 Rawls, who had already suffered devastating loss of both of his brothers in childhood when they fell ill with diseases they separately contracted from him, published a book called *A Theory of Justice*. In it Rawls advanced a critical theory that reached beyond our normal complicated political balancing act between extremes. In this thought experiment, instead of trying to decide on political and social matters from an existing position coloured with the inevitable bias of that position, Rawls proposed that we should sit behind a 'Veil of Ignorance'. Behind this veil we know nothing about our own strengths or position. This veil puts us in something Rawls called the 'Original Position'. In the original position the power balance and our own position taking is put to one side. The original position ironically ditches any position taking. Rawls could see that power and position are the major influences on our outlook. It's an extreme version because we focus, not even on our own needs or our power, but on the needs of us all. What is great about this perspective is that our view becomes suddenly uncluttered with baggage so we can see clearly. From here, instead of maximising what we see through our perspective, we look at all and seek to maximise the advantages to all.

A client I worked with who was preparing for a difficult negotiation described this uncluttered front as the way he felt in as result of our preparation. Because he had done the necessary work to develop his strong core, he described how he felt going into the discussion was like having his hands in front of him free, but with the comfort of a backpack of all the things he needed. In the room, he listened, made suggestions, got what he needed and ended the negotiation on better terms with the other party than he went in.

In Chapter 7 we used the metaphor of the tennis court to better understand the interaction between two people. When we negotiate anything we are working with not one but at least two systems that face one another across a metaphorical net as such:

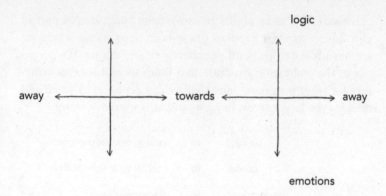

The trick is to know exactly where you are operating and to notice the things that influence the towards and away instinct; principally of the other person but also your own. In Chapter 7 Adam leapt over the net of the tennis court to play in his boss's half; he took the play to her, on her own terms. In Chapter 6, Liz learnt to control her judgement in a difficult feedback session and thus encouraged Alan towards her. We have seen that there are things we do that move us towards others but there are also things that move us apart. Every time we externalise and voice blame, express anger or judgement we take a step back. If the other stands well away from us we have to choose whether to make the generous move forward to build trust. Such a move may be courageous or make us feel vulnerable but it can be what breaks the deadlock. Sometimes, it can be almost like a game of counters where each action moves us one way or another (with the odd snake and ladder to take us up or down more swiftly). Above all we need to notice these things and act on them to achieve the coming together that we need for our negotiations to be successful. At the same time we have to have first built the strong core that allows us to do this. Going to the meeting without the backpack would have yielded a different result. The young woman at agricultural college in Chapter 4 found that simply going towards was not the answer either. We have to move forwards in confidence with inner strength. Doing so having built our strong core changes everything.

Ultimately, it is an ability to move from being simply part of and subject to what happens towards an open stance where we see our ability to respond proactively to the drama. We get up out of the embracing structure that holds us and see that structure for what it is, something that we can act upon by small and then maybe larger steps. In going towards we move from:

conflict	to	valuing our differences
blame	to	accepting responsibility
assumptions	to	observable facts
cleverness	to	wisdom
answers	to	questions
putting down others	to	helping others
objects	to	people

A model for negotiation

As a model of negotiation we can place each of the main areas we have talked about roughly on this bodily inspired grid. In negotiation, the core skill explored in Chapter 2, of moving away from position, or 'Knowing the Mountain' becomes a focus on identifying our 'Needs'. The ability we explored in Chapter 3 to see power and to maximise our own becomes a focus on our ability to 'Empower'. Together these build our strong core consolidated in Chapter 4. Both needs and power are also not just relevant to us but also to the others we relate to, as we seek to understand the other's perspective as well as we know our own. This brings us to our crucial engagement at front, where we face others. Here our ability to observe what is actually there and to listen fully is explored in Chapters 6 & 7 and becomes our capability to be fully 'Aware'. As we saw in Chapter 5, this can be achieved by going towards others more and building stronger 'Relationships'.

Together these form the phrase 'Needs Empower Aware

Relationships' or NEAR. This becomes a quick way to remember these four key components and to check with ourselves what we might focus on in any given situation.

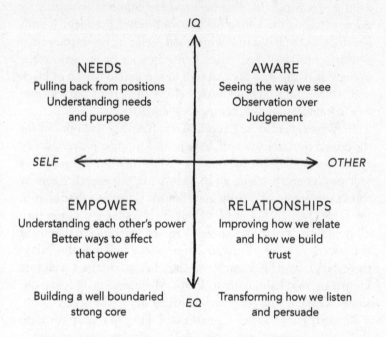

The clarity of the strong core or the backpack is all about clearing our front to allow us to move towards others. Making a clear appeal outward to 'other' works in many situations, not only in our negotiations but also in our wider communications. In one of the world's greatest speeches, Robert F. Kennedy took on the task, on the day that Martin Luther King was assassinated in April 1968, of breaking the news to a predominantly black audience in Indianapolis. Kennedy, then Senator for New York State and candidate for the Presidential nomination, had been warned by the local police not to make a speech on the basis that they would not be able to control any ensuing riots. Against this backdrop, Kennedy spoke from his heart from the back of a flat-bed truck, improvising with his notes in his hand. What Kennedy does first is, to audible cries of disbelief, acknowledge the news. He then recognises in clear language how the largely black audience must be feeling and ensures that, as he moves out to embrace the feelings of the audience, he creates a definition of a 'tribe' to which he also belongs. He connects with this by acknowledging the killing of his own brother, President John F. Kennedy, at the hand of a white man. Once he has membership of this group and their trust, Kennedy goes on to set out the options available and his vision of how a united nation of black and white could pick up King's effort to move from violence towards understanding, compassion and love.

To rising cheers as he pauses, Kennedy, still giving options for the crowd to move towards, asks people to say a prayer as they return home, both for the family of Martin Luther King and for 'our own country, which all of us love'. In this speech Kennedy shows the mettle of a truly great leader. He shows that he is in the same camp as his audience and he gives them a vision they all want to be a part of. Kennedy's speech worked. On that night there were riots in all major cities except Indianapolis. Sixty-three days later RFK himself was shot. In memoriam, a sculpture known as the 'Landmark to Peace Memorial' in Indianapolis shows Kennedy and King each reaching out to the other.

Kennedy ended with a request that I'd like to repeat: for us to dedicate ourselves to what the Greeks wrote many years ago:

> to tame the savageness of man and make gentle the life of this world.

What Aeschylus, 'the father of tragedy', hadn't experienced in his lifetime, around 500 BC, was the other extreme of man that had, by the time Kennedy spoke, been experienced in the Second World War and felt in the Cuban Missile Crisis. Just as we need to tame the savage we also need to tame our extremes of rational thinking. It is not just the savage who needs taming, it is also the logician; Doctor Strangelove. The combination of logic and self-protection is just as scary, if not more scary than emotion and self-protection. We can do far more damage wearing a suit than wearing a loincloth.

In Britain, the House of Commons was heavily bombed during the Second World War. In the aftermath of the war the parliamentary chamber was simply rebuilt largely to the original plan and reopened in 1950. The current two-sided plan in which the two main parties sit opposite each other was itself based on the original simple parliamentary assembly that took place down the sides of St Stephen's Chapel, also in the Palace of Westminster, between 1547 and 1834, when the chapel was destroyed by fire resulting in a move to a larger chamber.

Success and the resulting lack of change can become a problem. Jim Casey, who founded the delivery company that became UPS, strongly believed in 'constructive dissatisfaction', and this is still a core value of UPS. This is a method of always wanting to improve even when we win. If we follow this principle, we constructively spend time not just analysing the reasons for loss, but also working through a victory to see what it can tell us about a better future. This principle has also been applied to sport and is based on the realisation that what won you today's match will not necessarily win you tomorrow's; losers might be forced into reflection but winners should take time out to reflect also. If we learn from everything that happens to us and challenge ourselves to improve rather that resting on our laurels and citing past victories, then we can keep moving forward and constantly evolve. In Casey's model, reference to past successes will not suffice.

This was also a message poignantly delivered by German Chancellor Angela Merkel in her address to both of the British Houses of Parliament in February 2014 when, among other things, she quoted the words of the great British leader Sir Winston Churchill:

To improve is to change, to be perfect is to change often.

Taking these steps can be tough but just after Merkel gave this reminder to us all at Westminster, a highly successful company founder and CEO told me a story about his father that had, at the time, surprised him and, on reflection, had a life-changing impact on his own approach to business. He had returned home to find his father had cut down a large tree in the family garden. This was in direct contrast to his usual gentle gardening approach of tidying, trimming and mowing. His father, challenged to explain what he had done, simply stated that there is a time for all of us when we need to 'take out the tree'. Sometimes, for the sake of the rest of the garden which also needs to grow, we have to forsake what we have previously held dear. This means that sometimes it is time for even the most important of people to leave an organisation or for a principle that has long been held dear to be changed.

One of the answers to any challenge to end Punch and Judy-type conflicts would be to take up more of these 'take out the tree' challenges. The two-sided oppositional parliamentary chamber that that was bombed and burnt to the ground is now a good example of something that is overdue for review. The existing two-handed system is no different from the Punch Professor who places his Punch puppet on his dominant hand and faces the audience to perform a show where Punch gets to beat up his wife, a policeman, the justice of the peace and a jailor. Former Foreign Secretary, diplomat, founder of the SDP and author David Owen was once asked what his first act would be on becoming Prime Minister.[4] His answer was to rip out the existing opposing benches in the House of Commons and replace them with a semicircular chamber. Such an arrangement would assist in the discussion that is increasingly required between many diverse contributing voices towards a meaningful common purpose instead of following the model of a puppet show carried out in front of an audience for the purposes of entertainment.

Softly hard

As a word 'soft' has its own connotations for each of us. We might find softness in a cushion at home, we might find it in a field of grass in nature or, like Lao Tzu, we might find our ideal metaphor for softness to be water. The common factor that softness has is its ability to respond and to move fluidly with whatever acts upon it. The fur on the head of the cute dog is soft because it occupies more space than it strictly needs. The fur can then yield when we touch it, into available space. A cushion folds to our shape and supports us. At some point soft has strength, because it holds us. We do not fall infinitely through the give of a cushion.

Giving is the preferred medium of the soft. Yet what the soft gives up does not get lost in the yielding. The cushion is still a cushion. The dog's fluffy head remains cute. That softness is not lost. The physical boundaries of each remain intact. The hard rock insists on taking space for itself. Hard's problem is that on contact, its hardness allows only erosion; a reluctant giving up. Hard knows only strong. No initial accommodation occurs and thus no understanding follows. Thus what is structured to give and is expectant of giving remains more whole. If strength consists of a survival of integrity, then soft is indeed strong.

The Power of Soft builds on the advantages of each. It is a dual, front and core approach. We lead with the soft and combine this with the strength held behind. In this approach we have the ability to be fundamentally anchored and not blown about by the wind. At core we are principled, boundaried and powerful. Here we can borrow some of the more confident, rock-like qualities. At front then, we can be fluid and responsive, free to explore the available space. The knowledge that we are secure at core is what allows us to fully explore the soft fluidity of movement that is truly open to us.

One of the many reasons to crowd-fund a book is the engagement the process gives us straightaway between readers and author. The insights of others can provide invaluable points of reflection. Early on in the funding process of this book I met up with someone I once met in the reception of a client's office. Andy and I had shared a taxi back to the station and talked on the way. He later became an early supporter of this book, and what he said intrigued me. His reason for immediately pledging was that my words in an email to him had captured his imagination. All I had done, or so I thought, was to refer to the idea of the book as being about 'life's great negotiation'. For Andy, this drew him in. As the book has progressed this simple point has also grown significantly stronger and clearer for me. For the Power of Soft is, partly by chance and partly by design, crafted towards a whole life approach. There is in here a method of thinking about how we negotiate but there is also a philosophy that goes a lot wider. This is partly because, following the theme of this approach, if we understand things at core we have more options about how we behave within any given context.

Everything we do is in one sense a negotiation. It is a negotiation because by our actions we make choices. When we act we affect others. There is not always a person present who is obviously and directly affected by our actions, but if we take a wider view, most of what we do has external ramifications. The 'other' we affect can be the natural world, with which we are more connected than we usually acknowledge. For example, the disposal of the smallest and simplest piece of waste is a form of negotiation and has an effect. Just because we are not there to see the onward travels of our actions doesn't mean our actions have ceased to have an impact. We have come to see many of our actions as normal behaviour and thus apply little real awareness to them. Yet, at the extremes, even this seemingly simple disposal of an item reveals both a relationship with the world we live in and the negotiation of an outcome which will occur as a result of the choices we make.

This connects to a feeling in this softly hard approach that something far bigger is going on in the world, beyond even politics. This is that evolution itself may be our purpose in living; that we are part of an much larger evolutionary experiment. Unless we want to be replaced by the next stage of the experiment, we ought to understand this above all else. The success of such an experiment involves us handling a much more important negotiation with each other and with a planet and a system that, if it judges us at all, will only do so finally. This negotiation with our environment is aptly expressed in *The Giving Tree* where the boy takes much and gives back little. While that deal is available to us, it does not seem to be a fair or sustainable balance.

Ultimately, each of us can only progress by small changes that are within our influence. Sometimes our biggest joy is the realisation that this influence is wider than we thought. While writing this book I was heartened by one such story from a supporter. That story appears on the following page. It would be good to hear more of these stories.

A STORY

'I got on a train and sat down next to a man who had his feet on the seats. Early 30s, he seemed relatively well dressed and was playing a game on his phone. I quietly pointed to the sign that said "Please keep your feet off the seats" and suggested he follow it.

'He looked at me. And then sneered, "What the f**k has it got to do with you? You are a f**king prick." I raised my hands in a form of surrender and left it there. I didn't move and continued to read my book. I could sense the nervousness of the other passengers (it was a busy train) and wondered if I could or should have handled it another way.

'The guy continued to sit there with his feet up.

'Ten minutes later, he looked at me, took his feet off the seats and said, "Do you know what, mate? You are right. And I am sorry. You didn't deserve to be spoken to like that. I've just got a lot on my plate at the moment."

'I looked up and told him I appreciated the apology.

'He went on: "I am up at the Old Bailey at the moment. No idea if I am going to see my kids for a long time. I just don't know..." and he trailed off.

'He had a scar on his face, and then I realised his suit was a "defendant's" suit. For appearance. And when he got off at City Thameslink I noticed he had a pronounced limp. As if he had been hurt. I felt deeply sorry for the man who was presumably facing a spell in prison. And pleased that dealing with it quietly and considerately, we both got what we needed.'

Notes

Chapter 1 – Exploring Paradox

1. Taken from Stuart Cloete – a South African writer who fought in the Somme – from the first volume of his autobiography, *A Victorian Son*, published by Collins (1972).
2. Andersen Consulting changed their name to Accenture at the beginning of 2001.
3. Daniel Lyon, *The Complete Book of Pilates for Men: The Lifetime Plan for Strength, Power & Peak Performance*. Published by William Morrow Paperbacks, 2005.
4. The 'Feldenkrais' method was invented by Moshe Feldenkrais and is an approach that develops awareness of how we move our bodies.
5. 'ammonite fossils' – I am grateful to Jacquetta Hawkes's classic *A Land* for this insight. Published by Collins, 1951.
6. Paul Brickhill, *The Dam Busters*. Published by Pan Books, 1999.
7. Taken from an undated letter to Nicholas Hughes; reproduced in *Letters of Ted Hughes*, ed. Christopher Reid. Published by Faber and Faber, 2009.

   I also picked up on the idea of Strong Back and Soft Front and its effect on our awareness from reading an early draft of Khurshed Dehnugara's *Flawed but Willing: Leading Large Organizations in the Age of Connection*. Published by LID Publishing, 2014.
8. @paulgoldberger, tweet, 22 August 2014.
9. In his TED Talk in 2008, Jonathan Haidt first juxtaposed these two quotes from the Zen master and the ex-President.

Chapter 2 – Knowing the Mountain

1. Nan Shepherd, *The Living Mountain: A Celebration of the Cairngorm Mountains of Scotland (Canons)*. Published by Aberdeen University Press, 1977.

2. Patrick Kavanagh, *Collected Prose*. Published by Martin Brian & O'Keeffe, 1973.

3. Robert Macfarlane, in his introduction to Nan Shepherd's *The Living Mountain: A Celebration of the Cairngorm Mountains of Scotland (Canons)*. Published by Canongate, 2011.

4. Gavin Eisler, *Lessons from the Top: The three universal stories that all successful leaders tell*. Published by Profile Books, 2012.

5. Marshall Rosenberg, *Non-Violent Communication – A Language of Life*. Published by Puddle Dancer Press, 2015, is a great introduction to NVC. NVC is based on prioritising Observation, Needs and Unconditional Positive Regard; an idea originally founded by Carl Rogers.

6. Abraham Maslow's Hierarchy of Needs. First published in the paper "A Theory of Human Motivation", *Psychological Review*, 1943.

7. John Bowlby's Theory of Attachment is a critical theory for anyone interested in human behaviour. I recommend Jeremy Holmes's *John Bowlby & Attachment Theory* (Routledge, 1993) as a good introduction to Bowlby and his theory. The penultimate chapter of this book on "Attachment Theory and Society" explains from where the majority of our modern problems originate.

8. Jeremy Rifkin, *The Empathic Civilisation*. Published by JP Tarcher/Penguin Putnam, 2010.

9. Victor Frankl, *Man's Search for Meaning*. Published by Beacon Press, 1959.

10. For a development of this theme see Ian Nairn's *Outrage* (The Architectural Press, 1956) in which he blasts "Subtopia" and shows us, in terms of housing development, we are offenders as well as victims.

11. Taken from Ken Robinson's 2013 TED Talk.

12. I am grateful to Leadership Coach and Corporate Psychologist Peter Milligan for this story.

13. Tom Brown Jnr. as quoted in Charles Eisenstein's *The Ascent of Humanity – Civilisation and the Human Sense of Self*. Published by Evolver Editions, 2007.

14. Roger Martin, *The Opposable Mind: Winning Through*

Integrative Thinking. Published by Harvard Business School Press, 2009.

Chapter 3 – Harnessing Power

1. I can recommend both Robert Leach's book *The Punch & Judy Show: History, Tradition, and Meaning* (University of Georgia Press, 1985) and George Speaight's *Punch and Judy: History* (Studio Vista, 1970) for more information on Punch. I am also grateful to the many Punch Professors who answered my questions.

2. I am grateful to Conflict expert Neil Denny who introduced me to conflict stories and their prevalence in the press. Neil simply bought some newspapers into a workshop and was quickly able to demonstrate how the papers are full of essentially the same story.

3. Triangulation is a concept of Murray Bowen Theory.

4. Gavin Eisler, *Lessons from the Top: The three universal stories that all successful leaders tell*. Published by Profile Books, 2012.

5. I can recommend Michael Dobb's *One Minute to Midnight: Kennedy, Khrushchev and Castro on the Brink of Nuclear War* (Arrow, 2009) as a study of how the crisis evolved and resolved.

6. The talk was held at the Conway Hall, Red Lion Square, London.

7. Adam Kahane, *Power and Love: A Theory and Practice of Social Change*. Published by Berrett-Koehler, 2010.

8. This map stands on the shoulders of a much older (x) and (y) axis based graphical model called the Thomas-Kilmann Conflict Mode Instrument (or "TKI") which was introduced by Kenneth Thomas and Ralph Kilmann in 1974.

Chapter 4 – Strong Core

1. Schnarch's "Passionate Marriage" is primarily about how we can all keep sexual intimacy alive in long-term relationships. It contains some surprising truths that are applicable elsewhere. Differentiation is an important topic in its own right, best explored by family systems psychiatrist Murray Bowen. Carl Rabstejnek has written an excellent summary about Family Systems and the Murray Bowen Theory which is available online.

2. To read further about boundaries, I recommend Anne Katherine's book *Boundaries: Where You End and I Begin* (Touchstone, 2001). I have added The Strong Core analysis, along with my own thoughts about her example situation.

3. Theodore Zeldin, *Conversation: How Talk Can Change Our Lives*. Published by HiddenSpring, 2007.

4. I suspect Benjamin Hoff's *The Tao of Pooh* (Penguin Books, 1982) is an influence here.

5. As quoted in Joshua Kurlantzick, *Charm Offensive: How China's Soft Power Is Transforming the World*. Published by Yale University Press, 2008.

6. The term BTNA was coined by Roger Fisher and William Ury in *Getting to Yes: Negotiating an agreement without giving in* (Random House Business, 1981).

7. David Owen's *The Hubris Syndrome: Bush, Blair & the Intoxication of Powers* (Methuen Publishing Ltd, 2012) is a fascinating study of Tony Blair and George W. Bush.

8. Richard Olivier, in his book *Inspirational Leadership – Timeless lessons for leaders from Shakespeare's Henry V* (Nicholas Brealey Publishing, 2013), takes this play apart beautifully.

9. Malcolm Gladwell, *David and Goliath: Underdogs, Misfits and the Art of Battling Giants*. Published by Penguin, 2014.

10. Mark Earl's *Herd: How to Change Mass Behaviour by Harnessing our True Nature* (Wiley, 2009) is particularly good on this subject.

11. Keith Johnstone, *Impro: Improvisation and the Theatre* (Routledge, 1987). Some of my observations here are also based on a workshop with Keith in September 2014.

12. Dee Hock, *The Birth of the Chaordic Age*. Published by Berrett-Koehler, 1999.

Chapter 5 – Towards

1. The Arbinger Institute focus on this phenomenon and their books *Leadership and Self-Deception: Getting out of the Box* (Penguin 2007) and *The Anatomy of Peace: How to Resolve the Heart of Conflict* (Penguin, 2010) explain their approach and insights.

2. Stephen R. Covey talks about these in Habit 5 in *The 7 Habits of Highly Effective People*. Published by Simon & Schuster, 2004.

3. I have found a similar graph called the Managerial Grid that Robert Blake and Jane Mouton published in 1964. This contrasted 'Concern for Production' against 'Concern for People' on (x) and (y) axes.

4. David Allen's "Do Lecture" at Do Wales in 2010 is a great summary of his GTD (Getting Things Done) method. A recording is available online.

5. Kahneman, Knetsch, and Thaler, "Experimental Tests of the Endowment Effect and the Coase Theory". Published in *The Journal of Political Economy*, Vol. 98, No. 6. (Dec., 1990), pp.1325–1348.

6. Les McKeown, *The Synergist: How to Lead Your Team to Predictable Success*. Published by Pangrave Macmillan, 2011. This approach is also summarised by McKeown in *Do Lead* (The Do Book Co., 2014).

7. Daniel J. Siegel, *Mindsight: Transform Your Brain with the New Science of Kindness*. Published by Bantam, 2010.

8. headspace.com have this metaphor in an introductory video. Headspace is a helpful meditation tool and is available as a smartphone app.

Chapter 6 – Awareness

1. Thank you to the Moonriders who meet locally every Monday at 7pm for a night ride.

2. Richard Wiseman's Colour Changing Card Trick available online. His book *Did You Spot The Gorilla* (Arrow, 2004) is a good book on this topic.

3. Stuart Mittleman, *Slow Burn: Burn Fat faster by Exercising Slower*. Published by HarperCollins, 2000.

4. Ken Robinson made this point in his 2013 TED talk.

5. From Thomas Hanna's book *A Body of Life: Creating New Pathways for Sensory Awareness and Fluid Movement*. Published by Random House, Inc., 1980.

6. This approach came out of a conversation with Robert Poynton who shared a story of having seen this happen in practice. I am also grateful to Rob for the idea of observation and judgement as two parts of our binocular vision which seeded out of that

conversation. Rob also gave me the metaphor of the 'busy bartender' at the end of the chapter 6.

7. Susan Neiman: *Why Grow Up: Philosophy in Transit* (Penguin, 2014) is a useful philosophical look at these distinctions; looking at what becoming a "grown-up" might really mean.

8. Kathryn Schulz, *Being Wrong: Adventures in the Margin of Error: The Meaning of Error in an Age of Certainty*. Published by Portobello Books Ltd, 2011.

9. A great example of this rush to judgement is given by Dale Carnegie at the end of his chapter "A Sure Way of Making Enemies – and How to Avoid it" in the still very much relevant *How to Win Friends and Influence People* (Vermilion, 2004).

10. Eckhart Tolle, *The Power of Now*. Published by Yellow Kite, 2001.

Chapter 7 – Touch and Feel

1. Based on a Radio interview about Coates' exhibition: "The Sounds of Others: A Biophonic Line" at the Manchester Museum of Science and Industry in 2014.

2. Theodore Zeldin, *Conversation: How Talk Can Change Our Lives*. Published by HiddenSpring, 2007.

3. The work of Anders Ericsson refined and popularised by Malcolm Gladwell in *Outliers: The Story of Success* (Allen Lane, 2008).

4. David Allen's "Do Lecture" at Do Wales in 2010 is a great summary of his GTD (Getting Things Done) method. A recording is available online.

5. I am grateful to the Children's Charity "Place 2Be" for giving me an insight into their work and the way they train their volunteers.

6. Taken from Billy Connolly, as interviewed by Andrew Zuckerman in his book *Wisdom*. Published by Harry N. Abrams, 2008.

7. Wendy Sullivan and Judy Rees's book *Clean Language: Revealing Metaphors and Opening Minds* (Crown House Publishing, 2008) goes into this whole area in much more detail.

Chapter 8 – Connecting

1. I am grateful to Feldenkrias Practitioner Günther Bisges for these insights into the importance of the spine and pelvis, as well as the

idea that I might have a hand or a foot that was more giving or loving than the other.

2. The Dinosaur Experiment is an idea inspired by Don Juan in the philosophical conversation with the Devil in Act III of George Bernard Shaw's *Man and Superman* (Wildside Press, 2008).

3. I am grateful to John Stewart Collis's fascinating short study of George Bernard Shaw in *Shaw* (Jonathan Cape, 1925).

4. Taken from Robert Phillips, *Trust Me, PR is Dead*. Published by Unbound, 2015.

Further Reading

Abrashoff, Captain D. Michael. *It's Your Ship: Management Techniques from the Best Damn Ship in the Navy*. Business Plus. 2012. Print

Arden, Paul. *Whatever You Think, Think the Opposite*. Portfolio. 2006. Print.

Braungart, Michael and William McDonough. *Cradle to Cradle: Remaking the Way We Make Things*. North Point Press. 2002. Print.

Bull, Steve. *The Game Plan: Your Guide to Mental Toughness at Work*. Capstone. 2006. Print.

Burkeman, Oliver. *The Antidote: Happiness for People Who Can't Stand Positive Thinking*. Canongate. 2013. Print.

Carnegie, Dale. *How to Win Fiends and Influence People*. Vermillion. 2006. Print.

Collis, John Stewart. *The Worm Forgives the Plough*. Charles Knight. 1973. Print.

Covey, Stephen R. *The 7 Habits of Highly Effective People*. Simon & Schuster. 2004. Print.

Csikszentmihalyi, Mihaly. *Flow: The Psychology of Happiness: The Classic Work on How to Achieve Happiness*. Rider. 2002. Print.

Eisenstein, Charles. *The Ascent of Humanity: Civilisation and the Human Sense of Self*. Evolver Editions. 2013. Print.

Fisher, Roger and William Ury. *Getting to Yes: Negotiating an agreement without giving in*. Random House Business. 2012. Print.

Forster, E.M. *Howard's End*. Edward Arnold. 1910. Print.

Foster, Jack. *How to Get Ideas*. Berrett-Koehler. 1996. Print.

Gaarder, Jostein. *Sophie's World*. Farrar, Straus and Giroux. 1994. Print.

Gallwey, Timothy. *The Inner Game of Tennis*. Random House. 1974. Print.

Gendlin, Eugene. *Focusing: How To Gain Direct Access to Your Body's Knowledge: How to Open Up Your Deeper Feelings and Intuition*. Rider. 2003. Print.

Griffiths, Jay. *Kith: The Riddle of the Childscape*. Hamish Hamilton. 2013. Print.

Haidt, Jonathan. *The Happiness Hypothesis: Putting Ancient Wisdom to the Test of Modern Science*. Arrow. 2007. Print.

Hawk, Red. *Self Observation: The Awakening of Conscience: An Owner's Manual*. Hohm Press, U.S. 2009. Print.

Hock, Dee. *The Birth of the Chaordic Age*. Berrett-Koehler. 1999. Print.

Hoff, Benjamin. *The Tao of Pooh & The Te of Piglet*. Methuen Publishing Ltd. 1994. Print.

Hood, Bruce. *The Self Illusion*. Constable. 2012. Print.

Johnson, Steven. *Where Good Ideas Come From*. Penguin. 2010. Print.

Kegan, Robert and Lisa Laskow Lakey. *Immunity to Change: How to Overcome It and Unlock the Potential in Yourself and Your Organization (Leadership for the Common Good)*. Harvard Business Review Press. 2009. Print.

Kieran, Dan. *I Fought the Law*. Bantam. 2008. Print.

Kline, Nancy. *Time to Think: Listening to Ignite the Human Mind*. Cassell. 2002. Print.

Kohlrieser, George. *Hostage at the Table: How Leaders Can Overcome Conflict, Influence Others, and Raise Performance*. Jossey-Bass. 2006. Print.

Krznaric, Roman. *The Wonderbox*. Profile Books. 2012. Print.

Lencioni, Patrick. *Five Dysfunctions of a Team*. John Wiley & Sons. 2002. Print.

Lovelock, James. *The Revenge of Gaia*. Allen Lane. 2006. Print.

MacKenzie, Gordon. *Orbiting the Giant Hairball: A Corporate Fool's Guide to Surviving with Grace*. Viking/Allen Lane. 1998. Print.

Perls, Frederick. *Gestalt Therapy Verbatim*. Gestalt Journal Press. 1992. Print.

Poynton, Robert. *Everything's An Offer: How to do more with less*. On Your Feet. 2008. Print.

Redfield, James. *The Celestine Prophecy*. Warner Books. 1993. Print.

Rifkin, Jeremy. *The Empathic Civilization*. JP Tarcher/Penguin
     Putnam. 2010. Print.
Rogers, Carl. *On Becoming a Person*. Constable. 2007. Print.
Rogers, Jenny. *Coaching Skills*. Open University Press. 2012. Print.
Saint-Exupéry, Antoine de. *The Little Prince*. Reynal & Hitchcock.
     1943. Print.
Saint-Exupéry, Antoine de. *Wind, Sand and Stars*. Reynal &
     Hitchcock. 1939. Print.
Silverstein, Shel. *The Missing Piece Meets the Big O*. Harper & Row.
     1981. Print.
Simmonds, Jennifer. *Seeing Red: An Anger Management and
     Peacemaking Curriculum for Kids*. New Society Publishers. 2003.
     Print.
Stroud, Mike. *Survival of the Fittest*. Yellow Jersey Press. 2004. Print.
Tharp, Twyla. *The Creative Habit*. Simon & Schuster. 2003. Print.
Thomas, Evan. *Robert Kennedy*. Simon & Schuster. 2000. Print.
Tolle, Eckhart. *The Power of Now*. Yellow Kite. 2001. Print.
Trott, Dave. *Creative Mischief*. LOAF Marketing. 2009. Print.
Whyte, David. *The Heart Aroused*. Bantam Doubleday Dell
     Publishing Group. 1998. Print.
Wiseman, Richard. *The Luck Factor*. Arrow. 2004. Print.
Zuckerman, Andrew. *Wisdom*. Abrams. 2008. Print.

Plays and Films

Aeschylus – *The Oresteia* (first performed in 458 BC)
Bernard Shaw – *Man and Superman* (first performed in 1905)
*Doctor Strangelove or: How I Learned to Stop Worrying and Love
     the Bomb* (1964)
The Return of Martin Guerre (1982)
Love Actually (2003)
Sa som i Himmelen (*As It Is in Heaven*) (2004)
Crash (2005)

The Power of Soft Bibliography

Brickhill, Paul. *The Dam Busters*. Pan Books, 1999. Print.

Cloete, Stuart. *A Victorian Son*. Collins, 1972. Print.

Covey, Stephen R. *The 7 Habits of Highly Effective People*. Simon & Schuster, 2004. Print.

Eisenstein, Charles. *The Ascent of Humanity – Civilisation and the Human Sense of Self*. Evolver Editions, 2007. Print.

Eisler, Gavin. *Lessons from the Top: The three universal stories that all successful leaders tell*. Profile Books, 2012. Print.

Frankl, Victor. *Man's Search for Meaning*. Beacon Press, 1959. Print.

Gladwell, Malcolm. *David and Goliath: Underdogs, Misfits and the Art of Battling Giants*. Penguin, 2014. Print.

Hanna, Thomas. *A Body of Life: Creating New Pathways for Sensory Awareness and Fluid Movement*. Random House, Inc., 1980. Print.

Hock, Dee. *The Birth of the Chaordic Age*. Berrett-Koehler, 1999. Print.

Johnstone, Keith. *Impro: Improvisation and the Theatre*. Routledge, 1987. Print.

Kahane, Adam. *Power and Love: A Theory and Practice of Social Change*. Berrett-Koehler, 2010. Print.

Kahneman, Knetsch, and Thaler, "Experimental Tests of the Endowment Effect and the Coase Theory". *The Journal of Political Economy*, Vol. 98, No. 6. (Dec.,1990), pp.1325–1348. Print.

Kavanagh, Patrick. *Collected Prose*. Martin Brian & O'Keeffe, 1973. Print.

Kurlantzick, Joshua. *Charm Offensive: How China's Soft Power Is Transforming the World*. Yale University Press, 2008. Print.

Lyon, Daniel. *The Complete Book of Pilates for Men: The Lifetime Plan for Strength, Power & Peak Performance*. William Morrow Paperbacks, 2005. Print.

Martin, Roger. *The Opposable Mind: Winning Through Integrative

Thinking. Harvard Business School Press, 2009. Print.

Maslow, Abraham. "A Theory of Human Motivation", *Psychological Review*, 1943

Mittleman, Stuart. *Slow Burn: Burn Fat faster by Exercising Slower.* HarperCollins, 2000. Print.

Reid, Christopher (ed.) *Letters of Ted Hughes.* Faber and Faber, 2009. Print.

Rifkin Jeffrey. *The Empathic Civilization.* JP Tarcher/Penguin Putnam, 2010. Print

Schulz, Kathryn. *Being Wrong: Adventures in the Margin of Error: The Meaning of Error in an Age of Certainty.* Portobello Books Ltd, 2011. Print

Shaw, George Bernard. *Man and Superman.* Wildside Press, 2008. Print.

Shepherd, Nan. *The Living Mountain: A Celebration of the Cairngorm Mountains of Scotland.* Aberdeen University Press, 1977. Print.

Shepherd, Nan. *The Living Mountain: A Celebration of the Cairngorm Mountains of Scotland.* Published by Canongate, 2011. Print.

Siegel, Daniel. J. *Mindsight: Transform Your Brain with the New Science of Kindness.* Bantam, 2010. Print.

Tolle, Eckhart *The Power of Now.* Yellow Kite, 2001. Print.

Zeldin, Theodore. *Conversation: How Talk Can Change Our Lives.* HiddenSpring, 2007. Print.

Zuckerman, Andrew. *Wisdom.* Harry N Abrams, 2008. Print.

Acknowledgements

Three people helped me kick off this book. Spencer Whitbread asked me what I really wanted to do; coach Nick Hastings asked me to characterise what I felt and then, when I started talking about a book idea, writer Neil Denny inspired me to get on with it because, as he said, 'nobody would ever read it anyway'. Thus all the usual blocks to writing, including not being a writer, fell away.

At the Do Lectures in 2011 I took a significant big leap (literally; a group of us jumped in the river largely unclothed and shot the rapids) and came back with a resolve and a confidence to do what I needed to do. I met many people at the Do Lectures but in particular have to thank Rob Poynton for the sheer variety of inspiration and his generosity, both with his time and with his experience. The work he started in creating Parenthesis, which we have carried on together, has also been a crucial part of my journey.

From my time in industry I would like to thank everyone I worked with, particularly on the big deals we did – even the ones we lost, which were often the most revealing. At Accenture, Paul Cramer and in particular Charles Barker, his co-founder in CMI Concord, opened my eyes to what good negotiation skills really meant. At Capgemini, I'd particularly like to thank Derek Crates who just let me get on with it.

Through the development of the idea and the book, Tom Hunt, John-Paul Flintoff, Steve Chapman, Kay Scorah, Lizzie Palmer, Lucy Taylor, David Culling, Justin Verdeber, Dave Manchester, Catherine Stavrakis, David Wyer, James Wilson, Gideon Todes, Mark Goodyear, Anne Scoular, Paul Gilbert and the Blackwater River all gave me great feedback and some crucial help. Thank you also to Neil Drew, Jules Gapper, Tim Fisher, Katie Raw, Carole and Brian Littlechild, Joanne Marsden, Neil Randhawa, Peter Milligan, Jodi Singfield, Matthew Mezey,

Michael Chissick, Robert Shooter, Jason Bates, Craig Hunter, Mark Lloyd, Hugh Morris, Andy Solman, Chris Hay, Magdalen Evans, William Warren, Tracy Edwards, Ellie Taylor, Viv Green, Vanessa Berlowitz, Les McKeown, Adrian and Kirsty for your invaluable contributions and to Malgosia Stepnik for being a special and trusted friend.

A crucial part of the process of writing has been knowing when to go for a walk. This is where Pip and now Lola come in. I even invented a new method called 'DWD' or 'Dog Walk Download'; the capture of a few key ideas pumped up to the surface on a circuit of the local fields. Much of what is written here has also emerged serendipitously; a chance conversation or a clue has led elsewhere. So, though I can't always credit these seeming small (though important) connections, I'd like to acknowledge their critical value; the joy of doing what you love is that it seems to love you back.

Throughout this process Ina, my wife, has taken the brunt of my daily meanderings and experienced first hand – in the way only a partner can – the cogs grinding as they work out possible ways forward. So, I'd like to say a particular thank you to Ina for the patience, love and understanding throughout. Not jut for the writing, but also for partnering me through a continuously changing life.

I was fortunate some years ago to meet John Mitchinson and Dan Kieran, both of whom have reviewed versions of the book and given me helpful advice and invaluable editorial perspective. Thank you both! Mathew Clayton in his role as Unbound's Commissioning Editor provided me with pitch-perfect focus when he took me round Foyles' Charing Cross Road bookshop and made the book real. Mathew also plucked the title out of the thin air that passed between us, brilliantly, in the style of all good coaches, crediting me with the idea. That is not all the help I have had from the Unbound team: thank you also to Isobel, Phil, Justin, Jason, Charlie, Caitlin, Lauren, Emily, Amy, Christoph, Rachael, DeAndra, Jimmy and Laurie; also to Tamsin Shelton, Christian Brett, Alice Smith and James Jones. To do an experience-based project like this with the help of its own readers seems, for me, to be the perfect answer.

Thank you lastly to every one of the people who pledged for this book: you made it happen. By this clever ruse you, the reader, have a book in your hands.

Hilary Gallo, December 2015

Subscribers

@HopeGraceFury
Rebecca Abrams
Lawrie Alderman
David Anderson
Victoria Andreae
David Appleton
Peter Ashley
Simone Baird
Nick Ball
Jason Ballinger
Rick Barnes
Elizabeth Barrett
Jason Bates
Jacqui Bell
Antonin Besse
Richard Boyce
Jo Bradshaw
Erasmus Bread
Julie Brettell
Aleksander Bromek
Dave Brown
Jay Bryan
Jeremy Burke
Tom Burton
Michael Butler
David Camacho
Xander Cansell
Nicky Carew
Sue Carpenter
Petra Čechová
John Chasty
Michael Chissick

Marina Citus
Mary-Louise Clark
Nigel Clarke
Emma Clayton
Mark Cole
Stevyn Colgan
Tom Condon
Edward Lewis Cook
Emma Cox
Adam Craig
John Crawford
David Culling
Deborah Curtis
Tom Curtis
Chris Dale
Avalon de Paravicini
Mike Dean
Khurshed Dehnugara
Hannah Dell
Miranda Dickinson
Leanna Dobson
Andy Doddington
Jane Dowsett
Katie Driver
Chris Duddy
Angus Dudgeon
Keith Dunbar
Tony Dutton
David Eagle
Kester Eastman
Anthony Eldridge-Rogers
Graham Elson

Liz Emmerson

Timothy Entwisle

Hattie Erdal

Clemency Evans

Magdalen Evans

Paul Farmiga

Tom Farrand

Paul Fisher

John-Paul Flintoff

Dr Henry Ford

Kate Fox

Aldo Framingo

Jamie Fraser

Christopher Freeman

John Frewin

Alex Gallo

Ina Gallo

Linda Gallo

Marcus, Sally, Daniel,
   William & Adam Gallo

Rosemary Gallo

Jimmy Garnier

Paul Gilbert

Mike Gillespie

Angelique Golding

Paul J Goodison

Mark Goodyear

Keith Grady

Voula Grand

Viv Green

William Hackett-Jones

Sophie Hall

Kate Hammer

Chloe Hankwell

Leigh Hatfull

Christopher Hay

Andrew Hearse

Dave (hedgecutter.com)

Alex Heffron

Terry Henry

Simon Herrick

Jan Hildebrand

Tom Hockaday

Emma Hoddinott

Andrew Hodson

Becky Howard

Jo Howard

Adam Humphrey

Stephen Humphrey

Tom Hunt

Craig Hunter

John Inman

Ros Innes

Daniel Jackson

Wendy Jago

Jean-Marc Jefferson

Paul Jenkins

Daniel Bressel Jensen

Erin Johnson

Adele Jolliffe

Meghan Jones

Arpit Kaushik

John Keep

Patric Keller

Hilary Kemp

Dan Kieran

Don Koulaouzos

Keith Krasny

Andrew Kumar

Sarah Lafferty

Leticia Lago

Jon Lang

Jimmy Leach

Sue Leeson

Craig Lewis
Helge Lippert
Brian Littlechild
Mark Lloyd
Alexandra Lloyd-Jones
Gemma Lodge
Iain Lorriman
Sophie Mackley
David Manchester
Gill Mansfield
Graham Marshall
Sarah Massey
Alan Mathers
Huon Matthews
Alistair Maughan
Anita Mckiernan
Mohit Mehta
Mekalav Mekalav
Ute Methner
Craig Mill
Peter Milligan
Pete Mills
James Milner – Founder of
    EmberPSS consulting
Steve Mitchell
John Mitchinson
Michelle Montgomery-
    Knappett
Stewart Morgan
Beth Morris
Hugh Morris
Richard Moseley
Alex Musson
Thomas Negovan
Al Nicholson
David Nolan
John O'Brien

Julius O'Dowd
Sean O'Hare
Derham O'Neill
Wouter Oosthuizen
Mark Owen-Ward
Lizzie Palmer
KT Parker
Sarah Peacey
Sam Peters
Steve & Karen Pettyfer
Gary Phillips
Robert Phillips
Sam Phillips
Andy Polaine
Justin Pollard
Piers Pollock
David Pomfret
Neil Randhawa
Andy Randle
Valerie Read
Simon Reap
Stuart Reid
Ellen Richardson
Megan Ringer
Žarko Ristić
Mari Roberts
Josy Roberts-Pay
Malcolm Rogerson
Nick Rose
Julian Roskill
Lizzy Rudd
Marc Rupasinha
Ruth Sack
Ella Saltmarshe
Christoph Sander
Frank Martin Schmidt
Adam Scott

Laurence Shapiro
John Sheridan
John Shirlaw
Robert Shooter
Jodi Singfield
Jonathan Smith
Mike Smith
Robert Smith
Matthew Solle
Andy Solman
Julian Sowry
Dave Sox
Libor Špaček
Henriette B. Stavis
Catherine Stavrakis
Jason Stevens
David Steward
Charlie Stewart
George Stirling
Rachel Stirling
Kim Stockdale
Magnus Ström
Eleanor Sturdy
Jim Tatchell
Chris Taylor
Christine Thomas
Danson Thunderbolt
Adrian Thurston

Matthew Timms
Julia Tratt
Nihat Tsolak
Ana Maria Urrutia
Justin Verderber
Richard Visick
Steve Wadsworth
Anne Waldron
David Wall
Jon Walters
Colin Ware
Shelley Warnaby
Ruth Watson-Blumenfeld
Miranda West
Kevin Wheeler
Hannah Whelan
Christopher Whitton
Lloyd Wigglesworth
Richard Williams
James Wilson
Tobias Winterhalter
May Wong
Isobel & Doug Wood
Richard Woodruff
Scott 'Woolfie' Woolf
Rebecca Worthington
Ian Yates
Kevin Yuen

Index

A note about the typefaces

Jan Tschichold (1902–1974) was a German calligrapher, typographer, book designer, teacher and writer. This book has been typeset using a digital representation of his design, namely, Linotype Sabon.

Sabon-Antiqua, designed by Jan Tschichold for both hand- and machine-composition, was issued simultaneously by the Linotype, Monotype and Stempel type foundries in 1967. The designs for the roman were based on the type designs of Claude Garamond (c.1480–1561) and the italics of those by Garamond's contemporary, Robert Granjon.

The titling typeface used here was designed in 1916 for the London Underground by the Uruguay born calligrapher Edward Johnston (1872–1944), and has been in continuious use by the transport authority ever since.

It is difficult to overestimate Johnston's influence on the major lettering and type designers of the 20th century. One of his pupils, Eric Gill, reported Johnston's tutelage being 'struck as by lightening'. Gill was involved in the early development of the Underground type, for which he received 10 per cent of the over-all fee. A couple of decades later Gill revisited these designs to create his own typeface which went on to become one of the most popular sans serif types in history. The Underground type itself, was not commercially available until 2007, when the type-face was issued by the P22 Type Foundry under licence from the London Transport Museum.